DEATH IN ANCIENT EGYPT

DEATH IN ANCIENT EGYPT

BRIDGET MCDERMOTT

SUTTON PUBLISHING

First published in the United Kingdom in 2006 by
Sutton Publishing Limited · Phoenix Mill
Thrupp · Stroud · Gloucestershire · GL5 2BU

British Library Cataloguing in Publication Data
A catalogue record for this book is available from the British Library.

ISBN 0-7509-3932-X

Typeset in Garamond 11.5/15 pt.
Typesetting and origination by
Sutton Publishing Limited.
Printed and bound in England by
J.H. Haynes & Co. Ltd, Sparkford.

Contents

To Barbara and Chris,
Barbara-Louise and
John McDermott

Acknowledgements

I should like to thank the following people for their help and encouragement while I was writing this book. For permission to publish photographs: Dr R. Parkinson of the British Museum, Guy Rothwell of Ancient Relics and Dr M. Raven of the Rijksmuseum; to my editors Christopher Feeney, Clare Jackson and Lucy Isenberg for all their hard work. Thanks must also go to Dolores and Alec Charleson, Angela and Albert Barsford, Frances McDermott and Teresa Byrne. Much love and thanks to Sami Adib Gindi and Mohamed Hasan Ali, Lady Eloise, Raki and Jack Brown. A special thank you must go to the beautiful and talented Bethany and Mollie Marshall, and to Anne and Kenny. Thanks, as always, to Jason Semmens, Graham Ollerenshaw and David Orman for numerous insightful comments on the subject of magic, death and ancient lives – many of which inspired the writing of this book. Thank you to Dr Tim Hopkinson-Ball, for sharing your vast knowledge and amazing humour. Love and thanks as always to Mo Plume and Jo Beckett. A massive thank you to Pat and Barry Greenhalgh for saving this book. Thank you also to Ali, Paul, Poppy and Tom Chester, Merlin, Dorothy King, Chris Laing, Adrian and Flo; the late Verity Wood and Russell Dent; the extraordinary Alison Collier and to Jean and Lawrence Tebbot who taught me everything I know about Egyptian magic. Thanks to my father Christopher and my much loved grandfather Harold Dent, who first introduced me to Egyptian history. As always, thank you to Steve. Finally, much love and thanks to Delphi Anais Rose Kelly, for facing the battle with a Macedonian heart.

Introduction

DEATH AND HUMAN REMAINS

The ancient Egyptian landscape, dominated as it was both by arid desert sands and fresh flowing water, mirrored every intrinsic aspect of life and death for its inhabitants. In ancient Egypt land was scarce and people lived on and cultivated narrow tracts of fertile earth that lined the banks of the Nile. Even today, the visitor is often struck by the stark contrast between lush green vegetation and dry desert sand, the fine seams of rich black earth and the otherwise endless waves of barren desert that in ages past were a daily reminder that life was fragile and precarious. Wherever one travels in Egypt the senses are assaulted by violent contrasts such as these. Furthermore, her ancient sites comprise crumbling edifices and deathly relics – rendered all the more poignant because the imagery bequeathed by the ancient Egyptians is so abundant in colour, hope and spiritual vibrancy. So intense are Egypt's day-time heat and night-time cold, her hours of light and of darkness, her stillness and storms that they seem to act, as they did in the ancient past, as metaphors for life and death.

Standing in this kingdom of shadow, heat and decay one cannot help but wonder about the nature of death, not only of the grand civilisation that once thrived among these stones but of the individuals who lived and worked in this dramatic environment. In this book, I have attempted to answer the fundamental questions often raised in discussions of life and death in ancient Egypt, a task made the more problematic when one considers that ancient Egyptian burial practices evolved over a period of some three thousand years and that throughout this time occurred the transition from small desert graves to elaborate grandiose tombs, a process that can be traced now. We face similar difficulties of scale when we begin to assess the long periods of development in religious belief and the highly complex process of mummification. Fortunately for modern scholars, the Ptolemaic historian Manetho developed a system in which he divided each period of ancient Egyptian history into dynasties, enabling us to distinguish separate periods and events. By identifying phases in this way we are able to categorise important patterns and trends in a practical and efficient manner. Although this book deals with the subject of death, it also raises questions about how the ancient Egyptians saw time, practised their religion, celebrated life and prepared for the world beyond. As Egyptologists continue to study new evidence with regard to death in ancient Egypt we continuously review our opinions and beliefs. In this book I have attempted to present a comprehensive and modern analysis of this fascinating subject.

As archaeologists we are constantly trying to defeat time and decay and, in effect, wake the dead. For many of us, the quest can become both obsessive and deeply personal. My father died when I was six months old. From an early age I was aware of how a single death could change the structure of a family and how the choices made in response to the death could be complex and have far-reaching consequences. I realised that each death became a part of the 'butterfly effect' (a theory that suggests that miniscule events can alter the delicate structure of the whole) and had the capacity to change and mould the world in very subtle ways. As a child I never stopped asking questions about the dead and had an inexhaustible desire to root out the answers. When I read the book *Death's Acre. Inside the Body Farm* by Professor Bill Bass I knew I was not alone. In it, Professor Bass describes in what to me was all too familiar detail how he learnt as a small child to deal with the death of his father. His attempts to revive all the minutiae of his father's life resulted in a unique empathy with the bereaved and the victims of violent death. Professor Bass became an expert in Bio-Anthropology and now leads investigative studies at the University of Tennessee Forensic Anthropology Facility, or 'the body farm'. Here a large number of donated human corpses are left to decay in various places and under widely differing conditions so that experts may study the effect of disparate environments on decomposition. The studies conducted at the facility have produced innovative developments in forensic science that now help answer vital questions about a crime scene, the way a person died and time of death. Today, archaeology and Egyptology are part of a multi-disciplinary group that investigates or studies human remains. Increasingly, these specialisms overlap and many archaeologists often work alongside other specialists, particularly at crime scenes. In this way our knowledge is rapidly expanding. Although we deal primarily with the ancient Egyptian dead, we now broaden our researches to include the study of the cadavers of other cultures in an attempt to understand the diverse subjects of disease, death and embalming. Below, I shall often refer to the dead of other cultures in order to shed light on those of ancient Egypt.

When asked what first attracted them to ancient history most Egyptologists will say that they were influenced by one of the greatest archaeological events of all time, the discovery of Tutankhamun's tomb and the unwrapping of the king's mummy. We recall, with relish, the words of Howard Carter as he peered into sealed chambers that 'glinted with gold'. How many of us as children remember staring wide-eyed at an Egyptian mummy, torn between wonder and fear? Although the exhibition of human remains now evokes considerable debate and concern among religious and political factions, they are still the most popular and attractive items on display in public museums. Nothing can compare with coming face to face with the mummy of an Egyptian ruler such as Sety I or Ramesses II. Their sleeping countenances belie their awesome presence. It is a spine-tingling moment. Curiosities they may be but these mummies also remind us of our own mortality. While most ancient objects can be analysed, drawn or studied, we often remain puzzled by them – with mummies the impact is immediate.

The legacy of the ancient Egyptians is both complex and fascinating: funeral texts, temples, statues, paintings and papyri – and human remains. In this book we shall investigate their ancient funerary rites and try to establish why so many answers to Egyptologists' questions about death and its rituals are to be found within ancient Egyptian culture. The Egyptians mummified their dead from the earliest periods because they believed that the spirit resided in their physical remains, which had to be protected at all costs. They went to great lengths not only to preserve the body but also to protect it, fashioning elaborate coffins and casting magical spells. So important were the remains considered that the ancient Egyptians even made replica statues and heads to act as insurance in case the body was damaged. The tomb was viewed as a dwelling, equipped with everything a person would need in the afterlife. In this way the Egyptians demonstrated their belief that death was a continuation of life. After they left the mortal world families would be reunited; people would work, wage war and establish relationships. However, the dead were separated from the living, being placed in the desert regions and identified in the minds of the ancient Egyptians as those who follow the sun to the west. In death they became associated with two principal deities, Re the sun god and Osiris the ruler of the dead. Both gods were strongly connected to the concept of physical regeneration.

We derive such information from a vast and unique amount of ancient Egyptian materials and resources. Through the rich array of funeral goods, domestic and religious buildings we relate to the Egyptians as people and are able to connect with them. However, in doing so, we must remember that we view the ancient Egyptians through rose-tinted glasses. The upper classes employed elaborate burials and commissioned striking tomb paintings while the poor were buried with a few simple objects in graves in the desert floor. So it is important to understand that we see ancient Egypt primarily through the eyes of the elite. The upper classes designed their tombs as 'houses of eternity' and made every effort to secure them against robbery. Fortunately, the environment was conducive to their aims. The dry atmosphere ensured the survival of mummies, paintings and burial goods. These reveal much about the daily lives of the people; looking at them we experience a sense of intimacy based on familiar and shared experience, for here are representations of childbirth, sexuality, warfare and death. Despite all their state grandeur the Egyptians retained a feel for the natural world. One scene shows a calf with its mother; in another, party girls have lotus blossoms in their hair. This simple imagery of daily life is as poignant as the recovery of a child's sandal from the dust. Howard Carter knew the importance of these everyday objects. In the tomb of Tutankhamun he found and preserved not only the grand remnants of kingship but funeral bouquets, childhood garments and family heirlooms. These are the things that truly connect us, the living, with the dead. They also bring a deep-seated desire to fruition. The ancient Egyptians wanted their names to 'live'. In preserving and promoting their identity we have helped their cause, enabling the gods to grant them 'millions of years' – in effect, eternity.

We must never underestimate the power of the dead. Ancient Egypt was unified in an attempt to preserve the corpse of the ruler, for it was thought that the fate of the populace rested on the survival of the king's soul. The dead can also affect us on a personal level. Many times I have seen museum employees form deep attachments to certain Egyptian mummies while others, thought to harbour malice and ill-will, are shunned. In this way we are inexplicably linked to the dead, and some of us are changed forever by the experience. Indeed, a preserved body can become more powerful in death than it was in life for it provides us with a sense that it is possible to defeat the inevitable. In ancient Egypt death was an essential aspect of continuity. Since the succession of an Egyptian king was established only after he had provided the correct funerary rites for his predecessor, the ancient Egyptian funeral rituals had a multifaceted and far-reaching purpose, directly linked as they were to legitimate rule and ancestral continuity.

ARCHAEOLOGY AND HUMAN REMAINS

As archaeologists we view human remains with the utmost respect and employ considerable care in excavating them. However, archaeology is still in its infancy. We are still learning our trade and our methods will one day be viewed as primitive in the extreme. It is sobering to remember that during the early nineteenth century many people still adhered to the biblical view that the world had been created in 4004 BC. Today most Egyptologists remain in awe of the mummies we study and of the information we gain from them. Although we always remember that these were living individuals, someone's children and probably someone's parents, we also view the human body as a macrocosm of detail – a tapestry of threads. We long to unravel its secrets. Today, science and archaeology go hand in hand. The study of DNA, biochemistry and genetics will be the archaeological tools of the future. However, a human cadaver can still reveal many things to an experienced archaeologist. Examination of a well-preserved body can result in the identification of sex, height and weight. The weight of a mummy would be calculated at 25 per cent of its natural mass. Hair often survives. Archaeologists can gain much information from this organic material – including the identification of colour, the application of dyes, the presence of head lice and the cultural significance of hair styles. Studies can include an examination of hair adornments and the substances that were used to style the hair – these include beeswax, various oils and resins. Moreover, humans are invariably buried with jewellery. These objects are prized because they have religious significance and can often reveal a great deal about the social standing of the individual. Since the acquisition of jewellery is also linked to trade and foreign expeditions, a mummy can also reveal much about the community to which it belonged. It may bear important ritual scars, trauma wounds or tattoos. Clothing can also provide essential information. We can identify different social classes by the garments they wore. In ancient Egypt royal personages are easily recognised as they were dressed and adorned in clothes and jewellery designed especially for the pharaohs and their queens.

We can form impressions of the age of a mummy by examining its teeth. Scientists do this by looking at the eruption of permanent teeth and also by studying ridge growth. By studying teeth, experts can also deduce important information about diet. Bones too tell us a great deal about age. Bones fuse at various points in an individual's lifetime – for example, the collar bone at age twenty-five to twenty-six, the base of the spine at around fifteen to sixteen. The presence or absence of these fusions help us determine the age at death. In mummies the long bones are measured to estimate height. From the late 1980s, experts have begun to reconstruct the faces of the dead from nothing other than the measurements of the skull. Equipped with casts of the skull scientists and artists use pegs to determine the thickness of the soft tissue and then add clay to replace the superficial layers of muscle and skin.

Mummies also help us to reconstruct a person's lifestyle. They sometimes even reveal how they died, for trauma is frequently evident on human remains. Although many wounds, including slashed throats, can be identified on soft tissue it is the bones that reveal gashes and defence marks. While evidence of disease survives in the soft tissue, worms and parasites are often discovered in the body. Modern techniques allow us to study the mummies in non-destructive ways. X-rays have been used from the turn of the twentieth century while Xeroradiography, a technique that combines X-ray and photocopying, allows us to examine both soft and hard tissue in more detail. Mummies are now often taken into hospitals and passed through a scanning machine. Computed Axial Topography (CAT scans) allows parts of the anatomy to be viewed in sections or slices so that we can study the soft organs. Many scholars have employed a fibre-optic endoscope (a tube with a light on the end and commonly used by gastroenterologists) to pass through the body and examine the inside of the skull and abdomen.

Ancient human remains have modern relevance. The Mummy Data Base, Manchester, England, collects statistics and tissue samples from many different mummies around the world. Some ancient mummies shed new light on modern Egyptian diseases. We live in an amazing age. However, the world has changed forever. New developments in photographic imaging and cinematography mean that we have inevitably demystified our times. However, there is little doubt that we will continue to be inspired by mummies and the things they have to tell us. Without doubt, too, mummies will remain as relevant in the future as they are today.

In this book I have attempted to present a comprehensive study of ancient Egyptian burial customs beginning with an account of how the Egyptians measured time and viewed the ageing process. In many instances I have referred to the words of the ancient Egyptians themselves and have mined a rich vein of textual material to highlight ancient attitudes to longevity, disease, death and suicide. I have looked at mortality in the ancient world and examined many causes of death including childbirth, environmental dangers and death on the battlefield. Further, I have attempted to highlight the psychological effects of death on the community and to look in detail at what happens to the physical body when it dies, especially in a hot climate such as that of ancient Egypt. I have compared ancient Egyptian techniques with those used by other cultures and traced the development of the mummification process over several thousand years. I have also provided a chronological account of tomb building and examined the purpose of funerary architecture. Finally, I have traced the history of excavation in Egypt; introduced the early archaeologists and treasure seekers and described their discoveries in the Valley of the Kings. I hope this book will take the reader on a fascinating journey from the womb to the tomb of ancient Egypt. There is no other culture in the world where this journey is more exciting or rich in iconographic complexity, no other civilisation that is more beautiful to gaze upon.

ONE

Life and Death in Ancient Egypt

Re will withdraw from mankind, although he will rise at his hour one will not know when noon comes, for no one will identify his shadow.

From the prophecies of Neferti

MEASURING TIME

In Egypt one is always aware of the passage of time. As the haunting call to prayer drifts from the mosques and filters across the arid landscape it marks the hours of the day and tracks the movement of the sun. Furthermore, the ruins of the tombs and temples remind us that time erodes even the most magnificent of civilisations [Fig. 1]. However, it is the transformations, the rising heat and the ever-changing quality of the light that determine the hours of the day with pinpoint accuracy. In Egypt, populated tracts of land are flat and the journey of the sun stands out clearly against the horizon. During early morning the heat literally rises up your spine, it fattens your shadow and blazes above your head with remorseless intensity. During the afternoon, it mellows and softens and then, in the evening, as the temperature and light fall dramatically, a menagerie of birds appears flying low and parallel to the Nile. There is simply nowhere on earth where sunset provokes such a melancholic resonance, nowhere in the world where one feels such an immediate connection to the land. As in ancient times, the sun dominates the daily life of the populace. The sun is a 15,600,000kg mass of hydrogen and helium, is 149,600km from the earth and emits a phenomenal 386 billion billion megawatts a second. The sun is four and a half billion years old, and only now entering middle age. Although the ancient Egyptians were unaware of these staggering facts, their concept of this omnipresent celestial body nevertheless acknowledged its complexity and elicited their eternal reverence and awe.

Naturally, the Egyptians used the sun to mark the passing of the hours, measuring time by assigning twelve hours each both to night and day. They associated cycles of the sun and moon closely with agriculture, the hieroglyphic

1

Fig 1: The pyramids in shadow at sunrise, Giza. *(Photograph: Jason Semmens)*

sign for 'year' being 'renpet', a word carrying the image of a young shoot in bud [Fig. 2]. They also recognised three seasons: Akhet, or the Inundation, when the Nile flooded and fertilised the land (July); Peret, the season of 'emergence', when crops began to appear in the fields (November); and, finally, Shemu, the harvest (March).

Egypt is predominantly a desert region but along the banks of the Nile there are rich and fertile tracts of land that have been cultivated since earliest times. Then the Egyptians were entirely dependent on their agricultural resources and so observed the seasonal cycle of the river with great trepidation. By June each year, the river waters became swollen. At this dangerous time, while the Egyptians waited for the annual flood, it seemed as if all the hostile aspects of desert and water would engulf the community [Fig. 3]. It was a time of great anxiety. Would the flood come – and, if so, would it be too little or too much – would the land be starved or swamped? Even by Egyptian standards, the river god Hapi was an ancient deity. He was worshipped as a human male with pendulous breasts, his feet shod in sandals as a sign of wealth. Crowned with water plants and often shown before a table piled high with lustrous bundles of vegetables, grain and plants he was an effervescent symbol of fecundity. When the floods were due, peasants, priests and king united in their desire for a good harvest. They threw offerings into the river to encourage his bounty. The rising of the star Sirius, on about 19 July, heralded the floods, the season of the inundation. When, finally, the waters receded, but before the earth had time to grow hard, the Egyptians could plant and sow. Four months later, after the harvest, the cycle began once more. From the earliest periods, the Egyptians realised that the rising of the Nile waters corresponded with the rising of Sirius, a star found in the constellation Canis Major and often referred to as the Dog Star. They associated the star with the goddess Isis whose tears of mourning for her murdered brother and husband Osiris were said to cause the flooding.

The Egyptians divided the year by celebrating many important holidays and seasonal festivals that included dramatic re-enactments of mythological events with plays promoting a sense of ancestral continuity. Among these was the Opet Festival, celebrated at Thebes during the rising of Sirius. It lasted for almost a month. Lesser events such as the Festival of Tekhi (the festival of drunkenness) were also held on the first day of the second month. The Egyptians also recorded auspicious and inauspicious days, when they believed that particular abstinences or duties were required. The duration of the three seasons equalled four months, each month divided into thirty days. In this way the ancient Egyptians established a calendar year of 365 days, which included five additional days that were assigned to a special category known as the days of festivity.

Ancient societies adopted several methods of practical time-keeping. In Egypt, time-keeping was especially important in the temple

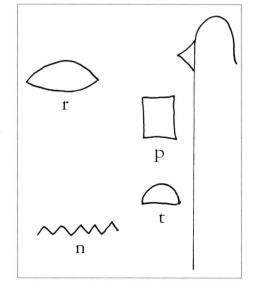

Fig. 2: The hieroglyphic sign for 'year' highlights the close associations between agriculture and the concepts of time. (Drawing: Bridget McDermott)

Fig. 3: Ancient Thebes and the Mortuary Temple of Ramesses III. The contrast between the vegetation and the desert sand is clearly visible from the air. *(Photograph: Bridget McDermott)*

where the priests needed to make specific calculations for religious practices that involved, among other rituals, the dawn ceremony during which the temple statue was bathed, anointed and worshipped. Early shadow clocks consisted of a bar that was designed with incised markings, each measuring a period of four hours. At midday when the sun was at its highest, the clock was reversed. The Egyptians also used water clocks and a water clock dating to the reign of

Fig. 4: A magnificent alabaster water clock from the reign of Amenhotep III. *(Egyptian Museum, Cairo/Photograph: Bridget McDermott)*

Amenhotep III [Fig. 4], is now on display in the Egyptian Museum, Cairo. It has twelve carved columns and a series of markings that correspond to the hours of the night. The water drips through a hole made in the centre of the base. To establish the time, the priests needed to look inside the clock and record the level of the water that remained above the markings. The clock is particularly beautiful. Its water contents drip beneath a figure of a seated baboon, a creature often associated with Thoth, the god of writing and wisdom. (Baboons, which traditionally greet the dawn with ear-piercing shrieks, naturally became associated with the sunrise.) The outer surface is decorated with figures and text that show symbols of planets and constellations while the middle register is occupied by the circumpolar stars in the form of animals and gods. The clock is also inscribed with a list of the protective spirits assigned to each day of the Egyptian week.

ASTRONOMY

The Egyptians' perception of time was further influenced by their knowledge of certain astronomical events. They identified their gods among the stars [Fig. 5].

Fig. 5: The ceiling of the burial chamber in the tomb of Sety I is decorated with celestial images depicting stars, constellations and the twelve hours of the night. *(Photograph: Bridget McDermott)*

For example, the god Sah, described as the glorious soul of Osiris, was recognised in the constellation now known as Orion. These deities were known as the 'imperishable ones', and in their locations, the Egyptians recognised the circumpolar stars in the northern sky. Among the clear and vivid patterns that can be seen with startling clarity in the Egyptian night sky, they identified, philosophised about and based their myths upon thirty-six groups of star gods or constellations. Each was known as a decon – rising above the horizon at dawn for a period of ten days every year. The star Sothis, or Sirius, was known as a decon and became the most important of these bodies. In the dark burial vaults of the Egyptian royal tombs, depictions of the night sky are often decorated with a party of star gods who travel across its circumference in a boat. The stars played an important role in the Egyptian psyche, with diagonal calendars or star maps being painted on wooden coffin lids of the early Middle Kingdom (2040–1674 BC) and the Late Period (747–525 BC). These calendars consisted of thirty-six columns which listed the decons and gave detailed information about the way the Egyptians viewed the night sky, the constellations and the stars.

The ancient Egyptians were skilled in various types of mathematical calculation. Since they needed to measure the annual flood of the Nile, the Egyptians built special stone Nilometers next to the river. Based on agricultural practices, they operated an efficient, and often brutal, tax system that required expert calculation. Specially trained military scribes accompanied large armies and were responsible for measuring distances, rationing food, issuing weapons and general army logistics. Temples were built to specific measurements, so that on certain days the sun would shine through corridors and passages and illuminate the faces of the statues of dead kings. Their knowledge of astronomy meant they knew the exact time to celebrate specific events in their history, while they venerated their ancestors in cultic re-enactments of ancient myths that referred to a primeval past, known as the 'first time', or the first heliacal rising of Sirius. Some Egyptian priests were employed as the 'imy wnwt' or 'hour watchers', and became the observers of stars and monitored the rising of the sun. Preparations for the dawn ritual included the arrangement of food, the bathing or purification of the priests, the presentation of a series of offerings and the organisation of ceremonial equipment.

AGEING

The physical decline of the human body takes a heavy toll. Briefly, from the age of thirty the spaces between the vertebrae begin to thin and height decreases by about 1⁄16 inch each year. Fat accumulates around the hips. The skin loses elasticity when exposed to sunlight, a problem seen today in the premature ageing of the skin of Egyptian men and women. The chest becomes weaker, and in dusty climates such as Egypt, lung problems are usual. In some Egyptian texts, a hacking cough is a common complaint of old age. Hair mass decreases and pigmentation of the skin fades. Wounds take longer to heal. Muscles lose strength, nerve cells in the brain begin to die and memories fade. Aching in the muscles and joints is another common complaint, as is disrupted sleep. The testicular functions decline and the sex drive weakens. As membranes in the ear deteriorate, hearing loss is common while exposure to direct sunlight affects the eyes and often results in cataracts. Artery walls thicken reducing the supply of blood to the organs. No wonder the Egyptians recorded a litany of complaints about the ageing process.

The Egyptians encouraged respect for the elderly. For example, one instruction text states: 'When you walk along the street, leave the way to him who is old. When you look at the feeble man, fear his fate and his weakness' while the Instructions of Ani charge their audience 'Never [to] remain seated if a man older than yourself is standing.' Some texts do reflect on the positive aspects of ageing – 'Old age is a good time in life because of its gentleness' but the process is rarely seen in an optimistic light. Old age is briefly discussed in the Instruction of Ptah Hotep, a text found on three papyri, although only one complete version has been discovered, dated to the Middle Kingdom; known as Papyrus Prisse it is housed in the Bibliothèque Nationale, Paris. It contains thirty-seven maxims that were meant to provide a code of moral conduct for Egyptian men.

> It has come, Age,
> Feebleness too, weakness grows,
> Like a child, one sleeps all through the day,
> Eyes grow dim, ears deaf.
> Strength is drained through weariness,
> The mouth is quiet, it speaks not,
> The heart, empty, remembers not,
> The bones ache.
> Good has become evil,
> What age does to people is evil through and through,
> The nose cannot breathe
> Painful is standing and sitting

Clearly, most Egyptians regarded old age as a time of emotional weakness as well as failing health. A gradual but increasing dependence on other members of his or her family was viewed by many as a loss of personal dignity. However, for anyone who reached old age and remained healthy, it was another matter. In ancient Egyptian texts, 110 years is an ideal age to reach. While enjoying mental and physical health, some elderly Egyptians were inclined to thank the gods for their good fortune. In the teachings of Neferkare is the remark: 'I spent a lifetime – until a hundred years among the living in possession of my faculties.' However, a healthy longevity must have been rare as mortality rates were high in ancient Egypt, and especially among the peasant workers, the few who lived beyond forty had much to be grateful for. The High Priest Romeroy admits he is blessed to have attained old age in the service of Amun. And there could be material benefits. Many elderly people of the higher classes were provided with pensions and endowments and some mature men who were valued for their wisdom retained important roles in the government.

The Three Tales of Wonder are a series of magical anecdotes that date to the Middle Kingdom in which King Khufu is being entertained by his son's stories. In one tale, Prince Hardedef asks permission to bring a real magician to the court. The magician, Djedi, was reputed to be 110 years of age. In the narrative Prince Hardedef travelled upstream to the magician's home town, Djed Sneferu: 'when he reached Djedi, his carrying chair was set to the ground. As he rose to greet him [Djedi], he found him lying on a mat in the courtyard of his villa. There was a servant beside him anointing him while another rubbed his feet. Prince Hardedef said, "Your condition is like that of one who lives above age – for old age is the time for dying, embalming and burial – one who sleeps until daylight free from sickness, without a terrible cough. Thus greetings honoured one!"' During the Old Kingdom the ancient Egyptians saw longevity as a royal reward; for instance, the Instruction of Ptah Hotep relates that 'The king was content with me, saying "May you have many years of life!" It was no small thing that which I did on earth, I had 110 years of life as a gift of the king.' During the later periods this concept would change and old age would come to be seen as a gift of the gods.

The Insinger Papyrus, dated to the Ptolemaic Period, makes many references to ageing. Here, the expectations of old age are pessimistically rendered:

> He who has passed sixty years, everything has gone
> If his heart loves wine, he cannot drink until he is drunk
> If he craves food, he cannot eat as he once did
> If he reaches for a woman, her moment doesn't come.

The same text also addresses the Egyptians' attitude to life expectancy:

The life that approaches its prime, two-thirds are lost.
A man spends ten years as a boy before he understands life and death.
Another ten years are spent being instructed on how to live.
He spends another ten years earning his living
He spends another ten years growing old, his heart grows wise.
Sixty years of the entire life which Thoth has assigned to the man of god
One in a million, god grant a blessing, to him who spends them with good fate
Neither the impious nor the godly man can alter the lifetime that was assigned to
    him.
He who is fortunate in his days thinks of death in them.
The one who thinks about death for the sake of corn, the riches will bring ruin
The chief demon is the first to punish him after the last breath
Cedar, oil, incense, natron and salt [embalming ingredients] are the remedies for
    healing his afflictions.

Since our knowledge of the ancient Egyptians is primarily gleaned through their funerary or religious practices, it is important to keep in mind that they were not as obsessed with death as one might think. Above all else, they prized order and tradition and the final resting place of a family member was planned and executed with great precision – the completion of their tomb ranked high on the Egyptian's list of priorities. It is often stated that it was a love of life, and a deep desire to preserve its positive aspects, that drove the Egyptians to make such elaborate preparations for the world beyond. An aversion to human decay is natural in all societies. The Egyptians, who daily struggled against a harsh environment, were more familiar than most with the realities of death. Their texts frequently express repugnance for and fear of cadavers, decomposition and eternal damnation.

Although a lucrative funeral industry dealing in both human and animal remains thrived during the later periods of their history, the Egyptians did not promote images of ageing, sickness or death on the walls of their tombs and temples [Fig. 6]. They believed that a crafted image was imbued with magical potency that could be activated by a ritual. In some paintings, weapons or

Fig. 6: The Egyptians portrayed themselves in their finest clothes and wigs, an image of youth and beauty that was essential if one wished to pass to the beyond in perfect physical condition. Fragment. *(Brooklyn Museum, New York/Photograph: Bridget McDermott)*

Fig. 7: A member of the Amarna royal family being blessed by the sun. The rays of the sun end in small hands which present the symbol of the ankh (eternal life) to the subject. Egyptian iconography is full of such symbols and magical potency. Fragment. *(Brooklyn Museum, New York/Photograph: Bridget McDermott)*

animals are shown bound, a precaution intended to prevent their powers being unleashed. In later periods, the nose or heart of a written, painted or sculpted image was susceptible to violation, for an antagonist believed that by attacking his or her likeness they killed the spirit of the individual. Such acts highlight the relevance their funeral iconography had for the ancient Egyptians, embodying as it did both functional and dangerous elements – for an image might help or hinder the tomb owner in the afterlife. Images were not revered for their beauty, but for their potential [Fig. 7]. An overflowing bowl of fruit or vegetables painted on the walls of an Egyptian tomb was seen as a food source; a chair or table had a practical role. Because of the magical potency the Egyptians attached to painted figures and their belief that these could be animated at will, the people who appear in tomb paintings and temple carvings are generally shown in their prime. With only a few minor exceptions, men and women are shown in radiant health. Like today's magazine models, the Egyptians never baulked at a little airbrushing [Fig. 8].

There is something highly erotic about tomb representations. Even those involved in the menial tasks of fishing and harvesting wear elaborate make-up

Fig. 8: A noblewoman holding a lotus flower to her face. She is dressed in her finest clothes, a linen dress that divides at the breast. Around her neck she wears a magnificent collar of beads and on her wrists and ankles she wears bands that were probably made of precious metals. Old Kingdom fragment. *(Louvre Collection, Paris/Photograph: Bridget McDermott)*

and jewellery. The tomb owners and their families are depicted in their finest linen garments that have a subtle transparency designed to entice and arouse the viewer. Standing on the red carpet of the ancient world the Egyptian elite pose and preen. The tomb pulsated with glamour. It is these images of fecundity that are designed to defeat the principles of death. Age, it seems, was a highly undesirable state. In some rare scenes where signs of imperfection are evident, it is usually the loss of hair that is hinted at, or a faint fold or crease in the face. Few Egyptians saw beauty beyond youth [Fig. 9]. Even today, youth is highly revered in Egypt – most girls marry young. In hieroglyphic texts, words relating to age are determined (characterised) by men bent at the waist or leaning on sticks. One rare scene shows a couple wearing wigs of white – one can only wonder why the owners made this highly unusual decision. However, their faces, clothes and make-up still portrayed the necessary degrees of vitality, youth and beauty – and it is clear that they are merely hinting at their age.

Fig. 9: The tomb of Kheruef at Thebes with some of the most elaborate and beautiful images of women in ancient Egypt. Women are shown as both youthful and desirable. *(Photograph: Bridget McDermott)*

Fig. 10: Akhenaten's 'favourite', the secondary wife Kiya in the company of a young princess. Both are being blessed by the Aten, the sun god. The ancient Egyptians formed strong family bonds and family unity was promoted in funerary imagery. Fragment. *(Brooklyn Museum, New York/Photograph: Bridget McDermott)*

Despite avoiding the subject of death in artistic representations, the Egyptians had no qualms about making plans for their funerals. First, the head of a noble family would outline his will. Although a person's estate was usually left to the eldest son, the inheritance could also pass to spouses and daughters. We have records belonging to Nakhtefmut, a priest of Amun during the 22nd Dynasty, who left his belongings to his daughter because she had taken care of her parents in their old age. In ancient as in modern Egypt, children were expected to look after their parents as they aged. In fact, parents often referred to their children as the 'staff in my old age' [Fig. 10]. Childless couples would adopt children so that they would be looked after as they grew old. The children, as descendants of the line, had practical and ritualistic duties to perform that served to establish the smooth transfer of inheritance. For example, it was the duty of the eldest son to make his parents' funeral arrangements. In a papyrus dated to year 39 of the Pharaoh Amenemhat III, from Lahun, a man tells his son that, in return for his support, he will secure a position for him in the temple administration. On the other hand, a deed of conveyance was issued by the lady of the house Nutnakht, who planned to disinherit her children because they had failed to take good care of her.

In modern times, it is not expected that children die before their parents. Unless they are faced with the demise of a close relative, the young nowadays do not often contemplate death. By contrast, in ancient Egypt people were reminded daily of their mortality. The historian Herodotus of Halicarnassus writing in the fifth century BC tells us that at feasts the Egyptians would pass round a mummyform statue to remind themselves to enjoy life – a custom reflected now in the biblically derived saying 'eat, drink and be merry, for tomorrow – who knows?' In the ancient world, young and old philosophised about the end of their existence. In Papyrus Anastasi, a man laments, 'No one returns from death from the grave to tell us how the dead behave or what they lack, in order to calm our spirits at the moment when we shall follow them.' A funerary stele in the British Museum carries this wonderful description of death:

> The West is a land of dreams and deep shadows, the resting place of those that are there. They sleep in swathing bandages and wake but to see their brothers. No more do they see their fathers or mothers, and their heart remembers not their wife and their children.

Apart from practical considerations – for example what type of tomb and funerary equipment they would need in the next life – the ancient Egyptians also needed to prepare themselves spiritually. Their trial in the Hall of Judgement clearly addressed the deceased's moral conduct in life. In the instruction of Merikare it is said, 'Do not believe that all will be forgotten on the day of judgement, and put not your trust in the length of years. The gods regard life as but an hour.' He continues, 'He that shall come without sin before the judges of the dead, he shall be there as a god, and will walk in freedom with the lords of eternity.' Parallels to this type of spiritual rhetoric can be found in many of today's religious texts.

Although religious texts can provide us with images, guidance and myths that describe the afterlife and its regulations in vivid detail, there is only one extant account of a living person conversing with the dead. An individual visits the underworld and then returns to the living. The story is based around a prince, Khamwase [Fig. 11], the fourth son of one of Egypt's greatest kings, Ramesses II. In life, Khamwase was an extraordinary figure. He was High Priest of Ptah at Memphis, a revered scribe and honoured as a sage who took a great interest in Egypt's past. Indeed, he is sometimes viewed as the first Egyptian archaeologist

Fig. 11: Statue of Khamwase, son of Ramesses II.
(British Museum/Photograph: Bridget McDermott)

because of his excavations and restorations of funerary temples and cemeteries in the north of the country. There he explored the magnificent underground tombs of the Apis Bulls at Saqqara and perhaps made his own tomb in the Serapeum.

In these morality tales, Khamwase, now known as Setne, has many adventures. One such relates how he learns about a book of magic written by the god of wisdom, Thoth. However, the book is kept in the tomb of Naneferkaptah at Memphis. After a long search Khamwase broke into the tomb and found the book; he converses and plays board games with the spirits of the dead tomb owner and his wife, who warn him of the perils of stealing the tome. The text deals with the subject of theft from the dead, a theme that had great relevance because it was written during a period when tomb robbery was rife. After stealing the book, Khamwase is bewitched – he is blinded by his love for a woman who goes on to murder his children. Horrified and restored to his senses, Khamwase returns the book to the dead. Indebted to Naneferkaptah for teaching him this lesson, he decides to find the resting place of his wife and son, and then has the whole family interred together. Another story tells how, after glimpsing the burial of a rich man, Khamwase finds himself at the funeral of a peasant, and falls into a deep sadness because the man has no mourners. He is taken to the underworld where, upon entering the fifth hall, 'Setne saw the blessed dead standing in their ranks. Those who had been accused of crimes were pleading and weeping at the entrance.' In the sixth hall Setne sees the gods of the tribunal and all the occupants of the underworld. He also witnesses 'the mysterious image of Osiris, the great god, sitting on a gold throne and wearing the "atef" crown. Anubis on the left, and the great god Thoth on the right, while the gods of judgement and all those of the underworld were beside him. The balance was in the centre, and they weighed the good deeds against evil deeds. Then Setne saw a rich man clothed in a garment of royal linen, standing where Osiris was.' It is a moral tale, for Setne learns that the man dressed in royal linen was the same who was interred in a pauper's grave, while the rich man, mourned by many, was among the individuals crying at the door.

FATE

The ancient Egyptians believed that the lifespan of an individual was preordained. Although the gods were thought responsible for mysterious diseases and deaths they were also seen as intermediaries, who, in special cases, acted on behalf of the living to sustain and protect human life. People believed in fate and prophesy. In several texts we see the gods arriving at the birth of royal children where they aid the delivery of the babe and decree their fate. Often the deities appear in the form of goddesses known as the Seven Hathors. In the ancient Egyptian fairy-tale 'The Doomed Prince', the Seven Hathors announce that the royal son will die by the 'crocodile, snake or the dog'. Morality also played a part. The seer Ptah Hotep says 'long lived is the man whose rule of conduct is in accordance with Maat [both a goddess and the principle of truth and justice] – but the covetous has no tomb.'

The Egyptians had a particular fear of foreigners and especially of dying abroad. The Insinger papyrus has a section that deals with the danger of dwelling in foreign lands.

> The ungodly man who goes abroad places himself in the hands of the enemy.
> He who dies far from his town is buried only out of duty.
>
> He who loves wrongful roaming is one who gets lawful punishment.
> The crocodiles make their meals from fools who love roaming.
> Such is the way of life of people who travel abroad.

The Story of Sinuhe deals in similar themes. Here an Egyptian refugee ponders his fate and wishes that he could return home:

> Whichever god decreed these events, have pity and bring me home. Let me see the place of my heart. What is more important than that my body be buried in the land of my birth.

In this story Sinuhe is offered the following advice. 'You shall not die abroad! Foreigners will not bury you. You will not be wrapped in goatskin to act as your coffin. Too long in a foreign land. Consider your corpse – come home!'

THE BURIAL SITE

In later periods, wills stipulated that a good burial must be provided for the deceased. It is clear that ancient Egyptians felt a deep psychological need to secure a burial site, to become familiar with it and to assure themselves that the necessary rituals and prayers would be conducted on their behalf once they were dead. Hordedef, an Egyptian wiseman, says 'Embelish your house in the necropolis, and furnish your place in the west.' The importance of family at a time of burial cannot be overestimated; the resonant images of the mourning wife and the rites of inheritance appear with notable frequency in Egyptian myth. In his earthly life, a wealthy man would go to considerable trouble to secure himself a fine burial. As we have seen, these preparations are often encouraged in the wisdom texts of the period. An ancient scribe writes, 'Do not go forth without knowing where you will rest. Let every place you love be

known, so you may be buried. Do it! Decorate your place in the valley, the burial place that will conceal your body. Make it important to you, as it is to the great ancestors who slumber in their tombs.'

Why, then, was a correct burial deemed so necessary? When a person died in ancient Egypt they believed they would enter the underworld or the beyond where their hearts would be judged by the gods. If they were found to be wanting, they would face a 'second' death, being devoured by a demon-headed monster. This concept of the 'second death' haunted the ancient Egyptians. It could occur for any of several reasons – if, for example, their name was forgotten, their sustenance denied or the funerary equipment destroyed. This explains why, as they resided in their houses of eternity, the dead required provisions, furnishings and the everyday equipment that they had used during their mortal life. The deceased also needed family members and lector priests to provide these food offerings and recite prayers for them. In this way the dead depended on the

living and a symbiotic if uneasy relationship between the two realms was cemented. Without their ties to the living the dead were doomed. Furthermore, the Egyptians feared that if their mummies or statuary – the living image of the deceased – were to be damaged, their spirit would cease to live. This concept is dealt with in the Coffin Texts where spells 'for not dying a second time' are placed in the tomb with the dead. The Egyptians had many views on the nature of the beyond; in such texts we see reflected a deep-rooted fear of death, seen not as a continuation of life, but as an apocalyptic image of destruction and decay. Death was an everlasting sleep, a life lost in the shadows; the absence of sunlight was an intolerable state.

The living were responsible for the preservation of the tomb and the upkeep of the funerary cults. The people of Thebes had close contact with their dead, and celebrated annually the festival of the dead when they visited the burial places of their families [Fig. 12]. Here they listened to musicians and feasted. The songs of the harpers were charged with emotion – they reminded the family of the joyous nature of life and reveal a deep affection for the dead.

Fig. 12: Behind the Ramesseum on the west bank of Thebes. The western necropolis, the burial site of kings, nobility and commoners can be seen in the background along with the temple of Hatshepsut and the 'pyramid' mountain that guards the Valley of the Kings. (Photograph: Bridget McDermott)

A generation passes, another remains
Since the time of the ancestors
The gods who came before us, rest in their tombs
Blessed nobles sleep in their tombs
Yet those who established the tombs are gone —
What has become of them?

the song ends

none comes from there [the underworld]
To tell of it
To calm our hearts
Until we follow, going where they have gone.

What exactly did the ancient Egyptians believe would happen to them when they died? Although some pessimistic literature deals with death as an eternal darkness most texts focus on a more optimistic ending. Having successfully passed through the Hall of Judgement the deceased would reach the field of reeds where there is an area known as the 't3 dsr' (pronounced char jeser) which was entered by a door protected by guards. Only the gods were able to open and close the ways. Here, the world of the living mirrored that of the dead, although everything seemed more elaborate – the river was wider, the crops taller and the food more abundant. People married, had sex, waged wars and committed crimes.

THE SOUL, SPIRIT AND SHADOW

The Ka was regarded as a restless spirit that was linked to the physical body. During the Old Kingdom the Ka belonged to the pharaoh alone. By the New Kingdom period the populace had developed a personal concept of the Ka and it was thought that in death, one 'went to their Ka'. The Ka, which is shown as a symbol of two upstretched arms, needed sustenance and had a strong connection to the funerary cult of the deceased. Food, drink and offerings were brought to special chapels that were dedicated to it.

From the 1st Dynasty onwards, Egyptian rulers had equipped their nobles with luxurious tombs that were arranged in rows around their own. During the Old Kingdom, the builder of the Great Pyramid, Khufu (Cheops), allotted his family and courtiers tombs that were arranged in streets and blocks around the Great Pyramid. Known as mastabas, these tombs were rectangular in plan and were designed with a burial shaft that descended deep into the rock. At the

Fig. 13: A Ka statue of King Hor. The hieroglyphic symbol for the Ka, the image of two raised arms, is carved upon his head. The statue was found at the 13th-Dynasty mortuary complex of Amenemhat III at Dahshur. *(Egyptian Museum, Cairo/Photograph: Bridget McDermott)*

bottom of the shaft there was a burial chamber. The mastaba was equipped with a funerary chapel that was designed to serve the Ka, the spirit of the deceased [Fig. 13]. It was here that people left offerings to the dead and magical formulae were evoked. Tomb scenes are finely rendered and the Old Kingdom is often regarded by scholars as the classical period of Egyptian art. The tomb walls are decorated with three major themes. The first shows the tomb owner viewing his estate – scribes are engaged in recording taxes and the servants of the Ka present utensils and funerary meals. Animals and birds are commonly depicted, agriculture being another dominant theme. The third theme often depicts the deceased before a mass of offerings or seated at a funerary meal.

In the latter part of the 4th Dynasty, funerary architecture encompassed fine rock-cut chapels that provided greater space – scenes from daily life became more elaborate and included boating parties, the cutting of statues and the hunting of game. The most important part of each chapel was a door for the Ka (a 'false door') carved into the wall of the tomb, through which the Ka could enter and leave. It was at this door that the priests, the servants of the Ka, left their daily offerings for the sustenance of the deceased. The Ka door, usually a deep niche in the stone chamber, was surmounted by an architrave, a massive wooden bar that supported the masonry above. The owner is often shown in this area, seated at a table layered with food that included an abundance of meat, onions, chicken and vegetables. In many of the chapels that date to the reign of Chephren, the builder of the second Giza pyramid, the architects designed two doors, that served the Ka both of the deceased husband and of his wife.

The Egyptians believed in several spiritual bodies. They believed that the Ba [Fig 14 and 46f], the divine nature, had a separate existence after death. The Ba could see, hear and speak. It could take several forms – for example, the Ba could be depicted as an animal with the hybrid features of a god. Therefore a crocodile might appear as the Ba of the reptilian god, Sobek. A person's Ba was the 'vital' element of the deceased, and it could be animated through imagery found in the tomb. The Coffin Texts present the dead as having lived in a symbiotic relationship with their Ba. The Ba could accompany the deceased when travelling. While the body remained earthbound, the Ba became a free, mobile element – it was able to travel through the walls of tombs and fly in the guise of a human-headed bird. The Instruction to Merikare describes it thus:

> the Ba comes to the place it knows
> It does not miss its former life
> no magic restrains it
> it welcomes those who give it water.

Fig. 14: A painting from the tomb of Irunefer dating to the 19th Dynasty accompanies Spell 92 from the Book of the Dead. It is entitled 'Spell to open the tomb for the Ba and shadow of (N) so that he may come out in the day and have power over both legs'. The shadow of the deceased can be seen within the door frame of his tomb, the Ba is shown twice – both leaving and returning to the tomb. *(Drawing: Bridget McDermott)*

In life, people identified with their Ba as if it had a separate intelligence. It could even persuade its higher self to make wiser decisions. In times of trauma, the Ba could leave the body. In a Middle Kingdom story the fugitive Sinuhe is brought into the presence of the pharaoh: 'My Ba was gone, my limbs shook, my heart had left my body, I knew not life from death.' Scrutiny of texts in which the Ba appears gives us the sense that it was often thought of as part of the psyche of its owner rather than an aspect of the soul. Its importance to the survival of the physical body after death cannot be overestimated. Spell 89 of the Book of the Dead, 'A Spell for Letting a Ba Rejoin its Corpse in the Realm of the Dead' was intended to be recited over the amulet of a human-headed Ba bird which had been laid on the breast of the mummy. It is said of the amulet, 'May it see my corpse and be placed on my mummy which will never be destroyed or perish.'

The Akh, shown as a crested ibis, is often described as a ghost or spirit. The Akh was activated by a special ritual 'to make one become akh' which was conducted by a priest called an Akh Seeker (Skhenakh). The Akh is also associated with the concept of 'effectiveness', namely the active force of an individual. For example, a king who traditionally builds monuments in the name of his father was said to be 'doing what is akh-effective'. Other spiritual elements are also described in ancient Egyptian texts but we know very little of their meaning. Some texts mention the Sahu, describing it as an imperishable spirit body that dwelt in the heavens and was associated with the mummy and the physical body. Others briefly describe the Sekhem, considered to be the life-force of a person when he or she dwelt in heaven with the Akh. In many primitive cultures the human shadow is regarded as a reflection of the soul or ego, a 'vital' force that often assumes a separate intelligence from its source. In ancient Egypt it was believed that the shadow could either help or hinder its owner, or could be violated or lost at death. In Egypt a portrait was believed to be highly charged, likewise the shadow, which was thought to encapsulate the darker side of the soul. The shadow moved freely and could enter the underworld and animate the dead. The Egyptians depicted it as an ostrich feather fan or a human silhouette. In Spell 92 of the Book of the Dead, entitled 'A Spell for Opening the Tomb to the Deceased's Soul and Shade so that He May Go Out into the Day and Have Power in His Legs', a man prays that the gods do not curb his shadow saying, 'Oh you aids of Osiris – do not restrain my soul or hold back my shadow'.

For the people of ancient Egypt, whether high born or lowly, the spirits of life and death were very real. They required constant service and duty from mortals in order to ensure not only their good offices for the living but also to maintain the latters' well-being in the afterlife.

TWO

Mortality in Ancient Egypt

Year 30, third month of the Inundation, day seven, the god ascended to the horizon. The King of Upper and Lower Egypt, Sehetepibre, ascended to heaven and united with the sun disk, the divine form yoking with its maker. The residence was silent, hearts grieved, the doors were closed, the courtiers were head on knee, and the people wailed.

Description of the death of King Amenemhat I, from the Story of Sinuhe

Take the king to the sky so that he may not die on earth among men.

A Spell from the Pyramid Texts

DEATH OF THE KING

The death of the king [Fig. 15] was a disastrous and dangerous event for the ancient Egyptians. The king was a symbol of continuity and order, an upholder of 'maat' the principle of chaos conquered [Fig. 16]. The smooth transition of power between the king and his heir was essential to maintain stability and for this reason many kings established a co-regency with their eldest sons in order to safeguard their inheritance. While ancient Egyptian history does offer some examples of women who took the title of Pharaoh, the most famous being the New Kingdom ruler Hatshepsut, for convenience, we will refer to the king as a man.

During the very Early Periods of ancient Egyptian history there is some evidence to suggest that important members of the king's circle were buried with him when he died. They were either buried alive in large earthen pits dug around the king's tomb or were poisoned, the features of these incarcerated individuals indicating that they died as a result of suffocation.

The seventy days between death and burial when the king's body dwelt in the house of mummification was a dangerous time, for Egypt was bereft of a ruler and a living god. The burial rites of an Egyptian king were not only conducted to aid the spirit of the deceased but were also carefully designed to legitimise the transfer of power from the dead Pharaoh to his heir.

Fig. 15: Ramesses II immortalised in stone. His prolific legacy, preserved in the form of countless monuments throughout Egypt and beyond, is testament to the Egyptian ideals of immortality and the preservation of the king's name for eternity. Broken statue from Luxor Temple. *(Photograph: Bridget McDermott)*

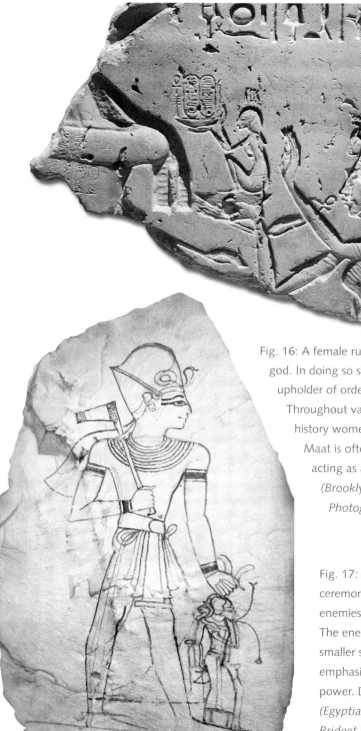

Fig. 16: A female ruler offers Maat to the sun god. In doing so she presents herself as the upholder of order in the land of Egypt. Throughout various periods of Egyptian history women took the role of pharaoh. Maat is often shown in her physical form acting as a symbol of truth and justice. *(Brooklyn Museum, New York/ Photograph: Bridget McDermott)*

Fig. 17: A Ramesside king in full ceremonial dress about to smite his enemies, whom he grasps by the hair. The enemy are always shown on a smaller scale than the king in order to emphasise his physical might and royal power. Drawing on a stone fragment. *(Egyptian Museum, Cairo/Photograph: Bridget McDermott)*

The Egyptian king was divine. He was always depicted on a larger scale than his subjects and enemies, his stature on a par with representations of the gods [Fig. 17]. His titles, too, reflect his relationship with the gods. The epithet 'Son of Re' attests to the role of the king as the son of the sun and 'the Divine Horus', the living manifestation of god on earth, his divine birth highlighted in scenes that show the union between the god Amun and the king's mother. Not only was the king born of the divine but he also served the gods in the temple and on the battlefield. He acted as a bridge between the gods and the populace and each would become dysfunctional without his intermediary acts. Some rulers such as Amenhotep III and Ramesses II proclaimed their divine status while seated on their earthly thrones, for they are shown making offerings to themselves as gods. At Abu Simbel the statue of the deified Ramesses II is constructed to the same scale as those of the deities Ptah, Re Horakhty and Amun. They sit side by side as equals [Fig. 18].

At death, the Egyptian rulers adopted a new role. They left behind their earthly one as 'the living Horus' and, as children of the gods, adopted divine status in the underworld. In the afterlife the king was identified with Osiris [Fig. 19] or Re, ruling the dead rather than the living [Fig. 20], his rule was carefully recorded in the ancient Egyptian king lists and he became part of the great ancestor cult. In his mortuary complex he is shown as a mummy with Osiride insignia, namely the crook and the flail.

Fig. 18: At Abu Simbel the southern temple of Ramesses II, the king is shown on a monumental scale. Although the small figures at his feet depict his chief wife and queen of Egypt Nefertari, the figure of Re (centre) is shown on an equal level to the king. *(Photograph: Jason Semmens)*

The king was also assimilated with the sun god Re. His tomb became a symbol of the solar energy and his earthly transcendence brought continuity and order to the land.

SUICIDE

How did the Egyptians react to suicide? Sadly, there is no clear-cut answer. Suicide, prevalent in every culture, was certainly known to them. Indeed, in extreme circumstances ritual suicide was practised. When a member of the elite

Fig. 19: Osiris, principal god of the underworld, seated on his throne. His name is spelt in hieroglyphics to his right. Fragment. *(Egyptian Museum, Cairo/Photograph: Bridget McDermott)*

was found to have committed a serious crime against the king they were not executed but allowed to drink poison. Clearly, the Egyptians were aware of final acts of desperation. The Admonitions of Ipuwer, a text dated to the 12th Dynasty, highlights psychological despair: 'Look crocodiles will feast on the catch, people will go to them of their own free will.' Suicidal connotations also appear in Middle Kingdom literature. In the 'Dispute Between a Man and his Ba' (Papyrus Berlin 3024), a discontented man tells of his longing for death. He laments, 'Death is before me today, like a man longing to see home.' As he considers suicide, his Ba threatens to desert him, an act that would mean eternal damnation for his soul. Terrified at this prospect, the man is brought into a dialogue with his Ba who successfully reasons with him. The text ends with an agreement between the two to embrace life. The Ba tells him that death will come at its natural time and says, 'I shall be with you when you are weary, and then we shall dwell together.' Scholars see the text as a philosophical treatise that mirrors many of our modern complaints. After all, how many of us can fail to relate to this man, who is bewildered by a world that has fallen into madness and moral decline.

DISEASE AND THE ENVIRONMENT

We know very little about ancient Egyptian mortality rates, and are unable to establish exact data regarding this subject. However, it is clear that there was a wide discrepancy between the mortality rates of the upper classes of Egyptian society and those of the peasants, who were considered to have reached a good age if they died at forty years, while members of the upper classes were clearly

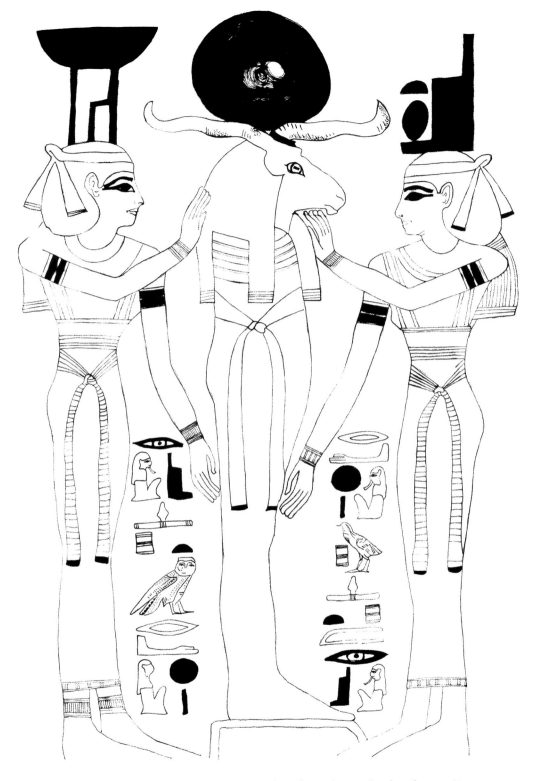

Fig. 20: Re being embraced by Isis and Nepthys, from the tomb of Nefertari. *(Drawing: Bridget McDermott)*

expected to live longer. Some of the latter are known to have reached advanced ages, albeit the achievement was rare enough to be noteworthy. Ramesses II, the New Kingdom ruler, is known to have been in his eighties when he died and to have survived many of his children. Mortality rates were high because the Egyptians were not only susceptible to various diseases, but also frequently succumbed to death in childbirth or from environmental hazards. The Egyptians were familiar with various types of disease, the most common of which took the form of parasites that burrowed into the body when a person bathed or paddled in the river. The climate was conducive to the spread of disease as was the abundance of insects and flies which would transfer bacteria from faeces and rubbish to humans. Eye infections were common and the Egyptians often suffered from trachoma which inevitably led to blindness. While mosquitoes spread malaria and sand affected the lungs and teeth, lice were a common irritant. Arteriosclerosis, a hardening of the arteries, occurred among many of the upper classes who enjoyed rich diets. While the Egyptians suffered from the highly contagious tuberculosis they were also familiar with

Fig. 21: A 5th-Dynasty fragment found at Saqqara showing emaciated individuals. *(Musée de Louvre, Paris/Photograph: Bridget McDermott)*

poliomyelitis, tumours and rheumatoid arthritis. Leprosy, which can be dated to
the Egyptian Ptolemaic Period, was probably known in Egypt even earlier.
Dental disease was common. For example, the grains of sand that inevitably
found their way into their bread caused catastrophic dental disease. However,
the people who lived along the Nile had a nutritious diet, eating vegetables,
grain and fish.

Despite its beauty the environment was harsh, and tending the land was often
dangerous. Snakes, the most despised of creatures, posed a constant threat. The
Egyptians were also heavily reliant on the annual flood of the river. Times of
drought are described in the ancient prophesies that say 'Dry is the river of
Egypt. One must cross the river on foot; one looks for water to sail on, its course
having turned into the shore.' At such times the Egyptians suffered terrible
famines. Their texts reveal how fear of hunger played on the Egyptian psyche for
the famine theme occurs in several pessimistic texts. An Old Kingdom fragment
shows emaciated figures that seem to be suffering from starvation [Fig. 21]
while the Famine Stele describes a period of seven years of hunger. One text,
dated to the Ptolemaic Period, may have been based on actual events. Here
Hapy, the river god, had 'failed to arrive'.

> During seven years – grain was not
> There was no food
> Every man robbed his brother
> Children wept, they fell
> The hearts of the old were weeping
> They fell to the ground – their legs drawn under them
> Their arms clasped them
> Nobles were wanting, the temples were closed
> Shrines were covered in dust
> Everyone was in distress.

The Nile attracted hoards of people. Among their numbers were fishermen
who worked from boats of papyrus and laundrymen who washed clothes on the
river banks. The Egyptians were plagued by two dangerous animals which
inhabited the river, the crocodile and the hippopotamus. Both were responsible
for many deaths in ancient Egypt. The crocodile is an expert hunter and can
silently approach a riverbank without being observed. It leaps suddenly from
the depths, grasping its victim and rolling it through the water until it drowns.
In the Satire of the Trades, a text designed to recruit young men as scribes, the

Fig.22: The wooden Meserheti Model showing a troupe of soldiers armed with archery equipment. *(Egyptian Museum, Cairo/Photograph: Bridget McDermott)*

author tells of a hidden menace to manual work – of the laundryman he hints, 'the washerman washes beside the river – with the crocodile as neighbour!'

Special attributes were accorded those who died in the river, some of whom are shown in the ninth hour of the Book of Gates, drifting restlessly through the primeval waters. In the Book of the Netherworld, the drowned reached the shores of the beyond directly from the Nile, and had a strong association with the god of the dead Osiris.

DEATH ON THE BATTLEFIELD

During the Old Kingdom the ancient Egyptians had established a fine array of weapons, many designed specifically to counteract those of their enemy. On the battlefield, Egyptian soldiers used staves and archery equipment [Fig. 22] as well as spears and short daggers. Although little is known of the injuries sustained during conflict, artistic representations show graphic scenes of carnage where decapitation, chest and head wounds are common. During the Middle Kingdom when the Egyptians experienced a long period of civil disturbance, we have a clearer picture of the types of wounds incurred by soldiers as a result of work on a group of mummies known as the soldiers of Mentuhotpe that were found at the site of Deir el Bahri in modern-day Luxor. Examinations of the bodies reveal a great deal about the nature of Egyptian warfare. It seems that these soldiers died after being trapped on the field – they had been assaulted with missiles and arrows that had been propelled from a precipice above their heads. Many of the soldiers lay dying on the ground while the army was forced to retreat. The enemy then plundered the field and finished off the dying with bludgeons [Fig. 23]. The bodies had been attacked by carrion birds [Fig. 24].

Fig. 23: The soldiers in this typical military scene dated to Middle Kingdom are being finished off with bludgeons and javelins. *(Drawing: Bridget McDermott)*

Fig. 24: The Battlefield Palette. Carrion birds and a lion feed on the enemy that were left strewn over the battlefield. *(Drawing: Bridget McDermott)*

Fig. 25: Nubians with their typically heavy features and thick gold rings in their ears. The traditional enemies of Egypt, the Libyans, Asiatics and Nubians, were all depicted with stylised features making them easily identifiable. Fragment. *(Brooklyn Museum, New York/Photograph: Bridget McDermott)*

While arrow tips had become entangled in the soldiers' hair, arrows had pierced their arms, ribs and necks. Stone missiles had crushed their skulls. When the comrades of the soldiers had returned to collect their bodies, they wrapped them in a coating of sand which they stuffed into the wounds and head cavities. The sand dried the flesh of the soldiers. Although there were no signs of embalming, the features, hair, nails and tendons were perfectly preserved. The men were wrapped in linen bandages while still on the battlefield; several layers of sheet linen had been placed on each body. They were transported back to Egypt on carts or chariots.

Dating from the New Kingdom the Egyptians have left an abundance of military imagery that depicts their traditional enemies, namely, the Libyans, Asiatics and Nubians in various perilous circumstances [Fig. 25]. The Egyptians were always portrayed as the victors on the battlefield and their soldiers were rarely shown in danger. One remarkable exception is a scene that dates to the Amarna Period depicting an Egyptian soldier being garrotted by an enemy soldier as his comrades rush to his rescue [Fig. 26]. Images of physical contact were also rare, although hand-to-hand combat is often represented; the Egyptians preferred to depict the enemy as a carpet of dead bodies being trampled beneath the king's chariot. The carnage that would be left on ancient battlefields is almost too horrific to imagine. It is little wonder that Egyptian soldiers wore feathers in their hair – the feather was not just a symbol of archery, but of the vulture goddess Nekhbet, whom, for obvious reasons, the warrior sought to appease. Literature that relates to warfare avoids reference to the soldier in battle, and his vulnerability is rarely portrayed. Doctors travelled with the army to attend the sick and wounded and some of the remedies they

Fig. 26: An Egyptian soldier in danger, a rare scene. From the military Amarna Papyrus. *(British Museum/Photograph: Bridget McDermott)*

prescribed are found in ancient medical papyri, many of which deal with skull injuries and arrow wounds. Appropriately in this context in particular, the hieroglyphic sign for doctor, 'swnw', is determined by an arrow.

There were dangers for the military other than warfare. Although soldiers had many minor complaints, the most common being foot problems, living in large camps could have serious consequences. Diseases could spread quickly among groups of men living in close proximity in isolated conditions. Although many fatal wounds were incurred upon the field, mainly from staves and sword wounds, the enemies of the ancient Egyptians used barbed arrowheads that became embedded in the flesh – their removal must have caused great pain. Moreover, these minor injuries were likely to fester and subsequent infection could lead to fever and death. Although the condition of the mummies of the Soldiers of Mentuhotpe is often considered exceptional, it is highly likely that the Egyptians would have taken every opportunity to remove the dead and wounded and bring them back to Egypt whenever possible. Not only did they abhor the concept of dying abroad but also the inevitable desecration of the corpse filled them with revulsion – carrion birds are able to strip a human carcass within four hours of death.

EXECUTION

In the Middle Kingdom magical text the Three Tales of Wonder the magician Djedi decided to demonstrate a feat of magic to the king by attempting to replace the head of a decapitated animal. The king suggests that they should bring 'a prisoner from the prison that he may be executed' to which Djedi replies in horror: 'it is not permitted to do something of this kind to one of the noble cattle [the populace].'

Despite this instance of a moral stance the Egyptians were fond of executions. The earliest Egyptian images reveal ritual execution in the form of throat cutting [Fig. 27]. On the small fragment illustrated in Fig. 27 we see a man seated and bound, before him an individual who slashes him with a knife. A pot was placed on the ground to collect the victim's blood. History shows that during the early growth of a civilisation, ritual acts of extreme violence and even cannibalism were common. In Egypt, incidents of mass sacrifice quickly faded, however, themes of violence are evident in the Pyramid Texts where the dead king is encouraged to consume the bodies of his enemies in order to conquer or absorb their power.

The image of a king smiting his enemies in acts of ritual execution is the most iconographic in ancient Egyptian art. The image first appears during the Predynastic Period on a wall in Tomb 100 at Hierakonpolis. Armed with a mace, a priestly figure raises his weapon above the skulls of a group of bound prisoners. Several thousand years later, this image was still being employed by Ramesses II [Figs 110 and 28]. Ramesses the Great chose prime locations on his many magnificent temples to sensationalise this iconic representation of an all-powerful king. He stands astride the enemy, their hair clenched in his fist, and in his raised hand he holds one of the three classic weapons of war, the mace, the poleaxe or the sword. Although when depicting military scenes the ancient Egyptians avoid reference to contact, they nevertheless allow the viewer to

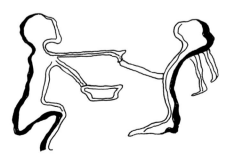

Fig. 27: Ritual execution from the Archaic Period. This label from the reign of Djer was found at the tomb of Hemeka, Saqqara. *(Drawing: Bridget McDermott)*

Fig. 28: An Egyptian pharaoh smiting the enemy. Rendered in the traditional manner in temple scenes, he clasps either axe, sword or mace and stands over his enemy whom he grasps by the hair. He holds the weapon above their heads in a theatrical display of dominance and power. The king would have been expected to execute his enemy in such a gruesome ritual spectacle. Ramesside block from Memphis. *(Egyptian Museum, Cairo/Photograph: Bridget McDermott)*

experience the full drama – a breathless moment before the might of pharaoh's arm falls upon the damned. We see the enemy, weakened by terror, on bended knee. Often the prisoner raises his hand in order to deflect the blow or appeal for mercy. Sometimes he looks over his shoulder, at us the viewer, pleading for his salvation.

The image is repeated on the walls of every temple the length and breadth of Egypt [Fig. 28]. It also appears on commemorative stelae and can be seen carved into the cliffs that border conquered territory. Ritual execution was not just an idle threat. The king was expected to make a public show of executing his enemy – it not only allowed him to flex his royal muscles but also enabled him to honour the gods who gave him victory. The New Kingdom pharaoh Amenhotep II is notorious for his cruelty. While it is likely that his policies were no different from those of his predecessors, Amenhotep II did not scruple to record his accomplishments with unprecedented relish. As the hour of Amenhotep's accession to the throne drew near, the court gathered to watch the ceremonial enthronement of the king. The sun was shining and it was a magnificent day. As Amenhotep settled himself on the throne the rebel leaders of the enemies of Egypt were brought into the arena where the king, as a sign of his newly assumed power, made a spectacle of personally beheading them. Later, Amenhotep would record the tough military campaigns he led into Asia. After the battles he would make examples of the enemy by burning large groups of them alive. After one gruelling campaign he returned to Thebes on his ship – all along the river the populace gathered to catch a glimpse of his majesty. On the prow of the ship he had hung the inverted bodies of the seven sons of the Asiatic ruler whom he had slain with his own hand. Later he would have some of them hung from the walls of the Theban temples while other of their corpses were despatched south to be displayed in Nubia. Although his policies were no different from those of the British, who hung the body parts of rebels like William Wallace on the walls of York and Westminster, Amenhotep is still viewed by Egyptologists as the 'bad boy' of his time.

During the reign of Ramesses III there was a disturbance at the royal palace that is now known as the 'Harem Conspiracy'. Records show that a Queen of Ramesses III, Tiy, began to plot to put her son on the throne of Egypt. It seems that the old king was dying and she had to move quickly. She engaged the help of royal officials along with high ranking army officers, all of whom had access to the king. She also sought the aid of magicians and had a number of wax effigies fashioned in the likeness of her enemies. Imbued with magic they were ceremonially destroyed. Fortunately for Ramesses III, she was no magician. Somehow the plot was discovered. The protagonists were arrested along with the queen and Ramesses ordered a trial. Records of the trial are highly detailed; they reveal many aspects of the Egyptian legal system and even list the judges who conducted the examination. Although we may learn various details about crime and punishment in the 20th Dynasty from this document, we know little of what happened to the rebels after they were found guilty. Furthermore, we learn nothing of the fate of the queen. The king was expected to set the punishment after the rebels had been found guilty. It seems that the instigators were even stripped of their names – a terrible fate, as we have seen, since names were essential for the survival of the spirit in the underworld. Furthermore, the criminals were branded with false names – for example, one was addressed as 'Binemwase' which means 'evil in Thebes'. The officers were condemned to exile and mutilation (their noses and ears were severed). Several members of the group, including the six women of the harem, were condemned to death. Those implicated from among the upper ranks of the Egyptian court were allowed to commit suicide.

THE DEATHS OF WOMEN AND INFANTS

The ancient Egyptians had no formal marriage ceremony. The union of men and women was known as 'establishing a house', its main objective to produce legitimate offspring. Traditionally sexuality was represented in very subtle ways, although erotic papyri and models are well known among tomb deposits [Fig. 29]. For all classes an abundance of children was highly desirable. Children provided an extended workforce for the men and women who worked in the fields while among the upper classes a large family was viewed as a symbol of fecundity. The ancient Egyptians took great pleasure in their children – family portraits depict young boys and girls with sweetness and affection [Fig. 10]. While children appear in a rich array of paintings and sculptures the Egyptian kings displayed their progeny on the walls of their temples and tombs. Clearly, childbearing was a highly visible aspect of Egyptian life [Fig. 30]. An ancient instruction text states: 'Take a wife while you are young, that she may make a son for you; she should bear for you while you are young, it is fitting to make people.' While fecundity was celebrated, infertility was regarded as an evil and men were entitled to divorce barren wives. Descriptions of attractive young women included the phrase 'one who has not given birth', i.e. a virgin. With the begetting of children a high priority, wisdom texts gave men instructions on how to treat their wives: 'Sweeten her heart as long as you live; she is a fertile field for her lord.'

It is not surprising that the ancient Egyptians avoided reference to child or infant death in their art and literature and such rare depictions as there are often prove poignant. The subject is touched upon in an ancient wisdom text, when a man named Any is told 'Do not say "I am too young to be taken", for you do not know your own death. When death comes he steals the infant who is in his mother's arms, just as well as he who has reached old age.' The Egyptians also

Fig. 29: A woman engaged in a sexual act. The ancient Egyptians produced various erotic representations in stone and on papyrus. Sculpture dated to the Old Kingdom. *(Brooklyn Museum, New York/Photograph: Bridget McDermott)*

produced medical papyri that dealt with the subject of infant death. In the Ebers Papyrus, the text states that 'if on the day a child is born it says "*ny*" it will live, but if it says "*mebi*" it will die.' An unfavourable diagnosis was also given if the infant's cry reached a certain pitch, or if it continued to hold its head in a downward position. It is clear that the ancient Egyptians viewed pregnancy and childbirth as times of great anxiety, and many texts suggest that Egyptian women went to extensive lengths to safeguard their health and that of their unborn children. Human remains have shown that Egyptian women wore tattoos like a belt around the abdomen as if to protect the contents of their wombs.

Fig. 30: A Ptolemaic queen gives birth to a divine child helped by two forms of the same goddess, Hathor. Fragment from the temple of Dendera. *(Egyptian Museum, Cairo/ Photograph: Bridget McDermott)*

Fig. 31: A mother or wet-nurse helps herself to a bowl of figs while breastfeeding a child. Saite relief from Thebes. *(Brooklyn Museum, New York/Photograph: Bridget McDermott)*

The dangers to the foetus or child were many. The health of the mother, her nutrition and lifestyle were important [Fig. 31]. The life of an Egyptian peasant woman was fraught with difficulties. They ate little meat and there is a strong likelihood that many suffered from anaemia and exhaustion. The Egyptians often married cousins and other close relations – a practice that may well have resulted in genetic abnormalities among their offspring. Diseases and heart defects are probable and hydrocephalus is known. A lack of antenatal care meant infection was common, a factor that may have led to many infant deaths. Haemorrhaging was often noted in gynaecological papyri and vaginal bleeding was associated with miscarriage. A condition known today as placenta preavia, which obstructs the passage of the baby along the birth canal, would in ancient times have resulted in profuse bleeding and certain death. Caesarean sections were unknown in ancient Egypt, so women died in childbirth when the infant's head proved too big to pass through the pelvic girdle. While multiple births were known in Egypt, the successful delivery of twins or triplets was rare. However, the birth of triplets is described in a text known as the Three Tales of Wonder. Ruddedet, a woman of the royal household, was pregnant with triplets fathered by the god Ra. Her children were destined to be the first three kings of the 5th Dynasty, Userkaf, Sahure and Neferkare.

One of those days Ruddedet felt the pains and her labour became difficult. His Majesty of Re, Lord of Sakhbu said to Isis, Nepthys, Meskhenet, Heket and Khum: 'Please go, deliver Ruddedet of the three children who are in her womb.' Isis placed herself before her, Nepthys behind her, Heket hastened the birth. Isis said: 'Don't be so mighty in the womb, you whose name is mighty.' The child slid into her arms, a child of strong bones, his limbs overlaid with gold, his headdress of true lapis lazuli. They washed him, having cut his navel cord, and laid him on a pillow of cloth.

Although some forms of contraception were known, married women conceived regularly. It is generally believed that one in three children died. As women aged they were more likely to miscarry, especially when they had brought numerous pregnancies to term. Repeated pregnancies could result in kidney damage or a prolapsed uterus. The Kahun Papyrus, an ancient Egyptian text that deals with gynaecology and obstetrics, describes injuries to the perineum. A text known as the 'Mother and Child Papyrus' describes 'a lump of faeces as something that has gone into the vagina of his mother'. This condition was probably the result of a fistula between the rectum and vagina. In ancient Egypt this type of rupture probably led to infection and death.

Fig. 32: The traditional image of Hathor, in a large pleated wig, with bovine ears and voluptuous features. She was the patron deity of women, dancing, music and sex. From Hatshepsut's temple at Deir el Bahri, Thebes. *(Photograph: Bridget McDermott)*

Pregnant women took various measures to protect their unborn babies. Jars depicting women in various stages of pregnancy reveal naked figures with sealed genitalia. Tampons inserted into the vaginas of Egyptian fertility figures suggest that pregnant women wore these objects as a safeguard against the loss of their offspring. However, ultimate power over the unborn child rested with the gods. In ancient myth the evil god Set is said to have plotted the death of Horus while the latter was still in the womb. It is clear that women made religious petitions to the gods in order to protect their children. Magic also played an important role at the time of birth. Several gods were believed to attend the birth chamber of a royal child. In birth scenes, the mother is shown kneeling over a layer of bricks; while one goddess holds her upright, another kneels before her to receive the child. Bes, often represented in the form of a dwarf, was sometimes armed with dangerous weapons. Thought to repel evil spirits from mother and child, Bes is often associated with the hippopotamus goddess Taweret, who is commonly shown with a heavily pregnant body. These popular household deities appear with naked women on wall paintings, head-rests and ivory wands. Another popular household goddess was Hathor [Fig. 32], who was regarded as the mistress of music and sexuality and was closely associated with pregnant women. However, her bovine characteristics also connect her to the production of milk and her title, 'Mistress of the Vagina', was indicative of her role in the birth chamber. A group of deities, the Seven Hathors, were believed to predict the fate of a child at the time of its birth.

After babies were born, nutrition was provided by breastfeeding mothers or wet-nurses [Fig. 31]. Babies and young children were particularly vulnerable to infection and parasitic disease. The environment was harsh and contained many hidden dangers. Examinations conducted on the bodies of many ancient Egyptians have shown that parasitic worms passed into the intestines through Nile water. The symptoms of this condition, now known as schistosomiasis or bilharzia, include the passing of blood during urination. It led to anaemia and a loss of resistance to other forms of infection, a condition that left young children very vulnerable. And there were other natural dangers. Snakes and scorpions often found their way into Egyptian homes. While adults could recover from bites or stings, children playing at ground level would rarely be so fortunate. Adults and children who worked or played by the river were often injured or killed by hippopotami or crocodiles and references to this type of danger often appear in ancient writings. In the Westcar Papyrus, a youth finds his sister in peril. 'He said to her, "What is the matter?" Then she told him. Her brother said to her, "Is this a thing to do, to come to me so as to involve me in your tattle." He tore off a stand of flax and dealt her a blow. Off went the maid to draw a bucket of water, and a crocodile snatched her.'

Magical papyri provide a great deal of evidence about the esoteric methods used by the ancient Egyptians to prevent injury to unborn children. Several cases suggest that prayers were recited over the children or written on papyri and then put into cylindrical amulets that were placed around their necks. An inscription housed in the British Museum states:

> A spell for protecting the limbs
> to be spoken over a babe when the sun rises
> Rise, Re, Rise
> Have you seen the dead who has come for her
> N [name] born of N [name]
> to place a spell upon her
> devising stratagems to steal her son from her embrace
> 'May you save me, my lord Re'
> so says N, born of N
> 'I shall not give your charge
> to any male or female thief from the West –
> My hand is upon her, my seal is your protection',
> so says Re as he rises.
> Come forth! This is my protection.

Magical wands or knives made of ivory or clay were decorated with demons and inscribed with protective prayers. These objects were laid upon pregnant women or newly born children. The ancient Egyptians also placed various protective amulets in the hair of their babies.

There are very few literary or artistic references to the death of children in ancient Egypt. While living children were painted on the walls of temples and tombs in elaborate displays of family life, all indications of early death were omitted. However, dating from the 18th Dynasty a unique scene, found in the tomb of Akhenaten at El-Amarna, has come to light that shows the death of a princess in childbirth. Moreover, examinations undertaken during the excavation of ancient Egyptian cemeteries reveal a large percentage of infant burials. During the Early Periods of ancient Egyptian history infants were placed in pots that were buried under the floor of the house. Royal or upper-class children were buried in elaborate family tombs and were embalmed in the traditional way, being mummified and placed in a series of anthropoid coffins. In 1922 Howard

Carter excavated the tomb of Tutankhamun in the Valley of the Kings at Thebes. In the antechamber of the tomb he found a box which he labelled No. 317. The contents included two foetuses. The bodies had been wrapped with linen bandages and placed in shrouds. They were enclosed within two anthropoid coffins the outer parts of which had been painted and labelled with the name of the god Osiris, a designation used during the New Kingdom to describe the deceased. The remains of the first child revealed evidence of embalming. Carter left the body unwrapped, its face covered by a gilded death mask. The second child, believed to be female, measured 91.6 centimetres. She was examined and thought to be of seven months gestation. The eyes remained open and there were traces of hair on the scalp. The embalming process was still visible, indicating that the skull had been packed with linen which had been inserted through the nose. Lower down, there was a small incision above the groin, through which the embalmers had pushed linen strips into the abdominal cavity. Later examinations have suggested that the child suffered from a condition known as Sprengel's Deformity.

Child mummies are relatively rare [Fig. 33]. However, the body of a child was discovered in the tomb of Tuthmosis IV where it had been left, propped up against the wall in a side room. It is thought to have been that of the king's daughter Tentamun. The tomb of Princess Tia, sister of Ramesses II, contained seventy-five mummies and many of the bodies, dated to the New Kingdom, were of children some of whom had been mummified and placed in coffins. The mummy of a child was found in the tomb of Amenhotep II in the Valley of the Kings. Thought to be that of a close relation of Tuthankhamun, the mummy is

Fig. 33: A child mummy found by the explorer d'Anastasi.
The child is a young boy from the Late Period.
(© Rijksmuseum van Oudheden, Leiden)

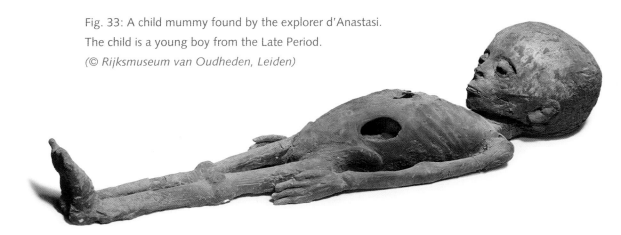

Fig. 34: Mummy of an unknown child from KV 35. The boy still wears the side lock of youth which indicates his young age. *(A photograph from* The Royal Mummies, *G. Elliot Smith. Reproduced: Bridget McDermott)*

remarkably well preserved and still bears the long side-lock associated with pictorial images of Egyptian youths. The boy was about nine or ten when he died [Fig. 34]. His hair had been shaved from most parts of the scalp. Plunderers had damaged the mummy in antiquity leaving a large gash in the left side of the neck and thorax. When Victor Loret excavated the tomb he said of the discovery:

> The second mummy, in the middle, was that of a child of about fifteen years. It was naked with hands joined on the abdomen. First of all the head appeared totally bald, but on closer examination one saw that the head had been shaved except in an area on the right temple from which grew a magnificent tress of black hair. This was the coiffure of the royal princes [called the Horus lock]. I thought immediately of the royal prince Webensennu, this so far unknown son of Amenophis II whose funerary statue I had noticed in the great hall, and whose canopic fragments I was to find later. The face of the young prince was laughing and mischievous, it did not at all evoke the idea of death.

GHOSTS AND MORTALS

The Egyptians were fascinated with the dead. The noble Nenoferaptah, believed to have lived during the time of Ramesses the Great, was said to have wandered around the Memphite necropolis reading aloud from the tomb inscriptions of the pharaohs and the stelae of his officials. The living could be haunted by vile apparitions but they also sent letters to the dead in order to solicit help from the beyond. In this excerpt a man asks help from his wife from beyond the grave and in return promises to embellish her tomb. 'How are you?' he asks. 'Are the dead taking care of you as you would like? I am your earthly beloved, please fight for me, act for my name.' He continues, 'Drive off the illness in my limbs. May you appear as a blessed one for me that I might see you fighting for me in a dream. Then I shall lay down offerings for you in the morning, and I shall erect an altar for you.'

The dead could also be seen as vicious and vindictive. They could appear in evil dreams and cause mayhem among the living as ghostly apparitions. The deceased could be addressed by the living who would ask them to petition or intercede with the gods on behalf of the sick. For their part, the dead would leave curses as a type of insurance against the living. For example the Egyptians often reveal negative views of the officials they employed to keep the funerary cult of their relatives; for those who breached their trust there were dire consequences. It was said: 'their wives shall be raped before their eyes; they shall not hear the words of the king when he is joyful. But if they keep good guard over the funerary foundation, may they enjoy all good. Amun Re, king of the gods, shall favour you with many days.'

In ancient stories the dead and the living were able to communicate. In the Setne Cycle, the hero Khamwase breaks into an ancient tomb to recover a book of magic. He is confronted by the ghosts of the tomb owner Prince Naneferaptah and his wife Ahwere. Ahwere reveals the history of the book, which contains spells that had been written by the god of wisdom, Thoth. A priest of Ptah told Naneferaptah that the book was hidden in a series of chests that lay at the bottom of the Nile near Koptos. Naneferaptah went to Koptos with his family. He made a magic boat and sailed to the place where the book had been submerged. The journey was difficult and he had to navigate $9\frac{1}{2}$km of serpents and scorpions before he could retrieve the book from the innermost chest. Naneferaptah shared his knowledge of the contents of the book with his wife. The first spell enabled them to enchant every creature on earth. The second spell gave them the power to see the true nature of the gods and learn all the mysteries of the underworld. In essence, they learnt all the secrets of magic. Thoth was angry at the theft of his magic and he sent an envoy to kill Naneferaptah's wife and child. After this, Naneferaptah committed suicide and was buried with the book of Thoth. The spirits of Naneferaptah's family try to warn Setne against stealing the book by recounting their terrifying story, but he ignores them. After he steals the book, the ghost of Naneferaptah sends a vile hallucination which forces Setne to return the forbidden book to its resting place in the tomb.

Death is also addressed in mystical stories and ancient fairy tales. In the story 'The Shipwrecked Sailor' the hero is washed up on the shore of a strange island that is inhabited by a snake. The creature tells him, 'It is god who had made you live, and brought you to this island of the Ka,' meaning that it is fate that has brought him to this spirit island. The snake then tells him of a tragic event that happened in that place: 'I shall tell you of something similar that happened on this island. I was here with my brother and there were children among us. We were seventy-five snakes, children and brothers, not including a little daughter whom I had begotten through prayer. Then a star fell, and they went up in flames through it. It happened that I was absent in the fire, I could have died when I saw them as a pile of corpses.' Finally, in the New Kingdom fairy tale 'The Doomed Prince' a child is given three fates at his birth. The Three Hathors announce that 'he will die by the crocodile, snake or dog'. In order to forestall the predicted tragedy, as a child, the prince's doting parents locked him in a house of stone and he was not allowed to go out. As he reached adulthood he begged his father for the freedom to face his fate. The young man must have prevailed over his parents, for the tale relates how he travelled to distant places where he met and fell in love with a princess who, in an example of a narrative parallel, had been locked in a tower. The story tells of the demonic forces of his fates who constantly try to devour him. Unfortunately, we do not know what happened to the doomed prince, for the ending of the story is lost.

THREE

Death and the Gods

Hail, great god, lord of the two truths,
I have come to see your beauty
I know you, I know your name.

The Book of the Dead, Chapter 125

FUNERARY GODS AND CREATION MYTHS

The ancient Egyptians had creation myths, many of which related to their funerary gods. Atum, the self-created primeval deity of Heliopolis emerged at the beginning of time and created the first gods – every living creature was therefore a fragment of his being. Connected with Re, Atum was an integral part of the sun god in his aged form when he set each evening and began his journey through the underworld and it is in this capacity that he appears frequently in mortuary literature. He is often depicted as an aged ram-headed figure in the New Kingdom royal tombs. In an ancient text, the god Re [Fig. 20] asserted that he came into being before the first moment of creation; at the end of the world he would 'recede into the chaos from which he had once sprung'. This concept of primeval chaos and watery realms has strong parallels in the teachings of Zen Buddhism, which explore similar ideas of being and non-being. The god Ptah [Fig. 35], patron of crafts, was said to have

Fig. 35: Ptah, often identified by his distinctive skull cap, carrying a staff that bears interlocking symbols: the Djed Pillar, the symbol of stability and the ankh, the symbol of life. *(Tutankhamun Collection, Egyptian Museum, Cairo/Photograph: Bridget McDermott)*

Fig. 36: The king presents his conquered enemies to the seated god Amun. Scene from Karnak Temple, Luxor. *(Photograph: Jason Semmens)*

been the one who 'gave birth to the gods' while Amun [Fig. 36], who came to prominence during the New Kingdom, was said to have 'begot the gods and men'. In yet another myth, the world was said to have been created through the tears of the sun god, while Khum fashioned people (and their Kas) on his potter's wheel. In her mortuary temple at Deir el Bahri, Khum is shown crafting the female pharaoh Hatshepsut in this fashion. As myths evolved over the centuries, the Egyptians retained important elements of their archaic beliefs and they were subsequently absorbed into evolving doctrines that are often complex and contradictory.

As for men, women and the animal world the creation of most Egyptian gods was attributed to a higher force. The gods too were subject to a hierarchy that had power over their fate. Thoth, the god of wisdom, was said to 'calculate the lifetime of the gods and men'. It is clear, then, that the Egyptian gods shared much of the human condition – they could wage war, become ill and die. Although the gods bestowed favour on those who worshipped them, once maligned they could unleash their anger on the mortal world, hence in some wisdom texts it is said that the people of Egypt were given magic as a weapon against the gods.

Most faiths employ symbols of resurrection and rejuvenation – in pagan communities the most popular deities are the corn gods who were annually cut down and reborn. The ancient Egyptians also worshipped these principles in the form of Osiris [Fig. 19]. In Egyptian myth Osiris was murdered by his jealous brother Seth and his body cut into pieces and thrown into the Nile. It was his sister-wife Isis who by her magic assembled the pieces and brought the body back to life. She is often shown hovering over the phallus of Osiris in the form of a kite. Their son Horus [Fig. 37] was conceived in this divine union between the living and the resurrected dead. While Horus became the embodiment of the earthly king, Osiris dwelt in the underworld and was worshipped as the god of the dead. Osiris was originally a fertility deity. His cult spread throughout Egypt and into him were absorbed the identities of existing grain gods such as Andjety and Khentimentu. He is sometimes described as the pavilion of the gods, a title that refers to the place of embalming. Like many fertility gods throughout history he symbolises victory over decay. He even goes on to judge the dead – and in this capacity he is known as lord of the living.

The Apis Bull [Fig. 107] was regarded as a manifestation of the soul of Osiris. Re, too, was deeply woven into his myth, and while Re retained a separate identity he is also inextricably linked to Osiris. In stories of the solar journey through the underworld Re unites with Osiris, who is, in effect, his own corpse. Egyptian myth is complicated, to say the least! Osiris has many funerary symbols. He is associated with the corpse and its mummy wrappings; he is sometimes depicted as an anthropoid mummy case or a Djed Pillar with human arms. Frequently he is represented accompanied by the tiny figures of the four sons of Horus who are shown on a table in front of him. Sometimes he lies on a bier, mourned by Isis and Nepthys. As the combined Re-Osiris he is depicted as a mummy with the head of a falcon, ram or beetle.

The people of Egypt were regarded as the 'cattle of god' or 'the divine herd' and the gods had absolute power over their fate. Fate was regarded as the time allotted to an individual at the time of his or her birth. However, the Egyptians could petition their gods for extra time on earth – in the story 'The Shipwrecked Sailor', the main character begs for 'fifty years over my fate'. Further, humans could become assimilated with the gods of the underworld. The brothers Peteese and Pihor were deified and worshipped in Dendur, near Aswan in the south of Egypt. During the Late Period they were venerated as the drowned ones and were associated with Osiris. In death the Egyptians called themselves 'the Osiris' and their tomb equipment included corn trays designed in his image. The trays were planted with seeds – their growth, however, went unseen by mortal eyes. Examples of such trays, exhibited in the Egyptian Museum, Cairo, have an eerie quality. They remind us of the hidden forces that operate behind the sealed doors of the tomb. Many gods were associated with Osiris, or were seen as an 'aspect' of his form. Neper, the grain god, is one such deity, the Coffin Texts describing him as 'living, even after his death'.

Gradually, tales of the gods were absorbed into more complicated and detailed myths and some deities were furnished with tombs at holy sites in Egypt. Gradually, too, they became humanised. In this way, they became vulnerable, and developed human weaknesses. Although some gods could age, become injured and die, some high-ranking deities such as Atum and Osiris remained imperishable. In the Coffin Texts the god Atum told Osiris that only the two of them would survive when the world reverted to the primeval ocean from which everything had come. The Egyptians believed that the world would founder – and the gods looked ahead to an 'end of time'. Tragically, in the Book of the Dead, Osiris acknowledges that at the end of time he would be imprisoned alone in eternal darkness.

In the Pyramid Texts the souls of Nekhen and Pe mourn the death of Osiris. After the murder of Osiris they urge Horus to take revenge on his uncle Seth. One can almost feel their despair as they 'come to Osiris at the sound of the mourning cries of Isis and her sister Nepthys. The souls of Pe clash sticks for you, they smite their flesh for you, they clap their hands for you, they say – "Come, wake from sleep, your life is everlasting!"' In the Book of the Dead there is an amazing testimony to the god Osiris in the form of Spell 154 'A Spell for not Letting the Corpse Perish': 'Hail to you Osiris. You who have your body. You will not be destroyed, you will not be infested with worms, you will not decay, you will not stink or putrefy.' This spell had a practical purpose, to ward off decay so that the deceased would become as Osiris. The petitioner goes on to utter the rest of the spell: 'I am Khepri, I will have my body forever. I will not be destroyed, I will not putrefy, I will not become worms. I exist. I am alive. I am strong and at peace. I have not decayed, my viscera are intact. There are no wounds, my eyes are safe, my skull is unbroken, my ears function and my head is attached to my neck. My tongue has not been removed, my hair is uncut, my

Fig. 37: Horus, the embodiment of the living pharaoh, and the son of Isis and Osiris. Statue from his temple at Edfu. *(Photograph: Bridget McDermott)*

eyebrows remain. My corpse is forever, it will not perish or be killed in this land forever.'

There were also many minor funerary deities in ancient Egypt that reveal archetypal features. In various religions the dead are rowed to the beyond. The best known of these myths is that of the Roman ferryman Charon who conveys his charges across the River Styx into Hades. This belief still flourishes far to the north, in Jutland, Denmark where fishermen even now wear coins in their ears: if they drown at sea, they can pay for their passage to the next world. The ancient Egyptians, too, had a ferryman. He was known as Her-ef, Har-ef, which means literally 'he whose face is behind him'. He is portrayed as a strange, solitary creature standing or sitting in his boat. Often he is shown being hailed by the deceased. Sometimes his head is depicted back to front. The Pyramid Texts relate how he ferries the deceased king across the shifting waterway to the field of offerings. In Utterance 481 of the Pyramid Texts the deceased summons the ferryman: 'O Her-ef, Ha-ef, ferry me across. The boat of the sky is set in place, that I may cross in it to Re in the horizon.' He continues, 'I cross in order that I may stand on the east part of the sky among the imperishable stars, who stand at their staffs and crouch at the east. I will be among them, for the moon is my brother, the morning star is my child. Put your hand on me in order that I may live.' In Utterance 270 of the Pyramid Texts it is the king who summons the ferryman:

> Awake, peace, you of the reversed face
> You who look backwards,
> The ferryman, Nut's ferryman
> Ferryman of gods,
> Unas has come that you may ferry him
> In this boat in which you ferry the gods.

Earth deities are also a universal phenomenon, of which the god Geb is an early Egyptian example. He is known as one of the children of Atum. Collectively they are the Ennead, who represent sky, moisture and earth. Geb personifies the grave. In the Pyramid Texts the king will not 'enter' into Geb [Fig. 38] nor will he sleep within his house. In this way, the king refuses to die and will be reborn. Other gods are linked to timelessness. The deity Heh embodies infinity. He is shown grasping a notched palm branch of the type that was used to note time or keep records in the temples. The sign was used to denote the sum of 1,000 in ancient Egyptian hieroglyphics. The palm also

Fig. 38: The separation of earth and sky is shown in mythological representations. The body of the sky goddess Nut is shown stretched across the heavens while her husband, the earth deity Geb, lies prone on the ground. The god of air, Shu, separates the couple after Nut swallowed the constellations and Geb became enraged at her 'devouring' of their children. Shu acts with oustretched arms to keep both elements eternally divided. *(Drawing: Bridget McDermott)*

became the symbol for the word 'year'. Female counterparts of this god exist. Renpet, a goddess who personified the duration of a year, was also recognised by a notched palm branch. There is a further category of gods; these are difficult to define and appear as essences rather than as substantial beings. Nun embodies the primeval waters which existed before the beginning of time. He was the father of the gods, being a hidden cavern or abyss where stillborn babies and condemned souls reside.

In ancient Egypt dogs or jackals were well-known graveyard scavengers so it is not surprising that the major funerary deity of ancient Egypt was depicted with canine features. This god, Anubis [Fig. 94], became a major deity of the Egyptian pantheon and the ruling god of the 17th Nome of Egypt. He was also worshipped at many shrines and chapels in the ancient Egyptian temples. Depicted with a long, prominent snout and pointed ears, Anubis's many epithets include 'he who is upon his sacred mountain' for Anubis is often shown on the edge of the mountain that overlooks the Valley of the Dead. His body is painted black, the colour of decay, and his eyes and ears are shown alerted to intruders. He is also called 'foremost of westerners' which means that he ruled the dead, and 'he who is in the place of embalming' which indicates his role as the mortician who attended the body of Osiris. As we shall see later, the chief embalmer was always closely associated with the cult of Anubis and was compelled to wear an awesome jackal mask as he conducted rituals upon the dead. In ancient representations Anubis conducts the ceremony of the opening of the mouth on the mummy of the deceased. He also plays an important role in the scenes that show the weighing of the heart in the Hall of Judgement.

FUNERARY GODDESSES

Hathor [Fig. 39] is one of Egypt's most ancient goddesses, her image appearing on predynastic objects that pre-date the pyramids. Women related to Hathor, the goddess of sexuality, and hoped to meet her on their journey to the west.

Fig. 39: The goddess Hathor, in her role as a bovine goddess, acts as protector for the young Ramesses II. 19th Dynasty fragment. *(Musée de Louvre Collection, Paris/Photograph: Bridget McDermott)*

Hathor took many forms. Sometimes she was a tree goddess, known as the mistress of the sycamore, who supplied food and drink to the deceased. She was also the Lady of the West, who welcomed the dead, offering them purifying water. Although Hathor was worshipped as a cattle goddess she also came to be associated with the excesses of life – drinking and dancing were celebrated in her name. However, like most Egyptian deities she had her darker aspects; she was often represented as the 'Lady of the Red Cloth', the mistress of blood.

Isis [Fig. 20] is the best-known female deity of the ancient Egyptian pantheon. In funerary texts she is said to protect the deceased along with their mourning relatives. She was also thought to have a special affinity with sick children and to use magic to aid their recovery. Together with her sister Nepthys [Fig. 20], she constitutes the archetypal image of the Egyptian mourner. Both women are shown as kites. Kites, as birds of prey, were known for their bitter and haunting call – a sound associated with the cries of grief-stricken women. Kites are also associated with carrion, and may have become connected to Isis in her role as healer when she wandered and scavenged the entire land of Egypt looking for the severed parts of her husband's body. Isis safeguarded the dead in the underworld. In Egyptian mythology she also used her magic to defend the gods. She is shown holding the ankh sign towards the nostrils of the dead – in so doing she offers them the breath of life. While Isis is often depicted as a mourning woman with one hand lifted to her face, she is also shown with enormous wings which she spreads protectively around the statue or coffin of the deceased.

Although Nepthys, the sister of Isis, was the wife of Seth she was also con-nected to Osiris and bore him a child. According to myth, Nepthys aided her sister Isis in searching for the lost body parts of Osiris, and in this role she assumes the same protective features that are connected to her sister. She became one of the four guardians of the canopic jars, vessels that contain the viscera of the dead. Like Isis, she is often depicted as a kite on sarcophagi, coffins and shrines [Fig. 20]. In funerary scenes Nepthys is placed at the head of the mummy, while Isis appears at the feet. Neith was an ancient warrior goddess who was identified by the sign of a pair of crossed arrows; in her role as a funerary goddess she is asso-ciated with mortuary rituals. She is often shown with her sisters, Isis, Nepthys and Serket at the four corners of the royal coffins protecting the dead [Figs. 40a and b]. In the underworld Neith is also a judge of the dead. She was said to be the inventor of weaving, and became closely associated with the bandages and shrouds that were placed around mummies. Tayet was also a goddess of weaving and was said to gather together the bones of the dead and to have woven the outer panels of the tent of purification in which the embalmers worked.

Fig. 40 *Right and below:* A gold statue of the goddess Selket, one of the four goddesses who guard the corners of the canopic chest of Tutankhamun. *(Tutankhamun Collection, Egyptian Museum, Cairo/Photograph: Bridget McDermott)*

Nut is shown stretched between the earth and sky [Fig. 38]. While her hands and feet are earthbound, her body arches through the stars. She is, perhaps, the most beautiful of the mythical figures of ancient Egypt. Nut is the embodiment of the heavenly expanse, and here she symbolises regeneration. Within her body, the dead become stars. Nut had a profound significance for the ancient Egyptians and became inextricably linked with caskets and sarcophagi. She is often painted on the lids of coffins. In this position, lying above the deceased, she is believed to have obtained 'unification' with the dead. Despite her sexual nature she also served as a reminder to the deceased. Looking up, it was believed that the deceased would merge with her celestial body as the spirit hungered for the stars. In the resurrection spells found among the Pyramid Texts (616) these words were addressed to the deceased: 'Nepthys has gathered your members in her name of Lady of the Builders, she had made them work for you, you having been given to your mother Nut in her name of "Sarcophagus". She has embraced you in her name of "Coffin", and you have been brought to her in her name of "Tomb".'

In the Book of the Dead, Nut, like Hathor, appears in the trunk of a sycamore offering water and nourishment to the recently deceased. Several goddesses were associated with the sycamore tree, which symbolised shade and respite. The tree is often shown with arms while the hands were heavy with offerings. The trees are also depicted with breasts which, as symbols of rebirth, were offered up to the dead.

The gods and goddesses of ancient Egypt moved between the worlds of the living and the dead and played an essential role in mediating between these two realms; each deity was imbued with a myth or emblem that could help the ancient Egyptians (the majority of whom were illiterate) understand the subtle moral codes, roles and answers they would need during the hazardous journey to the world beyond.

FOUR

Funerary Literature

Unas comes, an indestructible spirit like a morning star above the river.
Pyramid Texts, Spell 217

THE PYRAMID TEXTS

The earliest excerpts of funerary literature are known as the Pyramid Texts. They first appear carved on the walls of the pyramid of Unas, a ruler of the 5th Dynasty, and were subsequently used by his successors. They were designed to ensure the welfare of the dead king, nourish his star cult and promote the necessary daily rituals required in the tomb. Some scholars have pointed out the rhythmic feel one gets when reading the spells aloud. It is now thought that the Pyramid Texts were designed for this purpose. Further, it has been suggested that the spells correspond to the architectural design of the pyramid. They describe the descent of the soul before it rises to its new life. Old Kingdom pyramids were built with sloping corridors; one must first descend into the structure before meeting a corridor that rises and leads up to the burial chamber. The entrance to the pyramid faced the northern pole of the heavens allowing the king access to the circumpolar stars. These stars remained above the horizon and were deeply significant to the ancient Egyptians for they were a symbol of eternity. An abundance of celestial imagery was used in the Pyramid Texts and the night sky became closely associated with the regeneration of the king's body.

At this period in Egyptian history, there was little reference to personal survival of the soul of the individual after death. For this, the deceased was entirely dependent on the king for it was only through working for the survival of his soul that the individual could be saved. Therefore the correct funerary rituals and provisions were of the utmost importance with regard to the burial of a pharaoh. The Pyramid Texts are a series of funerary and magical spells designed to aid the king in the afterlife – they are at once violent and profoundly beautiful. The text comprises a series of speeches addressed by the king to the gods. Each spell deals with a specific theme, for example the survival of the king's body, his ascension and his requirements for food and prayers. There are vivid descriptions of the king uniting with the sun god, being ferried over the horizon or becoming a star. The Pyramid Texts make many references to the devouring or consuming of emblems of power – a whole section of spells are known as the 'Cannibal Texts':

> Unas [the Pharaoh] is the bull of heaven
> Rage is in his heart
> He feeds on all the gods.
> He eats their entrails
> For their bodies are full of magic
> From the island of Flame.

> Unas is he who eats men, and feeds on the gods,
> Lord of messengers who sends instruction.
> It is Horn-Grasper in Kehu who ropes them for Unas
> It is the Snake Raised-Head who guards them for him,
> It is the One on the Reeds who binds them.
> It is Khons, slayer of men, who cuts their throats for Unas,
> Who tears their entrails out for him.
> He is the one sent to punish.
> It is Shemu who carves them up for Unas
> And cooks them in his dinner pot.
> Unas eats magic, swallows their spirits.
> The big ones are for his morning meal,
> The middle one for his evening meal,
> The little ones for his night meal,
> The oldest males and females for his fuel.
> The Great ones in the northern sky light the fire
> The pots are filled with the thighs of the old ones
> The sky dwellers serve Unas
> And the pots are scraped with the women's legs.

The Cannibal Texts describe how the ruler devours the crown of Lower Egypt to gain dominion over his territory – he also devours the flesh of the gods, enabling him to harness their power.

Fig. 41: In the fifth hour in the Amduat, a pyramid of sand emerges in the underworld. Beneath it is the cave of Sokar, which is full of light to promote the regeneration of the sun. Khepri, the scarab beetle seen at the top of the scene, then pushes the sun through the gates of the horizon. Scene from the tomb of Tuthmosis III. *(Photograph: Jason Semmens)*

Resurrection is also a pervasive theme. In Resurrection Text 723 it says:

O king raise yourself upon your iron bones and golden limbs, for this body of yours belongs to a god; it will not grow mouldy, it will not be destroyed, it will not putrefy. The warmth which is in your mouth is the breath which is issued from the nostrils of Seth, and the winds of the sky will be destroyed if the warmth which is in your mouth be destroyed; the sky will be deprived of its stars if the warmth which is in your mouth be lacking. May your flesh be born to life, and may your life be more than the life of the stars where they live.

Although the Pyramid Texts are confined to the Old Kingdom period, they clearly influenced later funerary literature, namely the Coffin Texts, the Book of the Dead and the Book of Breathings.

The Coffin Texts first appear on coffins of the Middle Kingdom and their content shows clear influence from the Pyramid Texts. In certain sections of the Coffin Texts the dead speak of their lives in the underworld.

> Lord of light, creator of light who fills the sky with his beauty. I am he. I take his name. Make a way for me so that I may see Nun and Amun. For I am the Akh [ghost] who can pass beyond the guardians. They do not speak for fear of the one who is hidden [Amun] who is in my body. I know him. I will not fail to address him. It is fitting that I should open his door. As for any person who knows this spell, he will be like Re in the eastern sky, like Osiris in the underworld. He will pass through the fire and the flames will not touch him.
>
> Spell from the Coffin Texts

In the Coffin Texts the underworld is plunged into a 'painful' darkness. The descent of the sun brought a time of uncertainty and fear. In this place, everything seems larger than life, the roads stretch for eternity, and the expanse of the gates seems immeasurable. The Egyptians believed that the sun travelled unaccountable lengths throughout his underworld journey, and that this was a place of confusion where directions could be reversed and there were no straight lines. To the Egyptians, who were so partial to order, this seemed a nightmare world, where people had to walk on their heads or travel backwards.

Another important funerary text, and a variation of the Coffin Texts, is known as the Book of Two Ways. It first appears on coffins of the 12th Dynasty and it provided a map of the hereafter, highlighting routes that were both good and evil. Most funerary texts deal with the complex and bewildering scenes of the Egyptian underworld. The landscape of the afterlife, once understood, is a microcosmic model of the Egyptian afterlife. In essence, it is a blueprint of religious aspiration and primeval fear. If one could learn to interpret the images and texts that describe these realms, they would afford an unparalleled opportunity to penetrate the more obvious, outer layers of the ancient Egyptian psyche. The underworld is presented as a psychedelic panorama of strange landscapes, rivers and deserts. The changeling sun god is forced to become a snake so that he can navigate the hot sand of the underworld and enter the dangerous cave of Sokar. He must pass lakes of fire, evade thunder and tempest, brave the place that is shrouded in silence and make his passage through the caverns of darkness. In essence, it is the story of the heroic challenge, a myth that has its counterpart in most cultures. In some stories it is the fate of a maiden or a tribe that rests upon the shoulders of the challenged hero. In Egypt, the hero Re must perish in the depth in order to be reborn [Fig. 41]. The fate of mankind – both the living and the dead – rests on the triumph of the sun. For deep into the darkest hours of the night, the sun god must regenerate; his spirit must unite with his corpse so that the souls of the blessed dead may live again.

These myths also appear in the Amduat, a text that was first used by the New Kingdom king Tuthmosis I. The Amduat, divided into twelve nocturnal sections, describes the realms of the dead and its text is augmented by vivid imagery. It details the complete journey of the sun as it disappears beneath the horizon. Each hour represents a different phase of the sun's progression through the underworld. There are detailed accounts of the strange territories of the twilight hours. The zigzag pathways of the Sokar desert are revealed in the fourth and fifth hours of the night while the final hour leads us to the very edge of the netherworld which curves into a broad cartouche. Egyptian architects and tomb builders were influenced by these stories. They based the axial principles of the royal tombs in the Valley of the Kings on the jagged paths described in the Amduat, while some funerary chambers and sarcophagi were softly rounded to imitate the oval boundary at the edge of the beyond.

The Book of Gates is similar in content to the Amduat. It first appears during the 18th Dynasty in the tomb of the pharaoh Horemheb. Like the Amduat, the Book of Gates provides twelve divisions for the nightly journey through the underworld. Each section is sealed by a gate which is guarded by a snake that has the power to unbolt the door to permit the passage of the solar barque. Scenes from the Book of Gates are recorded in the tombs of Sety I, Merneptah, Sety II, Ramesses III and IV. They are also depicted at Abydos, where they show Horus as the creator of the human race. Snakes play both dangerous and protective roles in the underworld [Fig. 42].

In the Book of the Dead we catch glimpses of the way the Egyptians viewed heaven. They called this paradise the 'sacred realms' or 'the field of reeds'. However, the Book of the Dead also describes the gates of the beyond which lead to the realm of Osiris. The deceased would be challenged at each gate and on each occasion he or she would have to prove their knowledge of the words of power. At these gates terrible demons stood guard that would devour any who were ignorant of the words. The Book of the Dead, the texts of which have been found in coffins, on papyri and on leather scrolls, consists of a series of magical incantations that are illustrated with images called vignettes. Also inscribed on the

Fig. 42: The coiled snake Mehen protectively circling the king, from an 18th Dynasty funerary shrine. *(Tutankhamun Collection, Egyptian Museum, Cairo/Photograph: Jason Semmens)*

walls of Egyptian tombs, the Book of the Dead is a compilation of almost two hundred spells or chapters. There was a thriving industry in its manufacture and ready-made copies were available to the poor who could purchase individual chapters rather than a whole book. Judging by the numbers, the most popular sections included Chapter 1, 'The Coming Forth by Day after Burial', Chapter 17, 'Coming Forth by Day Triumphant Over All Enemies', and Chapter 64, 'Coming Forth by Day in Various Transformations'. The content of some chapters such as 174, 177 and 178 can be traced directly to the Pyramid Texts. Edited versions of the Book of the Dead were common. Some books are short, comprising only three or four chapters written on narrow pieces of papyrus. Others consist of numerous chapters that form rolls of papyrus several metres long. Although some of the earlier versions of the Book of the Dead were small, the chapters grew and their style evolved, their illustrations becoming richer and more elaborate. Traditionally, the illustrations were placed at the top of the text, but important images might fill a whole page. The inscriptions on the papyri were written in hieroglyphics with reed pens dipped in black and red pigment. Once it was dry the copy was rolled up and tied with linen. It was then sealed with mud and placed in or on the coffin. Sometimes, the papyri were stored in a wooden statue of Ptah Sokar Osiris or placed on a plinth in which the statue stood. Some were put on, or inserted into the mummy bandages.

Another funerary text, that known as the Litany of Re, was first introduced at the beginning of the New Kingdom. It consists of seventy-five sections that deal with prayers to the sun god and describes the dark and fearful elements of the underworld. As the deceased passes through the first gate of the underworld he enters a vast landscape that extends for 193km. The environment mirrors that of the Nile Valley. While it provides vivid descriptions of the realms of the dead, the Litany of Re's focus is on the spirit of the dead king and his

Fig. 43: Two lions representing the dual aspect of the sun god Re, being addressed as yesterday and tomorrow. Between them is the sun on the horizon decorated with an ankh, the symbol of eternity. Scene from the funerary sledge of Khonsu, from the tomb of Sennedjem, 18th Dynasty Thebes. *(Photograph: Jason Semmens)*

relationship to Re the sun god [Fig. 43]. Egyptian myths are explored in detail. For example, we are told how the goddess of the west transforms the ageing sun god into the form of a child; in this way, Re is reborn each morning. These solar journeys are illustrated on the magnificent ceilings of the late Ramesside tombs where a naked goddess swallows the sun in the evening and gives birth to him at dawn. The god is shown as a human child emerging from the womb of Nut or rising from the primeval waters. A striking sculpture from the tomb of Tutankhamun best illustrates this poignant moment of rebirth by showing the king's head emerging from a thicket of lotus flowers.

Although the majority of the ancient Egyptian population were unable to read, most chose to be buried with these books. The text's esoteric role is clearly defined in the context of a royal burial, however their function in the tombs of women and peasants, the majority of whom are thought to have been illiterate, is more complex. Here the presence of the texts must have acted as a talisman that served in a magical rather than practical sense. Whether the texts from the papyrus were learnt or memorised by the individual during their lifetime is a matter of academic debate, but for students of Egyptology these texts are invaluable in that they enhance our understanding of how the Egyptians viewed the underworld by revealing much of their complex religious ideology.

JUDGEMENT OF THE DEAD

Earthly justice continued in the world beyond. The most famous representation of the Judgement of the Dead appears in Chapter 125 of the Book of the Dead, where the heart of the deceased is weighed against his deeds. Attending the ceremony is Anubis, the god of embalming, and Maat, the goddess of truth and justice. Osiris is witness to the proceedings which are judged by a tribunal of forty-two judges. Here the deceased must vindicate himself before the gods:

> Hail, gods who dwell in the house of Maat
> I know you, I know your names.
> Let me not fall under your slaughter knives
> And do not bring my evil ways to Osiris, the god you serve.
> Let no evil come to me from you,
> Declare me righteous in the presence of Osiris
> Because I have done what is right and true in Egypt.
> I have not spoken evil of the gods
> I have not suffered evil through the king who ruled my day.

As the heart is weighed on a scale, it is accompanied by a hybrid monster with the head and jaw of a crocodile, a creature that will devour the petitioner if he fails to pass the test. The successful candidate was known as 'one who has been vindicated' and becomes Osiris. The deceased could then join the souls of the dead on their solar journey through the underworld; until this point, the dead are represented as mummies. In scenes that show the return of the sun and the triumph of death, light floods the dark chambers in which they sleep and they are depicted casting off their bandages. As the spirit or Akh is freed, the dead appear to dance with joy.

A JOURNEY THROUGH THE UNDERWORLD

As the deceased entered the underworld and successfully passed through the Hall of Judgement he or she joined the ranks of the blessed dead on their nocturnal barque sailing through the twelve hours of night [Fig. 44]. At the end of the 18th Dynasty a revised version of this journey appears in the Book of Gates, with the sun entering each hour of the night through a portal guarded by spitting serpents. Each hour has a name that had to be uttered by the dead. The first hour is known as the 'Smiter of the Heads of the Enemies of Re'. This section describes how the sun god and his crew of blessed dead encounter a company of baboons. These creatures, associated with the god of wisdom Thoth and known for making vociferous greetings by shrieking as the sun appeared above the horizon were considered as harbingers of the successful rising of the sun. Baboons were also said to 'make music for Re when he enters the underworld at the evening time'. It is for this reason that images of baboons are painted on the walls of Egyptian tombs.

The second hour is known as 'the Intuitive One Who Guards Her Lord'. During this hour the sun god sails through the fields of reeds accompanied by four sacred boats, one of which bears the moon. During the third hour, 'She Who Cuts the Ba', the sun rests in the fields before moving downriver to find himself on desert land where the boat must turn into a snake in order to journey down narrow channels until it reaches the 'cavern of Sokar'. In the fourth hour, 'Mighty is Her Strength', the sun god follows the desert path called 'the Mysterious Channels that Anubis Entered to Hide the Body of Osiris'. The fifth hour of night is known as 'the Guide Who Is in Her Boat', while the sixth is described as the 'Watery Depths of Those Who Dwell in the Underworld'. This last is the dwelling place of the king's royal ancestors and their servants. At this point, the entire populace is waiting to be reborn through the triumph of the

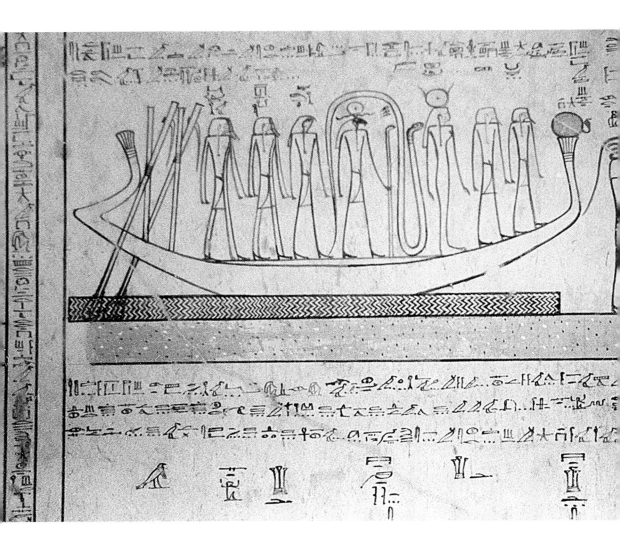

sun, which is depicted with a coiled snake, a universal symbol of eternity. In the seventh hour the king does battle and annihilates his demons in the form of Aapep; this is his moment of triumph, an hour known as 'She Who Turns Back Chaos and Beheads the Savages'. Here the sun god rests and watches the execution of his enemies. This is a metaphorical journey celebrating the eternal cycle of birth, triumph, rest and rebirth – universal symbols that have been used in storytelling from the dawn of time. Here, at the midpoint of his journey, the sun god is challenged by his demons and faces a sacred mystery that was re-enacted in the temples by the king. The Ba of the sun god joins with his inert persona, namely, his corpse. It is a celestial fusion that allows the sun to regenerate, rest and rise – and so another day may dawn and all the blessed dead

Fig. 44: The sun god Re, in the form of a ram-headed deity, in the centre of the solar boat. During the eleventh hour of the Amduat the gods travel on a solar boat through the final phase of the underworld. Scene from the tomb of Tuthmosis III. *(Photograph: Jason Semmens)*

are reborn. However, to arrive at this point the boat must pass through the eighth hour, the 'Treasury of Her Gods', during which the deceased and his fellow dead must navigate a landscape of caves where the most ancient and secret gods reside. Here the sun god rests during the ninth ('Protector of Her Lord'), tenth ('The Powerful One Who Cooks Alive the Rebels') and eleventh hours ('The Learned One of the Sacred Bark Who Emerges to Punish the Rebels'). Many of the events that are described as occurring in the underworld were familiar to the ancient Egyptians in life. The highly ritualised punishment of the damned was practised not just in the underworld but also in the temple. As the sun's journey comes to its end, the procession reaches the twelfth hour, 'Seeing the Perfection of Re', and the rebirth of the sun is complete.

FIVE

Ancient Egyptian Burial

A night is made for you with ointments and wrappings from the hand of Tait. A funeral procession is made for you on the day of burial, the coffin is made of gold, its head of lapis. The sky is above you as you lie on your bier, oxen draw you, the musicians go before you. The dance of the Mu is done before the door of your tomb and the offerings are presented to you. A sacrifice is made at your libation stone.

The Story of Sinuhe

THE ARCHAIC PERIOD

In both Upper and Lower (northern and southern) Egypt the earliest excavated cemeteries date to the Neolithic–Badarian Period. Here the dead were placed in the desert sand – the perfect medium for dehydrating the soft tissues of the body. However, corpses were often exposed in the grave due to the actions of sand storms or scavenging animals and birds. When this happened the Egyptians noted the finely preserved and lifelike features of the disturbed corpse; they would have abhorred the desecration of the grave and would have sought safer ways of burying their loved ones. The need to avoid desecration and maintain the safety of their dead clearly influenced ancient Egyptian burial practices.

During this period, the body, often first dressed in fine linen and jewellery, was wrapped in reed mats in preparation for burial. The dead of the Badarian Period were buried at some distance from the village in egg-shaped graves and while multiple burials have been found, most appear to have been buried in single pits. The grave was several feet deep, and the body was placed in a flexed position on its left side, its head turned westward to view the setting of the sun. Small mounds of stones were placed over the grave. These mounds came to symbolise the original moment of creation when land first emerged from the primeval waters of chaos, hence the image of the mound became an enduring and iconic symbol.

Fig. 45: A typical Old Kingdom mastaba tomb site.
(Photograph: Jason Semmens)

Often the dead were buried with jewellery, combs, cosmetics, pots and carved slate palettes. Excavations have also revealed caches of weapons such as mace, arrowheads and axes. In 1902, Georg Moller excavated an area around Abusir el-Melek where he discovered 900 graves that were dated to the Naqada III phase. The graves consisted of oval and rectangular pits lined with mud brick in which contracted bodies had been placed in coffins of pottery or wood. Many new developments occurred during this phase, the most significant being the erection of the 'grandiose' tomb. The building of elaborate tombs often heralds important new developments in urbanisation and foreign trade. During this period, the Egyptians added a superstructure to their graves. A room, placed above ground, would house the funerary equipment and goods of the deceased, now coming to include Asiatic objects and semi-precious stones. Some of the grave goods provide Egyptologists with important information about early religious practices for they contain amulets fashioned in the shape of animal gods that were worn for magical protection. Fecundity figures were found in the graves of males and females and include small models of naked women lying on beds of clay or stone. Their purpose is still unclear, but as fertility symbols one would expect them to act as magical objects to promote regeneration or rebirth. Pots were commonly found in graves. Their purposes are unclear. They may have been used as everyday domestic utensils, but in Africa pots are often buried with corpses as they were seen to contain the soul. In Egypt they were often decorated with boats and exotic animals. Several scenes that were painted on these objects illustrate hunting and dancing.

THE EARLY DYNASTIC PERIOD

While the lower classes continued to be buried in simple pit graves, the cream of Egyptian society were designing their tombs as 'houses of eternity'. The burial pit was now a residence that was divided into a series of chambers, the central area being used for the interment of the deceased. The roof of the tomb was supported by planks and walls were decorated with mats that imitated the woven reed curtains used in domestic houses. Above ground, the tomb was surrounded by a wall of brick panelling that is often likened to a fortified structure; it was also guarded by an enclosure wall. Boat burials are also dated to this period. The sun god was believed to journey across the sky in a boat and ships were often found as a part of the funerary equipment of the king. Many of the royal tombs of this period were accompanied by subsidiary burials of male and female courtiers and studies of their remains indicate that they were interred at the same time as their king. Their pained expressions and contorted bodies show signs of a violent death. Although scholars have suggested that these servants took doses of poison, it is most likely that they were buried alive. This sacrificial practice – often associated with communities in the early stages of economic and political development – was mercifully brief. In ancient Egypt it is associated only with the early phases of the Archaic Period.

Egypt's early rulers were buried in a series of tombs known as mastabas, 'mastaba' meaning bench [Fig. 45] in Arabic. The word may also refer to the slab of stone that replaced the early rubble mounds on Egyptian graves. During this period the Egyptian economy flourished and their burial customs reflected the growing status of their leaders, acting as elaborate displays of their wealth and power. We have already noted that the earliest burial pits had been little more than mat-lined graves in the desert sand. Now these were replaced by large fortified structures that contained several rooms and subterranean burial chambers. Several mastaba tombs are of particular interest. That of King Hor Aha was surrounded by the graves of young men and lions while that of King Djer, the largest grave of this period, was surrounded by 318 graves of courtiers, relatives and dwarfs. These early kings built their cenotaphs or burial sites at Abydos where they were positioned below an incised mountain cliff that may have symbolised a gateway to the horizon. Their tombs were replica houses constructed with mud-brick superstructures that included twelve or more chambers, incorporating a central burial area and magazines. As time passed, the burial chambers were cut deeper underground. The dead may have been lowered into place from the surface while a wooden shrine was built around the structure. The Egyptians placed large pairs of stelae outside the facade.

By the middle of the 1st Dynasty the tombs had significantly increased in size. Descending stairways led to burial chambers that were now being protected by a great stone portcullis. Crenulated walls, often decorated with cattle horns, were built around the tomb. (The same startling design is used today in the Tandroy tombs of Madagascar, off the east coast of Africa.) The walls became smoother as the Egyptians began to abandon the use of recessed panelling, preferring to construct niches or install false doors at the east end of the tomb. Here the Egyptians built a false entrance where offerings would be placed for the king's Ka. A mud-brick temple was now added to the north side of the tomb. During the 2nd Dynasty these tombs became increasingly impressive, being designed with numerous rooms that served the same functions as those found in upper-class houses of the period. These included washing and toilet facilities and a servants' hall.

The deceased was wrapped in linen and placed in an elaborate sarcophagus which was housed in the burial chamber. Unfortunately, these tombs were heavily plundered in antiquity and we have little information with regard to royal burials of the Archaic Period. However, what evidence there is suggests that the body was laid flexed on its side with the head facing north. The burial chambers were annexed by rooms containing everything the deceased would need in the afterlife – burial goods included clothes, furniture and jewellery. Some rooms were used as storage chambers for grain, meat, wine and bread.

Although smaller by contrast, the tombs of the royal servants were similar in design. Each featured a central chamber, while their funerary equipment, which included tools, models, combs and jewellery, was limited to one or two rooms. The burial chamber consisted of a small oblong pit. Its roof was made of wood and this was covered with a round-topped superstructure. The contracted body was placed in a small wooden coffin. Peasants, by contrast, could not expect grand burials. Their dead were placed in pits in the ground, the body first wrapped in a reed mat and then interred with simple everyday objects such as pots and tools.

OLD KINGDOM BURIAL

During the Old Kingdom the Egyptians appear to have had no concept of personal salvation. However, when the king died it was expected that he would be rewarded with eternal life. It was at this point that he joined the sun god Re on his journey through the heavens in a solar boat [Figs. 53a and b]. The royal descendants and the nobles were dependent on the dead king's favour for the survival of their souls. In life, it had been the king who had provided them with earthly endowments such as a tomb and funerary equipment, and now they sought his favour again, wishing to share in his eternity. In the same way, the people who worked on the king's tomb hoped to acquire their salvation by working in his service. When the land was under flood, the peasants were recruited to build the king's pyramids, and for a time the country was unified in a single purpose. Therefore, during the Old Kingdom, the state controlled an enormous workforce who laboured with a single vision. It is not surprising, then, that the Old Kingdom is often regarded as the unsurpassed and classical period of ancient Egyptian building.

PYRAMIDS

In the Old Kingdom text the Autobiography of Weni we learn of the great expeditions undertaken by soldiers and labourers in order to equip the pyramid with stone. Weni records, 'His majesty assigned me to Ibhat to secure the sarcophagus together with its lid, along with the magnificent pyramidion of the pyramid Merenre-appears-in-splendour. His majesty sent me to Yebu to obtain a granite false door and its libation stone and lintels, to bring granite portals and libation stones for the upper chamber of the pyramid. The party went north to the pyramid in six barges and three pulling boats – a single expedition.' He continues, 'His majesty sent me to Hatnub to find a great altar of alabaster. I brought this altar to him in seventeen days – it too was taken to the pyramid.'

From the Cairo suburbs one catches many strange and distorted glimpses of the Giza pyramids. However, it is at sunrise that they seem most haunting. On winter mornings they appear on the skyline shimmering like dismembered bodies above the rim of the desert. Here their outlines rapidly change from hues of pink to a brilliant indigo blue. It is at times such as these, and viewed from a distance, that their mystery seems most intense. To the populace, living far from the desert, they must have seemed of another world. Moreover, to foreign visitors, the pyramids were a symbol of Egypt's might and in this respect were unprecedented emblems of power. They became, and remained, the architectural symbol of a society that was rapidly expanding its borders, trading with foreigners and defining its military strength. To the ordinary citizen the pyramids were a reminder of continuity; through them, the spirits of their ancestors were united with the circumpolar stars. The Egyptian people placed their faith in the ascension of the king, and in return, they sought salvation.

Over ninety pyramids were built in the north of Egypt, each endowed with a special name that revealed its solar functions. While Egyptologists are accustomed to view these edifices as royal tombs, none of them has yielded sufficient evidence to prove that they were used in this way. Archaeologists believe that the Egyptian pyramids were associated with the Ben-Ben stone at Heliopolis, the cult centre of the sun god Re. The Ben-Ben stone, which was capped with a small pyramidion, was a symbol of rebirth. Capstones found on ancient Egyptian pyramids have also survived. Inscribed with the names of dead kings, some reveal symbols of the sun disk, while others are carved with eyes. These eyes can also be found on Middle Kingdom coffins [Fig. 85] and were designed so that the deceased could look out and survey his domain. Some scholars believe that the pyramids were designed to imitate the rays of the sun, while others see them as ladders by which the king could ascend to the stars, a theory lent substance by a passage in the Pyramid Texts which alludes to the staircase by which the king ascends to heaven.

The practical function of the pyramid was to serve the domestic needs of the king in the afterlife; it was a house that had private chambers, a cult temple and storage magazines. The pyramid also served to reflect the ideology of ancient Egyptian myth – the belief that at the first moment of creation, a mound of earth rose from the primeval waters and acted as a bridge between earth and sky. The image of this mound of creation is still visibly influencing the funerary architecture of the ancient Egyptians during the New Kingdom period. The pyramid performed many functions – it acted as a royal tomb and a cenotaph, and it also served as a working temple employing priests and officials who laboured for the Ka of the king. As a large collection of pyramid complexes were built throughout the Old Kingdom, their construction and maintenance placed an increasingly heavy strain on the country's resources. The huge cost of employing staff and of the general upkeep of the compound is likely to have contributed to the political and economic decline of the Old Kingdom.

ARCHITECTURE

The ancient Egyptian pyramid was just one component of a large funerary complex. It was joined to a mortuary temple which was often situated at the eastern side of the building. The pyramid was equipped with a covered causeway that led to the river and a small valley temple where the body of the deceased was received and probably embalmed. It was in the mortuary temple that the daily rituals of the king's cult were conducted. The temple was carefully crafted, having colonnades, courts, pillars and decorated walls. While the structure was surrounded by satellite pyramids – which may have housed the king's Ka – smaller pyramids were designed for the wives of the pharaoh.

The pyramid complex was surrounded by the mass graves of courtiers. Being buried in the holy precincts of their king's funerary complex meant that these Egyptians were also assured of eternity. The Egyptians would say of the dead, 'When he is buried and the ground embraces him, his name does not pass from the earth, he is remembered for his goodness, that is the command of the gods.'

THE STEP PYRAMID

Scholars have long thought that the Greeks likened the shape of pyramids to their bread loaves or cakes and the word 'pyramid' is derived from a Greek word meaning 'wheaten cake' [Fig. 46]. The Egyptian word for pyramid '*mr*', is translated as 'place of ascension'. The designer of the first pyramid [Fig. 47], found at Saqqara in the north of Egypt, was called Imhotep. Imhotep, who was a High Priest of Re during the 3rd Dynasty, was associated with mysticism and wisdom for centuries after his death. He began with a basic plan for a mastaba tomb, then decided to extend it. It went through many stages of development that involved several significant changes. Originally, Imhotep planned to construct a raised mastaba, but then decided to add several layers of incised stone. The six layers were each shorter than the one below. An examination of his building plan [Figs 46c and 47] reveals the way that the first pyramid was

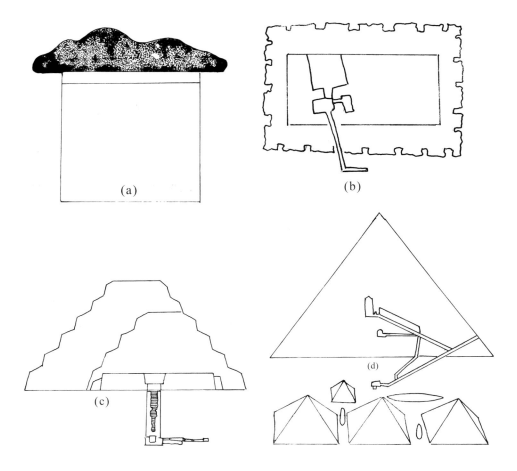

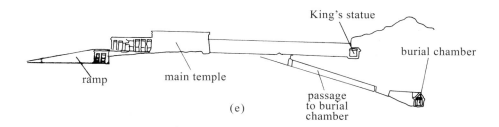

King's statue

burial chamber

ramp   main temple

passage
to burial
chamber

(e)

Fig. 46: *(Opposite and this page):* Egyptian burial rites can be traced through funerary architecture of various periods.

a) A simple burial pit was lined with matting and was marked by a mound that represented the first moment of creation when land arose from the primeval waters.

b) During the Archaic Period the Egyptians built mastaba tombs (named after the Arabic word for 'bench'). The mastaba consisted of a subterranean burial chamber and a raised superstructure – a continuation of the theme of the mound used in Predynastic burials.

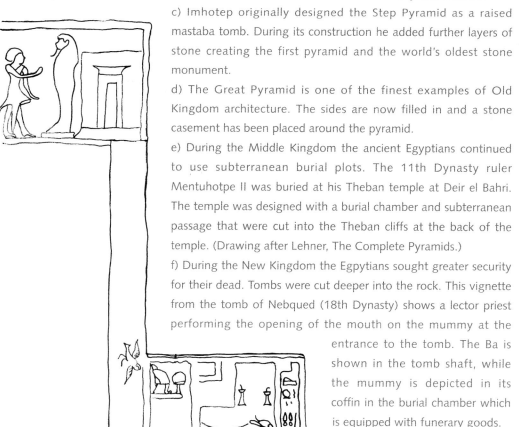

c) Imhotep originally designed the Step Pyramid as a raised mastaba tomb. During its construction he added further layers of stone creating the first pyramid and the world's oldest stone monument.

d) The Great Pyramid is one of the finest examples of Old Kingdom architecture. The sides are now filled in and a stone casement has been placed around the pyramid.

e) During the Middle Kingdom the ancient Egyptians continued to use subterranean burial plots. The 11th Dynasty ruler Mentuhotpe II was buried at his Theban temple at Deir el Bahri. The temple was designed with a burial chamber and subterranean passage that were cut into the Theban cliffs at the back of the temple. (Drawing after Lehner, The Complete Pyramids.)

f) During the New Kingdom the Egpytians sought greater security for their dead. Tombs were cut deeper into the rock. This vignette from the tomb of Nebqued (18th Dynasty) shows a lector priest performing the opening of the mouth on the mummy at the entrance to the tomb. The Ba is shown in the tomb shaft, while the mummy is depicted in its coffin in the burial chamber which is equipped with funerary goods.

(All drawings: Bridget McDermott)

(f)

Fig. 47: The Step Pyramid at Saqqara. *(Photograph: Graham Ollerenshaw)*

conceived and makes the Step Pyramid one of the most exciting buildings of the
Old Kingdom period. The building, made of Tura limestone or 'white stone',
was iconographic in that it was the world's first monumental stone building.
The pyramid was erected on the edge of the desert at Saqqara. It was enclosed
within a limestone wall that measured 10 metres high and 1,645 metres long
while the inner area of the complex measured 14½ hectares. The enclosure
contained a mortuary temple, storage magazines and courtyards. Next to the
mortuary temple, which was placed on the north side of the pyramid, the
Egyptians designed a Serdab chapel that served the king's Ka. It was equipped
with a room that housed the seated statue of Pharaoh. An incision was made on
the wall opposite the eyes of the statue so that the king could see the offerings

that were left for him in the chapel. Although the original statue was removed to the Egyptian Museum, Cairo, it was replaced by a replica model. Today, visitors may still take a glimpse through the slit in the wall and are caught off guard by the startling gaze of the king staring back at them.

The Step Pyramid complex was a virtual 'city of ghosts' that incorporated dusty pavilions, roofed facades, shrines and chapels. On the east side of the complex there were a series of buildings that were connected to the Heb-Sed festival, designed to celebrate the king's jubilee, a festival that may have ancient origins. Egyptologists believe that there may have been a time when the aged king was sacrificed as a part of a fertility ritual. This custom seems to have died out so that by the Archaic Period the king would prove his prowess by running the circuit of a courtyard that was adorned with dummy chapels and a dais. The buildings were constructed in pairs to represent the two regions of Upper and Lower Egypt – each with its own court, sanctuary and statue niches.

In the base of the pyramid, the architects decided to cut a shaft, descending deep under the desert floor. From here they built tunnels and underground chambers. The burial chamber was approached by a sloping ramp from an entrance in the north side of the pyramid. The substructure was divided into a series of rooms and subterranean passageways that led to the burial chamber. The excavators found eleven tombs, each with shafts and tunnels. However, little was found below the pyramid except a large alabaster coffin and the remains of a child.

PYRAMIDS OF THE 4TH DYNASTY

King Seferu of the 4th Dynasty built three grandiose monuments: the pyramid at Meidum, the Bent Pyramid and the north pyramid at Dahshur. Of these structures, the pyramid at Meidum is by far the most important for it reveals the first transition from the step pyramid to a true pyramid. The pyramid of Meidum began with the building of a series of seven steps that were later increased to eight. It remained a step pyramid for many years. Then, for reasons unknown, the shelves were filled with rubble and the craftsmen provided a smooth outer coating of limestone for the sides. The true pyramid was born. This pyramid reveals features that were incorporated in later funerary complexes, including a causeway, a satellite pyramid and a long sloping passage that was cut into the north side of the building. The corridor, which led to a corbelled burial chamber, was designed with large stone blocks that were used to secure the corridor against tomb robbers. After a period of ten years building at Meidum, the king abandoned the pyramid (although, as we have seen, he later returned) and decided to construct another edifice at Dahshur. Situated 32km from the site of Meidum, Dahshur is the traditional construction site for later pyramid builders of the Middle Kingdom. Here the king built two pyramids. The Bent Pyramid is unusual in that there was a drastic change in the angle of the pyramid. The lower area is built with an angle of 54 degrees while the upper is measured at 43 degrees. This pyramid is also unique in that it has two sub-chambers that were approached from two entrances. The first entrance is situated in the north face while the second lies in the east. The corbelled chambers lie directly above each other. The north pyramid is entered from the upper area via a long descending corridor that leads to a pair of antechambers with corbelled ceilings. A corridor runs up into the central part of the pyramid and leads to a burial chamber which was found to be empty except for a few fragments of bone.

THE GIZA PYRAMIDS

The three Giza pyramids that dominate the Cairo skyline were built by successive generations of Egyptian rulers. In the context of Old Kingdom mortuary architecture they are hailed as pure perfection. Each pyramid was designed with the standard features of a royal funerary complex that included the mortuary and valley temples. The causeways were measured at a kilometre long. Subsidiary pyramids and mastaba tombs surround these pyramids [Fig. 48]. The streets of tombs that line the Giza plateau house a phantom court of retainers and family members who, it was believed, would continue to serve the king in the afterlife. The most famous of these pyramids belongs to Khufu (*c.* 2551 BC), who named his tomb Akhet Kufu, which means 'the horizon of Khufu' [Fig. 49]. While the base of this structure measures 70 metres square, it rises to a height of 44½ metres square above the hazy skyline of Cairo. During construction, the pyramid was subject to a series of changes. The entrance was placed on the northern side of the building, where the craftsmen cut a long sloping corridor which was designed to terminate in the burial chamber. The Egyptians then changed their minds and decided to move the burial chamber up into the superstructure itself [Fig. 46d]. In order to do this they had to turn back into the corridor and create a new ascending tunnel in the roof. This horizontal shaft led to the so-called 'Queen's Chamber' which, confusingly, was originally designed to house the body of the king. This idea was abandoned, too. The Egyptians resumed construction of the ascending corridor which was then

Fig. 48: The subsidiary pyramids at Giza and the portico entrance to the tomb of a royal physician. *(Photograph: Bridget McDermott)*

extended. It is now known as the 'grand gallery' and is a magnificent architectural achievement, over 46 metres long and 8 metres high. It forms a corridor that leads directly to the king's burial chamber.

How was this pyramid used, and how does its architecture mirror the Old Kingdom funerary rituals? Unfortunately, we still don't have all the answers. When the king was brought to the pyramid he would have been accompanied by members of the royal household, courtiers, professional mourners and priests. He would also have been accompanied by Isis and Nepthys, who were known as the Kites, their roles acted out by priestesses. The funeral party would travel in a small group of boats that would be docked in the small harbour belonging to the valley temple of the pyramid. Later, these boats may have been dismantled and buried at the base of the funerary complex. Once the body of the king arrived at the temple, it would have been handed over to mortuary priests to tend. They would then conduct rituals that included embalming and

Fig. 49: The Great Pyramid of Giza. *(Photograph: Bridget McDermott)*

purification. Although some scholars are now questioning the location of the 'tent of purification' or embalming hall, many believe that the body was treated in the valley temple. When the body was treated and taken to the tomb other important rituals would be performed, the most important of which was 'the coming forth of the voice' when the dead received offerings, libations and censing. Another important ritual was called 'the opening of the mouth', a ceremony that allowed the soul of the deceased to be released and enabled him or her to breathe and speak. Finally, when the body of the king was placed in the pyramid tomb, it is thought that the Pyramid Texts were activated by the chanting of spells. The placing of the king's mummy in the funerary chamber was referred to as the 'landing at the cavern'. One final rite followed: the priests would leave and seal the chamber, carefully sweeping away any footsteps which they had left in the dust.

Khufu was succeeded by Djedfare who built his pyramid at Abu Rowash; little remains of this structure. Khafre (Chephren) was the next pharaoh to build at Giza [Fig. 50]. Although Khafre's pyramid appears larger than that of its predecessors, this is an illusion; in fact it was merely built on higher ground. The upper part of the building is still clad in the original limestone. The pyramid has two northern entrances, the upper door leading to a sloping corridor that levels out towards the burial chamber. The Sphinx [Fig. 51], Egypt's earliest large stone sculpture, is thought to be connected to this pyramid. Equipped with a temple that was built on a terrace below its paws, the Sphinx was designed with a central courtyard, colonnades and statues and was hewn from the natural rock at the edge of Khafre's causeway. The sculpture is in

Fig. 50: The pyramid of Chephren. *(Photograph: Jason Semmens)*

Fig. 51: The Sphinx. *(Photograph: Bridget McDermott)*

the likeness of a recumbant lion with the head of an Egyptian king. As a symbol of power and solar forces the lion has a close association with kingship.

The third pyramid, much smaller at 66 metres tall, belongs to Menkare [Fig. 52]. Two tunnels were cut into the pyramid, one below the other, so that the burial chamber could be extended. The chamber had an extra room that was probably designed to house the Pharaoh's canopic equipment. It was here that

Fig. 52: The pyramid of Menkare. *(Photograph: Jason Semmens)*

early excavators found a basalt sarcophagus, but it was later lost at sea while it was being shipped to England.

Pyramid building began to decline. During the 5th and 6th Dynasties inferior monuments were constructed with small stone blocks. The rubble core that supported these pyramids was inadequate so over time, the buildings crumbled. At the end of the Old Kingdom, pyramid building ceased altogether. It was revived briefly during the Middle Kingdom period, but these pyramids, which were built with a weak, mud-brick core, had nothing of the awe and grandeur of the classical Old Kingdom monuments.

THE GHOST SHIP OF KHUFU

As with the pyramids, no photograph can quite prepare you for the impact of seeing the solar boat of Khufu for the first time [Figs 53a and b]. The image of the ship is awe-inspiring – it literally takes one's breath away. One feels compelled to walk on it, to touch the rich cedar wood or explore the mysterious cabin whose interior is shielded from view. It takes a while to note the purity of

Fig. 53: Two views of the solar boat of King Khufu. *(Photographs: Bridget McDermott)*

the wood and the absolute simplicity of the design. And yet there is also something ghostly about the ship – something that hints at other-worldliness. Could this boat have been designed so that the king could navigate the heavens and the underworld in perpetuity? Was this celestial ship ever used as a funerary boat, or was it intended to be manned solely by the gods and the blessed dead? These are questions we still cannot answer with certainty.

Boats were an essential means of transport for the ancient Egyptians, who were unable to travel over inhospitable areas of desert landscape. From the Predynastic Period boats had been used as important symbols and served many purposes. From the Old Kingdom the Egyptians employed river ferries and fishing boats – they also used ships for expeditions, trading and transporting soldiers and military equipment. The king had a magnificent barge at his disposal from which to conduct official tours of Egypt, and the arrival and departure of the royal flotilla occasioned much ceremony. It is not surprising that the boats were the stuff of myth – they appear in the earliest tomb scenes and were etched on grave goods and pottery from the Early Periods. Iconic images show the sun god Re travelling through the heavens and the underworld in a boat. Excavations have shown that during the Archaic Period the Egyptians buried large boats within the precincts of their royal tombs. It is possible that these were designed to convey the king, the gods and their entourage on the mythical journey to the underworld. However, the precise purpose of the boat burials is still the subject of debate. Some scholars believe that the boats were those used to convey the body of the king to the place of burial; others view them as funerary objects and credit them with a practical function in the afterlife.

The solar boat of Khufu was discovered in 1954 after the Egyptian Antiquities Service began to clear debris from the south side of the Great Pyramid at Giza. At first the Egyptians thought they had found a boundary wall that had once encircled the pyramid. However, it soon became clear that there was something unusual about the structure. Kamal el Mallakh, an architect and Egyptologist, believed he had found a boat pit. Indeed, he knew of several boat pits that had been discovered in the area – although none had been found intact. Mallakh found a series of limestone blocks that were covering the pit, one of which was inscribed with the cartouche of Djedefre, the son of King Khufu. He decided to bore a hole in the stone. On 26 May 1954 he completed the task, claiming that he could still detect the fragrance of ancient incense rising from the pit beneath the floor. He used a shaving mirror to reflect sunlight into the pit. His ingenuity was rewarded – in the gloom he made out the remains of a dismembered ship. Shortly afterwards, a photographer from *Life* magazine was invited to Giza; he inserted his camera into the hole and took the first photographs of Khufu's boat. The images captured the imagination of the world.

Ahmed Youssef Moustaffa was an art restoration expert. An intuitive man who believed he had a spiritual connection with the objects he studied, Youssef Moustaffa, however, admitted that initially he had no knowledge of ancient ship building and the project caused him great concern. The Egyptians were beginning to think that it might be possible to reconstruct the boat, and samples taken from the wood had proved it was still in good condition. A make-shift tent was erected over the boat pit and large cranes were employed to raise the limestone blocks, a process that took several months. On 28 January 1955, the last stone was removed.

The boat had been covered by sheets of cloth. Beneath these, the Egyptians found layers of mats and ropes. Although the boat lay in pieces, the excavators recognised the prow, pieces of the stern and bow, the long oars, doors and decking. The Egyptians had to preserve, record and photograph each section of the boat, but it was not until December 1955 that they attempted to remove the parts. In the meantime Youssef Moustaffa began to study ancient boats. He looked at the model boats found in ancient tombs, and studied the numerous reliefs and paintings of Egyptian ships. Although there was a rich array of material, there was only one Old Kingdom tomb scene that depicted ancient boat building. This had been found in the 5th Dynasty tomb of Ti. As the 32.5-metre long pit was opened Youssef Moustaffa found layer upon layer of wood, rope and matting, 651 solid pieces of wood, including cabin doors, wall panels and decking. Most of the wood was identified as Lebanese cedar while some smaller features were made of acacia. There were also five pairs of oars of differing lengths, measuring between 6.5 metres and 8.5 metres in length. Only a few small copper staples were discovered. Thirteen layers of wooden panels were recorded so that Youssef Moustaffa could construct a series of models. From these he began to study and plan the reconstruction of the ship. The pieces were then soaked in a special solution to preserve the wood. By June 1957 the pit was finally emptied.

Youssef Moustaffa found himself with what amounted to a giant jigsaw puzzle of over 1,224 pieces of wood. But he was in luck. He realised that the boat had been buried in a systematic fashion, in the order in which it had been dismantled, and also that there were signs written on the wood that showed how the pieces fitted together. It would take five attempts to reconstruct the craft, now housed in the magnificent boat museum in its original location beside the Great Pyramid. The boat is 43 metres long with a deckhouse that consists of an antechamber and a main cabin with elegant palmiform columns that support the cabin's roof.

MIDDLE KINGDOM TOMBS

Rock-cut Tombs

During the Middle Kingdom period the Egyptian upper classes built rock-cut tombs that were hewn into the cliffs at important political or religious sites along the Nile. The tombs consisted of a portico with columns or a terraced courtyard which led into a columned hall. Inside there was a small room or niche which contained the tomb owner's funerary statue and where food offerings were presented as a part of the deceased's mortuary cult. The burial chamber was cut into the floor of the tomb.

Excavations of these tombs have revealed several important features. Many First Intermediate Period and Middle Kingdom tombs belonged to families with martial connections, consequently the decor was dominated by military themes. These scenes provide a great deal of information about the civil disturbances that occurred in Egypt during this period. The rock-cut tombs of Deir Rifeh in Middle Egypt were situated several kilometres from the warring city of Asyut. In the cemetery of Shas-Hotep, where the god Khnum was especially revered, archaeologists discovered a tomb that was said by Flinders Petrie in 1907 to be 'as fine as anything known from this period'. The tomb, which was described in a report called *Gizeh and Rifeh*, belonged to two brothers. It was also found intact. Today, its contents remain together and are on exhibit in the Manchester Museum, England. The cache was first examined by the Egyptologist Margaret Murray in 1908, and has undergone further examination under Professor Rosalie David, during which CAT-scanning techniques have shed some light on the manner in which the two brothers died. One, known as Nakht-Ankh, who is thought to have been a eunuch, died at about sixty years old, probably from heart disease. His brother Khnum-Nakht, who may have suffered from a growth disorder, was about forty when he died. Each male was buried in an anthropoid coffin set within a rectangular wooden coffin brightly decorated with floral collars, a series of red rosettes and gold bands. A panel down the centre of the coffin is decorated with inscriptions. Examinations conducted on the two brothers show that Khnum-Nakht was negroid while Naktht-Ankh was Caucasian. It is therefore possible that they were step-brothers.

Little remains of Middle Kingdom royal funerary architecture. The most important of these buildings was originally designed to house the body of the Middle Kingdom ruler Nebhetpetre Mentuhotpe II, a celebrated warrior and the first king of the 11th Dynasty, who had reigned for over fifty years. He named his mortuary temple Akh Sut Nebhetpetre, which translates as 'splendid are the places of Nebhepetre'. Foundation deposits found at the temple site reveal links to the cult of Montu-Re, a major deity associated with war, while other features emphasise the connection between the king and Amun Re [Figs 46e, 54a and b]. Situated in a dramatic arena below the Theban cliffs of Deir el Bahri, the temple is innovative in that it was built in multiple layers or terraces. Today it stands in the shadow of the New Kingdom funerary complex of Hatshepsut, the edifice it inspired. Sadly, it is mainly disregarded by the tourists who visit the temple of the female pharaoh, but the temple holds a particular resonance for Egyptologists, for it creates a visual link between the Old and New Kingdom funerary architectural styles. While it retains many features of the pyramid complex, it also has new elements, being the first edifice of this period that acted as both a tomb and a cenotaph. Its traditional features included a mortuary temple, sanctuary and hyperstyle halls, and a pyramid structure was once thought to have stood on a podium in the centre of the monument. Evidence now suggests that the podium was little more than a raised dais that was meant to imitate the first mound of creation. The podium was surrounded by a pillared hall, fronted by porticoes and approached by a ramp. It was encircled by an outer wall or ambulatory. The royal tomb was accessed via a passageway that was hewn into the rock at the back of the building. The burial chamber was lined with granite and equipped with an alabaster shrine. A processional causeway, traditionally used in the pyramid age and that measured over 950 metres long, was lined with statues of the king, who was shown in the Osiride form. The causeway linked the building from a valley temple to a tree-lined court. Here the Egyptians planted fifty-five tamarisk trees while two rows of four sycamores shaded a statue of the king.

It was at this site in 1900 that archaeologists discovered a large chamber that housed the bodies of six of the king's women. They had been placed in limestone shrines that were equipped with magnificent Ka statues. Each tomb contained an elaborate sarcophagus that was carved with scenes showing the royal women engaged in everyday activities. The distinct sunk relief carvings on the outer panels of the sarcophagi reveal fine details of their personal lives. The sarcophagus of Kawit [Fig. 55], for example, shows the royal princess attended by her hairdresser. As she is coiffed, she holds a bronze mirror in one hand, and a

Fig. 54: The Temple of Mentuhotep II seen from the side (top) and the Temple of Queen Hatshepsut from the cliffs above. *(Photographs: Jason Semmens)*

Fig. 55: The royal princess Kawit attended by her hairdressser. False braids are attached to her hair while she relaxes with her mirror and a drinking bowl. An image reproduced from her limestone sarcophagus found at the temple of Montuhotpe II at Thebes, Middle Kingdom. *(Drawing: Bridget McDermott)*

refreshment bowl in the other. Behind her, the hairdresser is shown weaving false braids into her hair. Little remains of the decoration of these shrines, although some small fragments depict the typical bold relief used by Middle Kingdom artists who portray their subjects with heavily rounded features and voluptuous figures. One fine image remains of the king's chief wife, Queen Mentuhotep Neferu, carrying a sunshade, while others show a procession of women holding hands.

12TH DYNASTY PYRAMID BUILDING

In an attempt to recapture the glories of the past the kings of the 12th Dynasty began to emulate the grand building programme of their ancestors and returned to pyramid construction. Ammenemes I built a pyramid at Lisht which was accessed via a harbour situated near the Fayoum. The design of the pyramid was heavily influenced by the Old Kingdom style; however, diminished resources meant that the economy could no longer support such grand building schemes. The core of the pyramid was now made up of small blocks of limestone, sand debris and mud brick. Blocks of stone were also 'borrowed' from the Old Kingdom monuments, including the Great Pyramid. The Middle Kingdom pyramid was built with open causeways and a series of terraces inspired by Theban funerary architecture. Members of the royal family were buried between two outer walls of the structure. Twenty-two tombs on the western side of the complex were designed for the royal women.

At Lisht, Sesostris I built a stunning complex, the largest edifice of its time. It was surrounded by a large group of subsidiary tombs that belonged to the king's officials. Nine small pyramids were also built within the enclosure, each equipped with its own chapel. Two of the pyramids have been identified as belonging to Neferu, the king's wife, and Princess Itayket. No coffins or physical remains were discovered. The pyramids of Ammenemes II at Dahshur herald a new phase in Egyptian architecture. The king had begun to experiment with several new features that included elongated enclosures and open causeways.

THE KAHUN PYRAMID

The Fayoum basin, an area with a plentiful supply of fresh water, provided the ancient Egyptian kings with a vast and exotic hunting ground. It was here that Sesostris II (1895–1878 BC) built his pyramid [Fig. 56]. The structure had a limestone core and a series of intersecting walls that were used to form a framework of compartments that were infilled with mud brick. The base of the building was set into a trench that was used to collect water. The entrance to the pyramid was difficult to find, as it was placed on the east end of its south wall. The burial shaft plunges to a depth of 16 metres and terminates in a horizontal

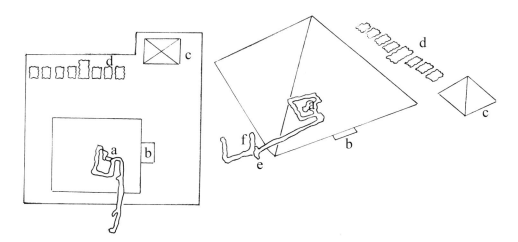

Fig. 56: The Pyramid of Sesostris II. The pyramid is surrounded by a boundary wall which marks the elaborate funerary complex: a) burial chamber, b) entrance chapel, c) Queen's Pyramid, d) subsidiary mastaba tombs, e) well, f) entrance shaft. *(All drawings: Bridget McDermott)*

corridor which leads to a hall with a vaulted ceiling. At the end of the hall there is a well. The outward corridor then rises to meet the burial chamber situated not in the centre of the pyramid but in an awkward position slightly to the side. The walls of the chamber are lined with granite. Inside, archaeologists found a red granite sarcophagus and an offering table. They also found the remains of a human leg bone and a gold uraeus (a snake emblem, usually worn on a royal crown) in a side room off the main burial chamber.

The complex had an outer wall of mud brick that was lined with trees. A series of additional tombs was found on the north side of the outer enclosure. In 1913 excavators led by Guy Brunton opened up the tomb of Princess Sithathoriunet, the daughter of Sesostris II, which yielded a vast array of treasure. Among the finds were lion-headed girdles, bracelets, mirrors and pectorals. Caskets were recovered from the tomb containing personal items such as razors, make-up dishes and ointment jars. The cache is now housed in the Metropolitan Museum of Art, New York, and is considered to be one of the finest collections of ancient Egyptian jewellery in the world.

THE TOWN OF KAHUN

Egyptologists have recovered only three town sites in Egypt, of which the community known as Kahun (or Ilahun) is the oldest. Although the town belonged to the pyramid builders of Sesostris II, it survived long after the edifice was completed. It was inhabited by those working for the king's mortuary cult. These sites are particularly exciting because their yields contribute a great deal to our knowledge of everyday life in an Egyptian settlement. The site of Kahun was known in ancient times as Hetep Sesostris, meaning 'Sesostris is Satisfied'. There were two periods of occupation at Kahun. Villagers lived there for a period of 100 years during and after the reign of Sesostris II. The population was dominated by soldiers, builders and priests. The soldiers conducted expeditions in order to retrieve stone for the pyramid structure, while builders worked on the edifice and its auxiliary complex. The priests were employed to perform the rituals of the king's cult, and would certainly have catered for the spiritual needs of the community. The other villagers would have included cooks, scribes and servants. Although the village was abandoned towards the end of the 13th Dynasty, and most finds are dated to this period, it was briefly reinhabited during the New Kingdom reign of Amenophis III.

Like most ancient Egyptian villages the site of Kahun was surrounded on three sides by a mud-brick wall. The one hundred or so houses seem to have been constructed in a dip. The overall area, excavated between 1888 and 1890 by Flinders Petrie, measured over 402 metres wide. Petrie made comprehensive drawings of the town, which was divided into sections on the east and west sides by a thick wall, a structure which may have served to separate the different classes of community members. An elevated area known as the Acropolis provided a grand view of the village. Here there was a large platform and a villa which may have been an official residence allocated to the king when he came to inspect his pyramid. The rooms of the villa were large – it had a kitchen, cellar, washing facilities and women's quarters. Generally, the large houses in the village were entered from the street through impressive doorways with stone lintels and had a doorkeeper's room. The houses had offices and servants' accommodation. The private chambers included pillared halls and colonnades. Ceilings were supported by columns made of wood and stone. The total area afforded to a house is estimated at 42.06 metres by 60.35 metres. The walls of the finest rooms were mud plastered and painted with a dado. A series of coloured borders were applied – a dark colour in the lowest area was followed by a series of black and red lines on a white background. The highest part of the wall was painted in a yellow wash. In some of the paintings we see depictions of the house owners and their servants.

On the western side of the town there were eleven streets of workmen's houses, each of four or five rooms. The houses were made of mud brick and were single-storey. They had large flat roofs that could be used for storage or for sleeping. On excavating the houses, Petrie found that many infants had been buried under the floors: 'Many new-born infants were found buried in the floors of the rooms, and, strange to say, usually in boxes made for other purposes, evidently, by their form. In short, unlucky babes seem to have been conveniently put out of the way by stuffing them into a toilet case or clothes box.' Such babies were often buried two or three to a box and archaeologists discovered that some of the infants were several months old and were adorned with beads and amulets.

Adult cemeteries at Kahun are situated in a number of areas around the town and the pyramid. Court officials of Sesostris II were buried here near the king. There were also a number of tombs at Kahun that were left unfinished. On an isolated mound known as the west hill, a number of 12th Dynasty tombs have been found the best known of which belonged to Anpy, the architect of Sesostris II who oversaw the construction of the king's pyramid. It is a magnificent tomb with four underground chambers that were reached by two shafts, one of which was vertical, the other sloping.

FINDS

A large array of interesting objects was found at Kahun and many are on display in the Manchester Museum, England. Several of these finds provide us with an insight into the daily lives of the villagers for they include many items of pleated linen clothing, simple jewellery and household furniture. The Fayoum was well known as an abundant hunting ground for it supported many species of animal and large bird populations. It is not surprising, then, that large bird nets, hunting sticks, bows, arrows and fire-sticks have been recovered from the village. Objects that relate to the everyday life of women were also found; these include alabaster cosmetic jars, ivory castanets and weaving materials. Household objects such as wooden chairs, headrests, walking sticks and sandals were also recovered together with a large number of children's toys. The village children played with clay animals, models, painted wooden dolls, balls of wood or leather and with board games. Aside from items of practical use, excavation also brought to light several important documents. Some legal texts reveal the manner in which inheritance was transferred, while other papyri have veterinary and mathematical inscriptions. Of these documents, Papyrus Kahun is perhaps the most important, dealing as it does with various medical complaints and their treatment.

NEW KINGDOM TOMBS

Royal Tombs

John Romer proposed that the function of the king was more important than that of royal figurehead. In ancient Egypt, the relationship between pharaoh and the masses was immediate; the king acted as a bridge between the people and the gods. He was expected to secure military victories for the gods who in return would authorise stability and fecundity for the land. The death of the king heralded a dangerous time. Rituals were required to secure a safe passage for the king through the underworld and to transfer the power of leadership from father to son. To ensure a smooth succession, the king often established a co-regency with his heir. At the time of burial, the prince would perform the ritual of the opening of the mouth for his dead father, an act that effectively established his legitimacy. During the seventy-day period when the body of the pharaoh was being embalmed there was enormous activity as the world of the living, and the dead, prepared themselves for the arrival of a new king. The tomb was a symbol of this continuity: it united the land, people and ruler in one purpose – to sustain the correct relationship with the gods, and to maintain and nourish the ancestor cult through offerings and prayers.

Although royal burial sites are known at Thebes from both the 11th and 17th Dynasties, it was during the New Kingdom that this area attained prominence as a burial ground for the Egyptian pharaohs. During the New Kingdom there were many developments in religious thought – religious practices reached a new level of sophistication while imperial expansion brought untold wealth. By 1390 BC Egypt had risen to the zenith of its power and its economic superiority was deliberately flaunted in an unparalleled building programme that would flourish for 500 years.

The royal tombs of the New Kingdom were situated in a narrow valley that lies under the shadow of a mountain dedicated to the goddess, the mistress of silence, Meretseger. It is known in modern times as el-Qurn, the horn [Fig. 57]. Today the area is known as the Valley of the Kings; consisting of more than one hundred burials of the New Kingdom pharaohs and their progeny, it is the most popular tourist site in Egypt.

While it was customary for the king to begin work on his tomb early in his reign, many tombs remained unfinished. Ramesses I and Tutankhamun were among the many rulers who died before they could complete their work, leaving small or hurriedly constructed tombs. On the other hand, the tombs of Sety I and Ramesses II, who lived to a ripe old age, were large and well equipped. As tomb building progressed, the Egyptians rarely discarded old ideas but rather elaborated upon them. Although new features were added to each successive tomb, the basic plan remained the same. Ancient Egyptian tomb plans such as that of the tomb of Ramesses IV, now housed in the Egyptian Museum, Turin, reveal how the Egyptians laid blueprints for their burial sites. Each royal tomb included an entrance, passageway, a transverse hall and subsidiary chambers [Fig. 58] that were cut at right angles to the axis. Throughout the New Kingdom, the style of the royal tombs varied. The earliest were designed with a curved axis that was almost certainly intended to reflect the uneven paths of the underworld. Soon the builders began to add a parallel axis, where the entrance hall forked at an angle. During the 18th Dynasty royal tombs were designed with four passages that were aligned with terraces and sloping ramps. These terraces were meant to symbolise the sun's journey through the different phases of the night. The walls of these tombs were incised with niches that housed statues, while some tombs contained a deep pit known as 'the Hall of Interference' that may have been designed to collect flood water or deter tomb robbers. The Egyptians then added a large chamber known as the Chariot Hall, and a large pillared room

Fig. 57: Medinet Habu from the air. The village of Gurna, the Ramesseum, the site of the tombs of the nobles, and the desert hills that surround the Valley of the Kings are visible. *(Photograph: Bridget McDermott)*

called the House of Gold; many storerooms were built around this chamber and were designed to house the king's burial equipment. During the late 19th Dynasty the Egyptian rulers abandoned the bent axis preferring to build long, narrow tombs. The architects added strong wooden doors to close the entrance, passages and storerooms. During the reign of Ramesses IV architects reduced the length of their tombs and began to omit the side chambers and to widen the corridors. The sloping floors were then abandoned, a modification that enabled the Egyptians to inter larger pieces of funerary equipment, including monumental sarcophagi, with ease.

NEW KINGDOM TOMB SCENES

The tombs were hewn and decorated by craftsmen who lived and worked in the village of Deir el Medina at Thebes. The tomb workers who lived here were divided into two gangs each led by a foreman. The gangs worked in ten-day shifts and lived in camps on the side of the mountain. They worked with hard stone mauls and bronze chisels cutting rough passages in the underlying limestone and marked the ceilings of the tomb in order to indicate the route of its axis. Simple baskets were passed from hand to hand by rows of labourers to remove the stone. Oil and twisted linen tapers were used as candles to illuminate the tomb. While workers burrowed into the cliffs artists prepared and smoothed the walls, polishing the stone and plastering it with gypsum. The scribes followed with their cakes of red and black ink, making careful outlines of the religious scenes required by the king's Ka. Later, the artists would arrive and lay down the preliminary drawings; after supervisory inspection they would etch out the scenes with their chisels on the soft plaster or stone. The images would then be painted in a variety of colours.

The tomb scenes were influenced by fashion and popular theology, principles that clearly affected the art and architecture of each generation. The evolution and representation of these principles enable Egyptologists to date a tomb and note the religious and political changes that affected the tomb decoration. In this way each royal tomb has its own character – each feels incredibly individual. The ancient Egyptians used no machinery – everything we see of their culture was fashioned by the human hand. It is often this sense of texture and

Fig. 58: The decorated corridor of a Ramesside tomb in the Valley of the Kings. (*Photograph: Jason Semmens*)

detail that makes a deep impression on the modern visitor, who can often detect fingerprints, lantern smoke and miscalculated outlines on the walls of Egyptian tombs. Often, the eye is drawn to the simplicity of detail, or the uneven grains of paint that lovingly depict the feathers on the hieroglyphic symbol of an owl. In a tomb designed for a living god, these are the details that seem to affect us most deeply – but even so, one cannot avoid the fact that the tombs were clearly crafted through brutal hard work. Standing in the Valley of the Kings with its eerie acoustics it is easy to imagine the scraping sounds of chisel on rock that echoed around this otherwise silent valley for 500 years.

TOMBS OF THE NOBLES

The mountain peak of el-Qurn towers above the Valley of the Dead and casts its awesome shadow over the arid landscape. Beneath it lie numerous ancient Egyptian tombs dating to the New Kingdom period. In this narrow desert plain where a fine seam of cultivated land marks a stark contrast with the desert floor, the finest warrior kings of ancient Egypt built their funerary monuments. The desert road that branches to the steep rise of the Valley of the Kings is lined with the mortuary temples of Ramesses II and Sety I. To the far right one can see Medinet Habu, the temple of Ramesses III, and behind that the remains of Amenhotep III's mortuary temple – perhaps the largest and most elaborate building Egypt has ever known. Here, visitors queue to visit the magnificent temple of Hatshepsut which lies adjacent to a series of tombs that belong to the officials of the New Kingdom. They are known as the tombs of the nobles.

The people of Gurna, who live among the tombs, believe they are direct descendants of the pharaohs' tomb builders. In the recent past, the people of Gurna housed their livestock in the tombs. The cohabitation of the modern villagers with the ancient tombs is complicated and the situation has been aggravated by several attempts to remove the people from the area. Despite recent resettlement in houses equipped with modern facilities, the inhabitants of Gurna returned once again to the village. Today, they still live in their houses among the tombs.

The tombs of the nobles at Thebes are of great importance for our understanding of life in ancient Egypt. For obvious reasons called T-shaped, the tombs consist of a forecourt, transverse hall and an elongated passage that leads to an inner room. The rear room was often designed with a niche where the statues of the tomb owner were placed. The tombs had a subterranean burial chamber and were meant to imitate the domestic dwellings of the ancient

Egyptians; like the royal tombs, they were intended to house the Ka of the deceased. Priests and relatives would bring food to the tomb and place beer and loaves before the false door through which they believed the Ka would pass and dine on their offerings.

The nobles were able to decorate their tombs in a more individual fashion than their royal masters. However, the most dominant figure in the tomb is not the tomb owner, but the king. The king was always the largest figure in the tomb and was given a prominent position on the doorway leading from the transverse hall to the inner rooms. The deceased and his family portray themselves not as the primary figures but as subjects of the king and highlight their role as his servants. The tomb owner also appears on each side of the doorway, where, together with his wife or family, he is shown making offering to the gods. While the painted scenes of agricultural life include harvesting and cattle counts, scenes that show the production of beer and wine were very popular. The Egyptians also placed great importance on the pilgrimage to Abydos, a holy city associated with Osiris. The Egyptians were expected to visit Abydos at least once in their lifetime. Here they would set up stelae or leave small pots of hair in shrines that were dedicated to the god of the dead.

These tombs provide Egyptologists with a great deal of information about daily life in ancient Egypt. Scenes from the tombs of the vizier Rekhmire are invaluable because they reveal a multitude of images of ancient craftsmen at work — metal workers, sculptors and artists — every aspect of their trade illustrated in painstaking detail. The tombs of the nobles are decorated with images of foreigners, men of Crete, Syria and Nubia paying tribute to the king. Alongside them, we see the harbour masters, their ships and the soldiers of Pharaoh's army [Fig. 59]; some of them are shown with their heads being inspected for lice. Scenes of the natural world dominate and Egyptians are shown fishing and fowling [Fig. 60]. Often, these images carry deep religious significance. Shown in their finest clothes, the Egyptians are depicted on skiffs [Fig. 61]. The tomb owner, often accompanied by his wife, is shown about to spear tilapia fish. When threatened tilapia hide their young in their mouths — spitting them out when the danger has passed. The Egyptians saw this action as a symbol of fertility and frequently used this image in their tombs.

Although erotic imagery is a dominant motif in tomb decoration the Egyptians portrayed their sexuality in very subtle ways. Most tombs are decorated with banquet scenes in which beautiful young women are depicted in transparent clothes. They often hold exotic flowers or fruits to their noses and lips. Because of its shape the mandrake has specific sexual connotations and is

Fig. 59: Soldiers man the ships of the king in the tomb of Khons at Thebes. *(Photograph: Bridget McDermott)*

Fig. 60: Two men carrying spears and fish. Scene from the tomb of Kenamun at Thebes. *(Photograph: Bridget McDermott)*

1. The king is seated before the sacred ished tree. The gods inscribe his names and regnal years on the leaves of the trees, and in so doing establish for eternity a record of the king's reign.

2. In the most iconographic image of New Kingdom rulership the king is shown bringing death and destruction to his enemies who are being crushed under the hooves of his chariot team. The enemy are traditionally shown as a mass of chaotic and twisted bodies. The viewer is meant to be gripped by the image of this breathtaking moment. As protector of his land and people the Egyptian king is the single, all powerful force that wields revenge on those who refuse to pay homage to Egypt and her gods.

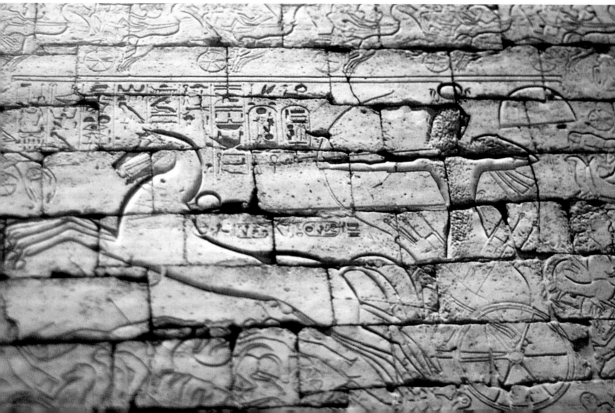

3. This illustration from the Book of the Dead shows a final ritual at the tomb of Hunefer, the deceased. Here we see the Sem-priest dressed in the traditional robes of his office which were made of cheetah or panther skin. Before him a group of priests raise implements to the face of the mummy as they conduct a ceremony known as the Opening of the Mouth. Hunefer's mummy is held by a funerary priest who wears the jackal mask of Anubis, and

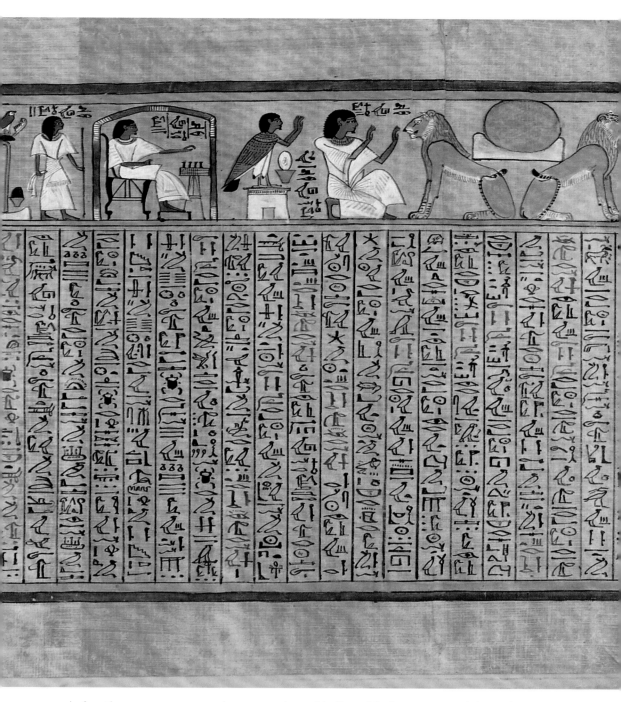

before the mummy a group of mourners dressed in fine white linen weep and throw dust on their faces. Hunefer is about to be buried in a pyramid tomb chapel which is fronted by a large stele. Below, the leg of a calf has been severed as a part of the traditional rituals conducted during Egyptian funerals. *(Courtesy of The British Museum)*

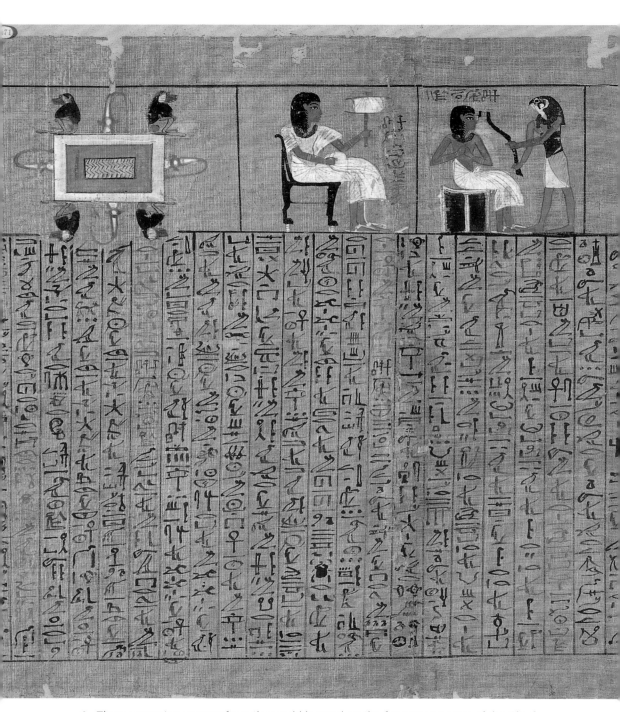

4. There are various scenes from the world beyond on the funerary papyrus of the Chief Military Officer Nakht. The deceased, Nakht, has passed the lake of fire, guarded by baboons and decorated with flaming braziers. He is shown seated with a sail in his hand. This tiny sail is a symbol of air and breath in the realm of the dead. A second image of Nakht follows. Here the Opening of the Mouth is performed upon the deceased by a

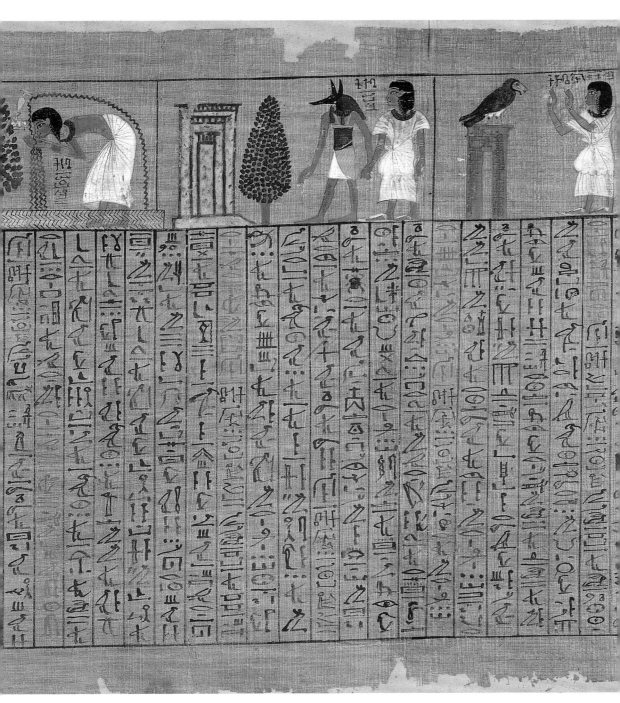

falcon-headed god, allowing Nakht's senses to regenerate. The following scenes show him being attended by a tree goddess who offers him food and water as he arrives in the west. He is then led by Anubis to the door of his tomb and is finally depicted worshipping a falcon-headed deity. *(Courtesy of The British Museum)*

5. This illustration from Spell 125 is the most well-known scene from the Book of the Dead. It depicts the Weighing of the Heart. Hunefer is led to the weighing of his heart by the funerary god Anubis. His heart is placed on a scale and its deeds are measured against the feather of truth. If his heart fails to pass the test it will be devoured by a hybrid monster

who can be seen crouching beneath the scale. In the last scene, Hunefer has passed the test and is seen being led by a falcon god to a ceremonial booth. Here he is brought into the presence of Osiris who is shown sitting on a throne that is guarded by Isis and Nepthys.
(Courtesy of The British Museum)

6. In 1989 an important cache of ancient Egyptian statues was discovered beneath Luxor Temple and were placed in a special exhibition hall in Luxor Museum. They are among the finest statues dated to the New Kingdom. Among the collection is this statue of Hathor, a goddess who represented all of life's pleasurable excesses. She was also known as the Lady of the West, and is often shown on the edge of the desert greeting the dead and welcoming them with food and water.

7. This Predynastic mummy from the British Museum dates to the Badarian or Naqada Period. The body was dried in the desert sand; his golden hair, finger and toe nails have been well preserved. This adult male was buried in the foetal position, presumably in preparation for his new life in the next world. He is exhibited with the tools and decorated pottery that he would have needed in the afterlife. *(Courtesy of The British Museum)*

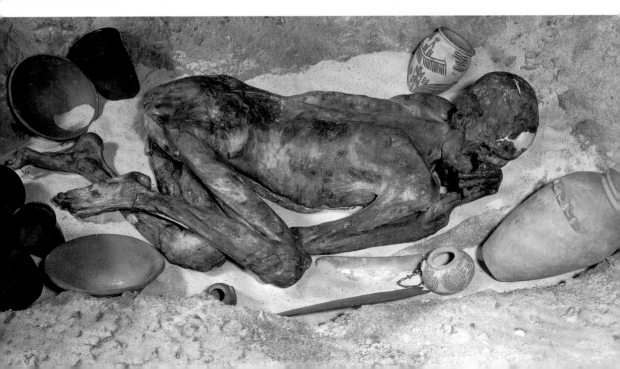

Fig. 61: A man and his family dressed in their finery as they sail out into the marshes to hunt game, from a detailed and vivid wall painting, with strong erotic connotations, from the tomb of Nebamun at Thebes and dated to the reign of Tuthmosis III. Fragment. *(British Museum/Photograph: Bridget McDermott)*

often shown in the hands of upper-class women in party scenes. Female acrobats are depicted dancing before the tomb owner. They wear nothing but a belt around their hips. The women are shown in thick, heavy wigs made of human hair. Hair had a deep sexual significance and texts dated to this period highlight the erotic significance of the wig. A man says coyly to his lover, 'Don your wig and let us spend a happy hour.' The banquet scenes also reveal that the Egyptians revered scent and other sensory pleasures. They also let us glimpse the excesses of ancient Egyptian life – they depict Egyptians eating and drinking until they are sick.

Scenes of grief and mourning were also important. In ancient Egypt there were few representations of fresh corpses and these occur only in military scenes. Rare images from the Ramesside tomb of Amenemopet, or 'the mystical tomb', so called because of its religious imagery, show a funerary workshop and the manufacture of burial equipment. While they seem to have avoided images of corpses, the Egyptians often depicted funeral parties. These included phyles of mourners who were often rendered in procession, walking towards the inner rooms of the tomb. In scenes of grief that have echoes in many cultures, the widow of the deceased is shown tearing at her hair or throwing dust over her face; sometimes she is depicted embracing her husband's coffin. The funeral procession is perhaps the most significant of these tomb scenes. Every element is carefully placed to conform to religious tradition. From the moment the coffin left the embalming house we can observe the procession in fine detail: we see the catafalque being dragged to the tomb followed by mourners; we witness the grief of the family, the elaborate rituals of death, the priests fumigating the dead; and, finally, the ceremony of the opening of the mouth.

TOMBS OF THE RAMESSIDE PERIOD

The Theban tombs of the Ramesside period can be distinguished from those of the 18th Dynasty. Most tombs of this period are T-shaped. Interspersed with pillared halls and passages, the tombs appear rigid but elegant, their sculptured reliefs cut into gypsum rather than the stone. A new wave of spiritual fervour can be felt in the tomb paintings of this period, which rely heavily on religious scenes rather than those of daily life. Vivid glimpses of life in ancient Egypt are replaced by scenes of the underworld and from the Book of Gates and the Book of the Dead. The surfaces of these tombs are decorated with images of the deceased in the company of the gods. Some walls are animated with tree goddesses sustaining the dead with their breasts. Others show Hathor waiting for souls at the edge of the cultivated land, welcoming them with water from the Nile. With their strong emphasis on theology, these tomb scenes seem less frivolous than those of the

Fig. 62: The deserted streets of Deir el Medina on a winter morning. *(Photograph: Jason Semmens)*

18th Dynasty. Even the textures and colours of the paintings seem more serious and severe, executed as they are in a predominantly stark mixture of red and yellow ochres.

DEIR EL MEDINA AND THE WORKMEN'S TOMBS

The village of Deir el Medina is situated behind the hill of Qurnet Mura'i and consists of 7,500 square metres of arid land that was inhabited at a distance of about 3km from the river's edge. Although the construction of the village is often associated with Tuthmosis I, it may have been built during the reign of his father Amenophis I (1526–1506 BC) who, together with his wife, was revered as

patron of the village. A shrine was built for the royal couple at the local temple and during special festivals a statue of the king would be carried around the village and consulted as an oracle. The village was divided into two areas, known respectively as the eastern and western sectors [Fig. 62]. It was surrounded by a boundary wall. While an entrance gateway was built on the northern side of the village the southern side was used as a rubbish dump by the occupants. Initially, the village consisted of fewer than twenty-five houses; however, during the long reign of Ramesses II, it was enlarged and went through a period of great prosperity as its inhabitants were employed building royal tombs and crafting elaborate funerary equipment.

The houses were built in narrow claustrophobic units. They were furnished with shrines that were decorated with household gods such as the popular dwarf deity, Bes. Each house had a main door that led out onto the street. Here, there was a table or bench that was used for socialising with other members of the community. Generally, the houses consisted of four rooms. They were equipped with a kitchen, storerooms, cellar and an outside oven. The rooms were painted with a whitewash to keep the house cool. The most important room in the house often had a single central column and was equipped with a raised platform on which a bench was placed. The storerooms and kitchen were situated at the rear of the house. Here, the Egyptians built a flight of stairs that led to the roof where the family would sleep in the heat of the summer.

The villagers, who were called 'servants in the place of truth', were entirely dependent on the outside world. All supplies, including grain, were transported from the temples while water was brought by cart from the river. Aside from those directly labouring on the tombs, scribes held an important position at the village for many of the people were illiterate. The scribes would write their letters and religious petitions. The scribes of Deir el Medina were also responsible for organising food supplies and rations for the workers and their families. Members of the community included priests, stonemasons, artists and their families. Servants, employed by the wealthier families, were expected to cook, wash and keep house. The villagers were often related, with the result that everyone knew everyone else's business. Positions in the village were hereditary and a man's eldest son would inherit his estate and his profession. Being so overtly linked to the cult of the dead king meant that the villagers observed strong religious traditions. While they endowed the temple with stelae and statues as offerings to the gods they also sent petitions asking for divine intervention in times of trouble. Many such petitions were made by childless couples who left offerings of stone phalli to Hathor the goddess of sexuality and childbirth. Letters and documents found at this site highlight the numerous disagreements and feuds that occurred among pharaoh's workforce: texts describe lawsuits that involved adultery, prostitution and inheritance disputes. Since generations of families worked on the royal tombs, their burial sites yielded a great deal of information about the lives of these ancient people. Artistic representations provide information about what they ate and the type of clothes they wore. Fragments of their lives are revealed not only in their tombs but in scenes from daily life sketched on sherds of pottery and in graffiti inscriptions found on the cliff faces that surround the village.

When not working in the Valley of the Kings the community built, furnished and decorated a number of their own tombs which they designed with mud-brick chapels in the shape of small pyramids [Figs 63a and b]. The pyramid, crafted from limestone, had a small stele set into the facade. The door jambs and architraves were sculpted. The workers also made their own funerary equipment including their coffins. Predictably, the tombs of the villagers were much smaller than those of the nobles. They consisted of an upper chapel and an underground burial chamber – men were buried with their wives and other members of their families. The scribe Ramose, one of the wealthiest inhabitants of the village, built a tomb to house the bodies of the nine women of his household.

The burial chamber was often constructed with a vaulted ceiling. Just as in the more ornate tombs of their superiors, the workers' brightly painted tomb scenes often reveal lively glimpses of everyday family life. The burial shaft was excavated from the courtyard, while the chapel was partly cut into the hill. In the underground chambers a vaulted ceiling was a common feature, decorated in vivid detail. The solar cult dominated the tomb and particular attention was paid to the sun god Re Horakhte who was reborn each morning. The tomb owner appears in many scenes. In some he is depicted with the gods as he travels through the underworld, in others he harvests fields of abundant flax. His family are shown attending the funeral, or worshipping the patrons of the village. Excavations of these tombs, two of which were still intact, have yielded important archaeological objects. The mummies of Senejem and his relatives had survived along with their funerary equipment. In his tomb excavators found a sledge that was used for dragging the tomb owner's coffin, while other goods included furniture such as a bed, table and chairs along with personal items such as sandals, food offerings and funerary garlands. The burial chamber of another worker, Kha the Architect, yielded other important daily-life items such as wigs, clothes, scented oils and opium unguent.

Fig. 63: The pyramid tombs of the workmen and their families at Deir el Medina. *(Photograph: Jason Semmens)*

ROYAL TOMBS OF THE LATE PERIOD

During the 21st and 22nd Dynasties the kings were buried at Tanis in the north of the country. The royal tombs were designed with subterranean burial chambers while mortuary chapels were built above the ground. The tombs were built within the enclosures of important religious buildings rather than in separate burial sites. High-ranking officials were also buried in these places of affluence, a practice that continued until the 25th Dynasty, a period known as the Nubian Dynasty, when rulers originating from the south of Egypt were once more buried in pyramid structures which were faced by small mortuary temples. Sadly, the private tombs of this period are mostly unrecorded. Most corpses were placed in shaft tombs that had undecorated burial chambers. The tombs of the Late Period were designed in various styles, many resembled the mastaba funerary complex. Family catacombs then began to appear. Over time, Egypt was conquered first by the Macedonians and then by the Romans. During the Graeco-Roman period a mixture of styles prevailed. Often bright and exciting, they were a strange mixture of cultural icons that included Greek and Egyptian religious images. Although a description of these types of burials must remain brief in this context, their strange combination of Egyptian, Greek and Roman styles is important for scholars because it reveals the manner in which ancient Egyptian traditions of building and decoration, and even religious practice, survived and became integrated with the cultures of conquering nations. For centuries ancient Egyptian buildings were broken down and reused; stone was recycled and crumbling temples were consumed by the dust. As the desert sand covered the last vestiges of these ancient monuments and tombs knowledge of the civilisation of ancient Egypt and its language faded and passed into the realms of legend.

SIX

Discovering the Dead

Who then discovered the dead? The science of Egyptology has conducted serious investigations for just over a century. Prior to that, an assortment of treasure seekers, artists and travellers had been at work in Egypt recording the ancient monuments of the pharaohs as they lay buried in the sand. Ancient tourists have also left important accounts of their visits. Herodotus of Halicarnassus, writing in the fifth century BC, left an impressive record of the ancient Egyptian funerary practices in Book II of his Histories. Egyptologists, however, have always viewed these writings as a mixture of fable and fact. In classical times the Greeks and Romans visited Egypt leaving graffiti on the monuments. Augustus, governor of Rome in 27 BC, had Egyptian objects shipped to his homeland, including an obelisk which now stands in the city's Piazza del Popolo. Interest in Egypt's past was revived in medieval times – the Jesuit priest Athanasius Kircher (1602–80) penned *Oedipus Aegypticus* (1652–4), arousing an interest in Egyptology among many of a scholarly disposition. Kircher's became the most widely read work on Egyptian history until Napoleon Bonaparte published a report of his expeditions almost 150 years later.

Tourists on religious pilgrimages to the Holy Land often visited Egypt. As most wished to make their way to Jerusalem they remained in the northern region, confining their visits to the pyramids and the Sphinx at Giza. The Venetian Pietro della Valle (1586–1632) went to Egypt to find mummies (two of these were housed in the Dresden Museum until they were destroyed by bombs during the Second World War), while the English scholar and astronomer John Greaves wrote an early study of the pyramids, *Pyramidographia* in 1646. Sir Thomas Browne in his *Hydriotaphia* (1658) described how mummia was crushed and taken as a liquid while Father Claude Sicard (1677–1726), a French missionary, was the first traveller to explore the south where he recorded more than fifty tombs. In 1705, Thomas Greenhill an English doctor published a book on Egyptian mummification called *Nekrokedeia or The Art of Embalming*. When the most celebrated adventurer of this generation, James Bruce (1730–94) first explored the tomb of Ramesses III, still known as 'Bruce's Tomb', public interest in mummies began to escalate. In 1798 Napoleon set sail for Egypt employing a great many scientists, cartographers and engineers to occupy and study the ancient land. Bronze medals show Napoleon addressing the troops on horseback – the pyramids are depicted behind him as emblems of legitimacy and power. Napoleon hired scholars to record the monuments of Egypt. They travelled south to Qurna with the intention of obtaining antiquities and mummies for which they paid large sums of money. Members of the campaign describe being knee-deep in mummies, broken bones and coffins while some scholars describe how they became stranded deep inside a tomb when the flight of a large group of bats extinguished their candles. However, after the battle of Alexandria, Egypt fell into British hands and the French were forced to hand over their collection of antiquities – the Rosetta Stone included. However, French interest in Egypt continued long after their military involvement; many pioneering Egyptologists were of French nationality including Mariette, whose remains were interred in a replica Old Kingdom stone sarcophagus in the garden of Cairo Museum.

Of the many who were attracted to Egypt, there was no more colourful figure than Giovanni Battista Belzoni (1778–1823), a circus strongman who had been drawn to Egypt through his love of engineering. Quickly drawn into the trade in antiquities, Belzoni is today much maligned for his excavation techniques which are considered extremely destructive. For example, on entering one tomb Belzoni declared:

> I sunk altogether among the broken mummies, with a crash of bones, rags, and wooden cases, which raised such a dust as kept me motionless for a quarter of an hour, waiting till it subsided again. I could not leave the place, however, without increasing it, and every step I took I crushed a mummy in some part or other.

With hindsight, Belzoni was a man of his time and painfully unaware of the careful techniques used in modern day archaeology. However much we cringe at his careless trampling of bones and his indiscriminate use of battering rams, we should not fail to acknowledge his achievements. Belzoni loved Luxor where he 'seemed to be alone in the midst of all that is most sacred in the world – and it caused me to forget entirely the trifles and follies of life'. Here he discovered several tombs in the Valley of the Kings, among them the magnificent tomb of Sety I. On 1 August 1817, he uncovered the great temple of Ramesses II at Abu Simbel and went on to find several statues of Amenhotep III behind the Colossi of Memnon on the west bank of ancient Thebes. Belzoni also discovered the entrance to the Second Pyramid at Giza; bronze medals were struck to commemorate this momentous event. On one side there is a depiction of Belzoni's head, on the reverse, the Giza pyramid. Belzoni, who married an equally interesting character, an Irish adventurer called Sarah, was a larger-than-life figure who was to die tragically young. After his work in Egypt ended Belzoni set out to discover the source of the Niger, but he died at Benin after contracting dysentery on 3 December 1823. He was buried beneath an arasma tree. Although he had accumulated a large collection of antiquities for the dealer Henry Salt, he died penniless.

Henry Salt (1780–1827) who had employed Belzoni also used the services of one Giovanni D'Athanasi (1799–1850). D'Athanasi was given a house in the necropolis close to the tomb of Nahkt. Here he entertained travellers and guided them among the mummy pits and ancient tombs in the area; however, he described their state of decay with notably less interest than the treasures which he found among them. John Garner Wilkinson (1797–1875) made two journeys to the Second Cataract and carried out several excavations in the Theban area. Based on his researches, he wrote a book entitled *Manners and Customs of the Ancient Egyptians* (1837) and is sometimes credited with being the founder of British Egyptology. G. Passalacqua (1797–1865) in his publication *Catalogue Raisonné et Historique d'Antiquitiés découvertes en Égypte* includes a three-page description of tomb paintings and mummy pits. He describes a corridor cut 45 metres into the mountain crammed with coffins and where he found a multitude of corpses that had been buried with artefacts such as tools, statues, bows and arrows. He states that many mummy pits were blackened by fire and piled high with charred fragments. Local Arabs, he said, had set fire to the corpses in their search for gold and precious metal. Lise Manniche in her book *The Tombs of the Nobles at Thebes* aptly describes the Theban necropolis as a 'battle ground for treasure seekers'.

The next great scholarly work was undertaken by the German Egyptologist K.R. Lepsius (1810–84). *Denkmäler aus Äegypten und Äethiopien* consisted of twelve folio volumes. Lepsius is highly regarded by Egyptologists as a serious scholar who made several expeditions to various sites in Egypt and Nubia. Amelia Edwards (1831–92) had been influenced by John Gardner Wilkinson's *Manners and Customs* when she took her first trip to Egypt. The result of this visit was the classic *A Thousand Miles Up the Nile* (1877). The book proved to be highly popular and Amelia Edwards was invited to America to talk about her adventures on the Nile. In March 1882 she was among a prestigious group of scholars who went on to found the Egypt Exploration Fund, an organisation that still exerts a considerable influence on British Egyptology. In 1885 she established the first chair in Egyptology at University College London which was later held by the archaeologist Flinders Petrie (1853–1942). During the nineteenth century the British travel company Thomas Cook made Egypt a popular and accessible tourist destination – it also became fashionable for the royal families of Europe to visit the country and gaze upon its illustrious past.

A.H. Rhind (1833–63) was a Scottish lawyer who spent the winter in Egypt in order to boost his health. He was horrified by what he saw and became greatly concerned at the manner in which the tombs had been violated by treasure seekers. His book *Thebes, Its Tombs and their Tenants* was published in 1862. The University of Strasbourg together with the Egyptologist P.E. Newberry instigated a clearance of the area. They went on to make a careful examination of seven private tombs on the west bank at Thebes. Petrie spent two months at Thebes in 1908/9 where he discovered several painted tombs. Scholars and treasure seekers flocked to the Valley of the Kings, which housed the tombs of the rulers of the New Kingdom and some of their most influential retainers.

The first known royal burial in the Valley of the Kings can be dated to Tuthmosis I in 1493 BC while the last king to be buried in the area was Ramesses X in 1098 BC. It is unclear why the New Kingdom pharaohs suddenly adopted this area as their traditional burial ground, but the site was considered both sacred and safe. The Valley of the Kings is situated on the west bank of the Nile, where each evening the setting sun dissolves behind the rim of a golden mountain. Behind this mountain lies the Valley's floor. Carved out of the rock by ancient rivers, the area is a series of high peaks, narrow rivulets and natural pockets of stone. Before it lies a vast plain where the New Kingdom rulers built their mortuary temples. The Valley is a remote area, a labyrinth of ravines that lie in the shadows of a great mountain that has a clear religious significance. It rises above the plain of the desert like an ancient pyramid. From the east bank it resembles the Akhet symbol, the 'gate of the horizon' – a similar mountain range inspired Akhenaten's choice of location when he moved his court to the desert city of Akhetaten, the 'new' holy city. The shape of the peak and the layout of the Valley resembled the landscapes found in the myths associated with the solar cycles and the crooked paths of the underworld. Indeed, the tombs also follow this design. The mountain peak was sacred to Hathor and the goddess Meretseger, 'she who loves silence', a fitting deity for the Valley of the Kings for the area affords the most incredible acoustics. At the close of day, when the last tourist bus rolls down the hill, an indescribable silence descends on the Valley broken only by the calls of the hawks that prey on the mountain ridges. Some, this author included, find the silence unnerving. The archaeologist Arthur Weigall commented, 'Sometimes when I have been sitting at work alone [in a tomb in the Valley of the Kings] . . . I have been oppressed by the silence and the mystery . . . and if, after this lapse of three thousand years, one is still conscious of the awful sanctity . . . one wonders what must have been the sensations of the ancient thieves who penetrated by the light of a flickering oil lamp into the very presence of the dead.'

Tutankhamun in the Valley of the Kings

At the end of his brief life the pharaoh Tutankhamun was buried in the traditional burial ground of the ancient Egyptian rulers in the Valley. As we have seen, it was well known to early visitors as a vast treasure pit that yielded an apparently limitless cache of priceless objects – in ancient times it was so badly plundered that many of the royal mummies had been removed from their resting places in order to safeguard them from violation. Because of this illicit practice most tombs in the Valley show signs of looting. Tutankhamun's tomb was unique in that it remained virtually intact.

Tutankhamun [Fig. 64] lived during the Amarna Period, the most fascinating phase of ancient Egyptian history. It was then that Egypt reached the zenith of its wealth and power, experienced a long period of economic stability and sustained a strong and profitable relationship with its neighbours. Power struggles erupted between the rulers of this period and the Theban priesthood who were trying to raise their patron god Amun to such prominence that the royal family were afraid that the power of the Amun priesthood would come to equal that of the king. It is for this reason that they began to counteract the position of Amun by promoting the cult of the Aten, a deity recognised in the form of the sun disk. In an unprecedented act, the pharaoh Akhenaten, who is generally regarded as the father of Tutankhamun, removed the royal court from Thebes and founded a new desert city called Akhetaten, the City of the Aten. Here he instigated the worship of the Aten, to the exclusion of all other gods. For the first time in their history the Egyptians embraced a monotheistic regime. For a short period, the Amarna Dynasty flourished and produced exciting and profoundly beautiful works of art that are highly distinctive and unique to this period [Figs 6, 7, 10, 16, 26, 35, 40, 64–7, 75–6, 80, 88 and 90]. Egyptologists continue to be fascinated by this evocative era. However, we

Fig. 64: The gold mask of Tutankhamun. *(Egyptian Museum, Cairo/Photograph: Bridget McDermott)*

still know little of the events and conspiracies that surround the move to this strange and haunting city. Tutankhamun's childhood is doubly interesting to Egyptologists because he grew up during the Amarna 'revolution'.

It is ironic that we know so little of this king whose tomb became one of the most famous archaeological discoveries in the world. Most Egyptologists accept that Tutankhamun was the son of the pharaoh Akhenaten, but his matriarchal line is more problematic. It seems that Akhenaten's chief wife, the beautiful Nefertiti, produced only female children. It is therefore proposed that Tutankhamun may have been a child of one of the king's secondary wives, possibly the royal favourite, Kiya [Fig. 10]. Tutankhamun came to the throne when still a boy in 1333 BC and ruled for approximately nine years. He was 'guided' by a series of influential and possibly sinister figures, the most prominent being the enigmatic soldier and politician Ay and the military general Horemheb, both of whom would succeed him. When he died, either through accident or by assassination, he was no more than sixteen or seventeen years old.

DISCOVERING THE TOMB OF TUTANKHAMUN

> Mr Carter, holding a candle before him, put his head in. Lord Carnarvon said, 'He did not say anything for two or three minutes, but kept me in rather painful suspense. I thought I had been disappointed again, and I said, "Can you see anything?" "Yes, yes," he replied, "It is Wonderful."'

An American lawyer, Theodore Davis, had been busy excavating the Valley of the Kings during the years prior to the discovery of the tomb of Tutankhamun in 1922. At this time, he was unaware that he had come frustratingly close to discovering the most renowned tomb in archaeological history. A member of his team had recovered several objects belonging to this elusive king, included a cup that bore the name of Tutankhamun. After uncovering a private tomb and burial pit, Davis concluded that he had found the final resting place of the pharaoh and famously said: 'I fear that the Valley of the Tombs is now exhausted.'

Howard Carter was born in London on 9 May 1874, the youngest of eleven children. Like his father before him Carter developed a keen interest in art and Egyptology. When influential friends introduced him to Percy Newberry, an Egyptologist working for the Egypt Exploration Fund, Carter was invited to go to copy scenes from the rock-cut tombs of the nobles at Beni Hasan in Middle Egypt. Carter fell in love with Egypt and developed an intense passion for its history and culture. He went on to spend six years in Thebes recording scenes from the mortuary temple of the female pharaoh Hatshepsut at Deir el Bahri and eventually took the position of Inspector General of the Theban Necropolis. He spent a great deal of time in the Valley of the Kings where he worked and socialised with the local Egyptians. A thoughtful, solitary man, he spent his time walking and familiarising himself with the layout of the area. His knowledge of the topography of the Valley would serve him well and he went on to conduct invaluable work on the royal tombs.

Like many men and women of his class and generation, Lord Carnarvon first came to Egypt for the good of his health. As a wealthy man he turned his interest in Egyptian history into a hobby and began to fund excavations at various sites. When he was introduced to Howard Carter the two men immediately formed a strong and enduring bond. It was history in the making. Carter and Carnarvon made a great success of their alliance and were able to dig at many important sites, the tombs of Amenhotep I and Amenhotep III being among their most interesting discoveries. A number of their finds were placed in a private collection at the home of Lord Carnarvon, Highclere.

By 1917 Carter had turned his attention to finding the tomb of Tutankhamun, but despite an extensive clearing programme conducted by Carter in the Valley of the Kings there was still no breakthrough by early 1922. Carnarvon was becoming restless and decided that he should turn his attention to other projects. He summoned Carter to his home in England to tell him that he had decided to abandon the search. Carter, desperate to continue, offered to fund the excavation himself. Fortunately his enthusiasm was infectious and Carnarvon, with renewed confidence, agreed to foot the bill. On 1 November 1922 the workmen, directed by Carter, resumed the search. This time they were lucky. On 4 November they found a sunken staircase below the entrance to the tomb of Ramesses VI. As members of the expedition cleared the steps, Carter realised that he had found what he was looking for. Carter despatched a telegram to Carnarvon in England. It said, 'At last have made wonderful discovery in Valley; a magnificent tomb with seals intact; re-covered same for your arrival; congratulations.'

Carter was forced to curb his excitement. He sealed off the area of the tomb until the arrival of his benefactor. Two and a half weeks later, on 23 November, Carnarvon arrived with his daughter, Lady Evelyn Herbert. Carter then cleared the stairs and revealed a seal impression that was inscribed with the name of Tutankhamun. The workmen forced their way through to the descending corridor which was packed with limestone rubble. By 26 November this too was cleared and a second door was revealed. Carter made a hole in the doorway and then inserted a candle so that he could take a glimpse into the beyond: 'At first I could see nothing, the hot air escaping from the chamber causing the candle flame to flicker, but presently, as my eyes grew accustomed to the light, details of the room within emerged slowly from the mist, strange animals, statues, and gold – everywhere the glint of gold.'

THE TOMB

The tomb consisted of a corridor, annexe, antechamber, burial chamber and treasury. The antechamber which is 2½ metres in height is measured to be at

Fig. 65: An elaborately decorated chariot from the tomb of Tutankhamun. *(Egyptian Museum, Cairo/Photograph: Bridget McDermott)*

7 metres below the Valley floor. In it Carter found a massive cache of ancient objects that included everyday items such as beds, chests, chariots, statues and large groups of household furniture piled up one against the other [Fig. 65]. The annexe, its walls unfinished and still marked by draughtsmen's lines, was so packed with treasure that the archaeologists were unable to work in the chamber for fear of crushing precious materials [Fig. 66]. They had to devise a system whereby they were suspended above the floor and could clear the objects in a painstaking but systematic fashion until all goods, such as beds, chairs, baskets, chariots, model boats and household furniture were catalogued and placed in safekeeping.

The burial chamber, which was $3\frac{1}{2}$ metres high, was plastered in gypsum and decorated with painted scenes, the walls still blackened with soot from the lanterns of the Valley workmen. On the east wall of the chamber there are scenes that show the mummified king on his beir being dragged by a group of men. On the north wall we see Ay, Tutankhamun's successor, as a priest performing the ritual of the opening of the mouth. Other scenes depict the dead king being welcomed by the sky goddess Nut while in another Tutankhamun and his Ka are embraced by Osiris and other members of the blessed dead. On the south wall the pharaoh is led into the underworld by Hathor, Anubis and Isis while

Fig. 66: Senet game set. One of many found in the annexe in the tomb of Tutankhamun, this wonderfully carved box is set on a sledge, and its legs curve into the shape of lions' paws. It consists of thirty inscribed ivory squares on which the tomb owner moved his pieces, and which were kept in a drawer below the board. On the walls of their tombs the ancient Egyptians are often shown playing Senet; the game is believed to have been based on the journey through the underworld. *(Egyptian Museum, Cairo/Photograph: Bridget McDermott)*

the western wall is decorated with scenes from the Amduat. Here the twelve hours of the night are depicted as twelve baboons.

As he entered the burial chamber Carter experienced the crowning moment of his career. For many archaeologists this moment is the stuff of dreams. One of his colleagues said that he (Carter) 'was nervous like a naughty schoolboy [and] naturally, very excited; although he knew a good deal about what was there he cannot have helped feeling that this was one of the very great moments that happen to few people'. The burial chamber contained over 300 pieces of treasure and would take eight months to clear. Inside, simple but exquisite objects such as the funeral bouquet, bows and arrows and ostrich feather fans rested among the magnificent gilded shrines that contained the king's sarcophagus. To Carter's amazement a further room, known as the Treasury, lay to the east side of the burial chamber. Its entrance was guarded by a ferocious and recumbant statue of Anubis who was shown mounted upon a large shrine, his great pointed ears alerted to intruders. Over 500 objects were recovered from this room, among them a religious icon in the form of a wooden model that depicted the cow-headed goddess Hathor. Here Carter found caskets, boats and the two mummified foetuses of Tutankhamun's children.

Before they began the systematic clearing the archaeologists equipped the tomb with electric lighting. For the first time a large group of specialists was employed to study an Egyptian tomb, including experts in botany, chemistry, engineering, architecture and photography. Suddenly, the attention of the world was upon the tomb of Tutankhamun, and people began to speculate about archaeology and to appreciate the importance not only of Tutankhamun's treasure but of the smaller finds, the household objects and, of course, the human remains. The world of treasure seekers and amateur Egyptologists had gone forever. The tomb was now the subject of national pride. The world was fortunate for it had in Carter a committed, professional and skilled individual whose unquestionable integrity was the perfect prerequisite for the type of work that lay ahead.

Carter was meticulous. He made sure that every object was catalogued; small beads scattered on the floor of the tomb were treated with the same respect as were the larger objects contained among Tutankhamun's burial equipment [Fig. 67]. Each object had a story to tell. Careful techniques were used to preserve the objects as they were transported from the tomb. The tomb of Sety II was employed as a safehouse and was used as the venue for photographing the excavated materials. Each object, or object group was given a number – the numbers can be seen written on cards in the excavation photographs. Furthermore, a sketch was made of each piece and listed on a record card. A plan was made of each room which shows each object placed in its original position. It was painstaking work that would take over ten years to complete.

Carter did not live to finish his work. He published a three-volume book, *The Tomb of Tutankhamun* (1923–33) but did not complete an overview before he died in 1939. His notes and photographs were presented to the University of Oxford, the Griffith Institute of the Ashmolean Museum. The collection of objects from the tomb of Tutankhamun is displayed in the Egyptian Museum, Cairo, its exhibition hall listed to this day as one of the most popular tourist destinations in Egypt.

Since the discovery of the tomb of Tutankhamun many other important finds have been made in Egypt. Muhamed Abd el-Rassul, who first discovered the royal mummy cache, also led the authorities to another important burial site. This tomb was discovered below the court of Hatshepsut's temple at Deir el

Fig. 67: The gold coffin of Tutankhamun. *(Egyptian Museum, Cairo/Photograph: Jason Semmens)*

Bahri. Here, Egyptologists Eugene Grebaut and Georges Daressy found a group of limestone slabs that covered the entrance to a burial shaft. The shaft, which measured 14 metres deep, was filled with limestone chippings. After making a hole in the debris, the excavators lit a candle and peered into the tomb. They realised that it was packed with varnished coffins and elaborate funerary equipment. The tomb was enormous. The corridor measured 2 metres wide and over 90 metres long. It continued for some 50 metres to the west, reaching a burial chamber and a single storeroom that lay beneath the lower court of Hatshepsut's temple. It was the burial place of the 21st Dynasty priesthood who served the chief Theban god Amun and its yield was astounding. Here archaeologists found 153 sets of anthropoid coffins, two-thirds of which comprised outer and inner containers and a coffin board. Other finds included

110 shabti boxes [Figs 81 and 82], 400 figurines, 77 Osiris statues containing important funerary papyri, 8 wooden stelae and 4 canopic containers. There were also domestic objects such as beds, boxes, baskets, floral garlands and sandals. Clearance of the corridor was completed within eight days. The contents of the tomb, which was left under armed guard, were carried to the government steamer and transported to Cairo.

In 1935 Walter Emery excavated the great royal tombs at Saqqara which date to the Early Dynastic Period, while the Royal Tombs of Tanis were excavated between 1939 and 1946. During the 1950s work was undertaken to rescue and reassemble the boat of Cheops at Giza and in 1975 the New Kingdom tombs at Saqqara were excavated by Geoffrey Martin where the tombs of Maya, the treasurer of Tutankhamun, and the lost tomb of Horemheb were discovered. Work continues on the study of the Egyptian dead and their tombs. Although these projects will never receive the same glorious publicity afforded to the discovery of the tomb of Tutankhamun, the finds continue to amaze and empower Egyptologists. Stunning discoveries continue. In 1987 members of the Theban mapping project rediscovered the tomb known as KV 5. Archaeologists were aware of its existence due to a brief comment made by the British explorer James Burton (1788–1862) on one of his handwritten plans, but little was known of the tomb that lay at the entrance to the Valley of the Kings. The tomb is dated to the Ramesside Period. Designed with 115 corridors and chambers it acts as a mausoleum for the sons of one of Egypt's greatest kings, Ramesses II. It is the largest tomb ever found in Egypt and is viewed as an archaeological wonder.

SEVEN

Festivals and the Temple

An offering which the king gives, Anubis, lord of the necropolis, first of the god's hall. May she be buried in the western necropolis in a good old age. May she travel on the fine road on which an honoured one travels. May offerings be made to her on the Feast of the New Year, the Feast of Thoth, the Feast of the First Day of the Year, the Wag Feast, the Feast of Sokar, the Great Fire Feast, the Feast of the Brazier, the Min Feast, the Monthly Feast of Saj, the Feast of the Month, the Half Month Feast, all feasts, every day for the royal daughter, the ornament, Nisedjerkai.

5th Dynasty funerary prayer, from the tomb of Nisedjerkai

Most societies celebrate a festival that honours the relationship between the living and the dead. Many share common features – for example, many rituals employ food and drink as symbols of the life-force. On the Day of the Dead Mexicans remember their ancestors whose spirits may visit the living on one day a year; in Britain, pagans and Wiccans celebrate Samhain, the night when the veil between the living and the dead is believed to be at its weakest point and one may feast with the dead. During these ceremonies, the living cook food that was favoured by their dead relatives. Light and aroma play an important part in these rituals; sweets and breads are particularly favoured, the latter being baked in human form. Music also plays a central role in the rituals. In Ireland hymns and laments are often played alongside wild reels and jigs that were composed to wake the dead. In ancient Greece, the Festival of Anthesteria was a time when the spirits of the deceased were said to emerge from the underworld. Modern Buddhists celebrate the festival of the Hungry Ghost. Zoroastrians celebrate Parsis with fire, incense and prayers. Catholics remember their loved ones on the Feast of All Souls. The Egyptians, who loved festivals, celebrated many that were connected to death and rebirth.

In Egypt, Min was considered the most important god of fertility and he is shown in a striking array of artistic representations as a mummified form holding an erect penis. His festival was held in the ninth month of the year, the celebrations beginning with the ritual cutting of a sheaf of corn by the king as a symbol of his reaping fertility for the people. The Feast of Wagi, which fell just after the New Year, is the oldest celebration in ancient Egypt and inextricably linked to the mortuary cults of the ancestors. The ancient Egyptians held the Beautiful Feast of the Valley (celebrated at least from the Middle Kingdom onwards) in the tenth month of the year. The festival was designed so that the people could commune with their dead. First, a great procession would depart from the Temple of Karnak; among the flock were priests who carried a large ceremonial boat that bore the statue of the god Amun. At the river the party stopped. The statue was ferried across the Nile and conducted to the mortuary temple of the king where it may have taken part in symbolic fertility rites conducted by priests and priestesses. The statue was also taken to various other mortuary complexes in the area accompanied by large groups of people enjoying a fine array of entertainments provided by dancers, acrobats and musicians. The

Fig. 68: The Temple of Ramesses III. From the air the large pylons, courtyards and temple walls can be seen. *(Photograph: Bridget McDermott)*

women carried the elegant sistra. This instrument, a type of rattle, had strong sexual connotations, as it was used to arouse the desire of the gods. The crowds would visit the necropolis where they would sit by the monuments of their dead. Here they would eat their favourite food, drink wine and hire musicians to play. Although this is the best known of the Egyptian funerary festivals, there were also many minor celebrations that were designed to ward off decay.

The Heb-Sed Festival derives from an archaic tradition and was usually held after the thirtieth anniversary of the king's succession. After that it was commemorated every three years. As the courtiers gathered at the opening of the festival they came to witness the king make a public show of his physical strength. Throughout history we have archetypal stories that tell of this type of trial; they are based on the principle that a king or hero was responsible for the fertility of the land and, even more importantly, that his physical body was a symbol of its fecundity. It is thought by some that the king ran a traditional course around the temple courtyard to prove his vigour. The temples of ancient Egypt are closely associated with these festivals – none more so than the mortuary temples which were designed especially for the enactment of rituals of regeneration connected to the dead king and his cult.

MORTUARY TEMPLES

> Rejoice Egypt to the height of heaven, for I am ruler of the two lands upon the throne of Atum. The gods have made me king over Egypt to conquer my enemies; they gave me this kingdom while I was a child, and my reign is full of plenty. Strength has been given to me by the gods of Egypt, from a heart of love.
>
> *Declaration of Ramesses III, from his mortuary temple at Medinet Habu*

Although the religious function of Egyptian temples was paramount these buildings also served other purposes. The temple was a fortress of the gods, its walls dominated by scenes of military prowess, and it was equipped with imposing pylons that were lined with flagpoles. In this way, the temple was viewed as a dramatic symbol of Egypt's military dominance overseen by the all-powerful deity Amun. Papyrus Harris describes the wall of a temple as having turrets, fortified gates and bastions. The most impressive feature of an Egyptian temple is the double pylon gateway that is often compared to the hieroglyphic sign of the Akhet – the gateway of the horizon [Fig. 57]. They were made from a series of large stones that were placed around an inner core of rubble. The pylon would be decorated with images of the king in his chariot trampling his enemy underfoot. Called 'Bekhnet' in Egyptian, the word pylon is translated as 'to be watchful', which would indicate another military connotation. In essence, the temples were forts of the gods, designed to uphold Maat (the emblem of truth and justice) and repel the forces of chaos. Brightly coloured flags were placed on either side of the pylons [Fig. 68]. The temple was a virtual city equipped with a palace, courtyards, granaries, treasuries and schools. Festivals and award ceremonies were enacted in the temple precincts where the Egyptians performed religious plays, combat displays and public executions. Mortuary temples were designed to serve the cult of deceased kings to which end groups of priests were permanently employed to work in the temple and perform a series of daily rituals intended to promote and safeguard the dead pharaoh as he took his place among the company of gods.

Although some Egyptologists now dispute the accuracy of the term 'mortuary temple', we shall refer to the buildings in this way for convenience while examining their basic function. Egyptologists recognise that the function of a cult temple, such as those at Luxor or Karnak, differs widely from that of a mortuary temple such as the Ramesseum or Medinet Habu, for the mortuary temple was used specifically for the funerary cult of the dead king. The two types of temple had different names, the cult temple was known as 'the mansion of the gods' while the mortuary temple was described as 'the mansion of millions of years'. The mortuary temples also had specific names; for example, the Ramesseum was known as 'United with Thebes', while Medinet Habu was called 'United with Eternity, mansion of millions of years'. While cult temples were built on the east bank of the Nile, the mortuary temples were established on the edge of the western desert, a barren landscape known as the City of the Dead. Mortuary temples were designed to sustain the king's Ka and in this way the rites conducted there also differed from those practised in the cult temples, where attention centred on maintaining and celebrating the living cults of the king and the gods.

When the building of the temple was instigated the king attended a foundation ceremony where he 'stretched the cord' or ritually measured the foundation plans. At this time he conducted a purification rite by pouring consecrated sand into the freshly cut trench. The king moulded the first brick and placed foundation deposits at each cardinal point; these deposits included tools and votive objects made of clay or wood and small pottery vessels inscribed with the names of the pharaoh and the gods. During its period of use, the temple may have seen various changes. For instance, the king's heir often repaired or added further buildings to his father's temple. Some temples were amalgamated into larger constructions, their stone blocks often re-used or adapted to serve other religious purposes. Egyptian kings were also capable of usurping the buildings of their ancestors and even of claiming the latter for themselves.

Both structure and decoration of the ancient Egyptian temple were carefully planned. The building was oriented to specific astronomical points; the mortuary temples had an east–west alignment, and for practical reasons were designed with full access to the river. It is important to note that the king visited his mortuary temple and stayed in the royal apartments that were built there. Here the king celebrated several important festivals. In some cases the king worshipped his dead or deified self. Each pillar, statue and inscription reflected various aspects of Egyptian myth. Even the sloping floors were designed to imitate the first mound of creation. At the southern temple of Ramesses II, Abu Simbel [Fig. 18], the main corridor was carefully designed so that on one day a year an influx of light penetrated the central corridor and illuminated a colossal statue of the king. The mud-brick temple of Mentuhotpe in western Thebes [Figs 54a and b] was also designed on a specific orientation so that it was aligned with the heliacal rising of the star Sirius. All temples are illustrated with the image of the chief god presenting the king with millions of years – in effect, eternal existence.

As the visitor entered the temple he or she found themselves in a large courtyard known as the open peristyle court. Wealthier members of Egyptian society commissioned stelae or statues that they would leave in the temple. They wanted their names to endure. The temple was built with a false door for the presentation of offerings while secluded areas were reserved for the worship of the ancestors. Subsidiary chambers, storerooms and crypts housed statues and ritual equipment. Enclosed and lined with columns, the hyperstyle hall was built behind the open court with an exit through a processional way that led to the most important room in the temple, the shrine. Here the cult statue of the temple god was housed. Every aspect of the temple architecture was deeply symbolic. For example, the rows of columns represented marsh plants, the ceiling, the vault of the sky. The terminals of these finely carved and painted columns were designed in the form of closed or open flowers, namely the lotus and the papyrus, the symbolic flowers of Upper and Lower Egypt. They terminated in an elegant architrave, while the ceiling was painted with azure blue and golden stars. Egyptian temples were based on a long processional way, made of mud bricks, that led to an outer wall which separated the local inhabitants from the estate of the gods, and may have measured an impressive 10 metres thick. Each temple had a landing quay built on the edge of the river so that goods could be conveyed straight to the temple; here, too, elaborate ceremonial receptions could be conducted for foreign dignitaries.

THE FIRST TEMPLES

Scholars now believe that early places of worship took the form of stone circles. These were later replaced by simple shrines. The most important Predynastic temple was found at Hierakonpolis, also known as the City of the Falcon, where the site had a court that measured 32 metres long and 13 metres wide. It was surrounded by a reed fence and may have contained a mound of sand. Wooden posts decorated with religious insignia were erected at the entrance. During the Old Kingdom the pyramids were equipped with mortuary temples that were annexed to the north or south side of the structure. The mortuary temple was designed with an entrance hall and a large columned court which led to a rear temple. The temple contained a sanctuary together with shrines or niches that housed statues of the king. While the majority of Middle Kingdom mortuary temples have largely been destroyed or dismantled, the temple of Mentuhotpe II at Deir el Bahri [Fig. 54] is, however, a magnificent example of this type of architecture. With its dramatic location, terraced colonnades and elegant statuary it became a source of inspiration to architects of the New Kingdom.

NEW KINGDOM TEMPLES

The earliest New Kingdom mortuary temples were magnificent. The most famous example of this type of building is the temple of Hatshepsut which was partly cut into the Theban cliffs at Deir el Bahri [Fig. 54]. Like the temple of Mentuhotpe II, its prototype, it was constructed as a series of free-standing terraces, its lower courtyard surrounded by trees, flowers and statuary. Highly decorated walls reveal images of soldiers and their foreign expeditions to Punt where the Egyptians traded exotic goods such as incense and ivory. The divine birth of Hatshepsut is also shown on the temple walls. The Divine Birth scenes were created in an attempt to legitimise the rule of the pharaoh by establishing a pictorial and written record of the romantic tryst between the ruler's natural mother and the god Amun. The Egyptians treated this matter with great subtlety. The Egyptian queen is shown being 'visited' by the god, who had taken the shape of her husband the king. Amun is then shown seated next to the queen, holding the ankh, the symbol of life, to her nose or lips.

He [Amun] changed his form into that of his majesty [the living king, Tuthmosis I]. He found her [the queen] as she slept in the beauty of her palace. She waked at the fragrance of the god which she knew from the presence of his majesty. He went to her then and he satisfied his desire and revealed himself in the form of the god. As he stood before her she rejoiced in his beauty, his love entered her limbs which were flooded by the fragrance of the god. Words spoken by the king's wife and king's mother Ahmose in the presence of this revered god Amun, Lord of Thebes: 'How great you are. You reside in splendour. You have united my majesty with your blessing. Your dew is in all my limbs.' After this, the majesty of this god did all that he desired with her. At this conception of Hatshepsut the god Amun says: 'Hatshepsut shall be the name of my daughter whom I have placed in your body. Behold this is my decree. She shall exercise the excellent kingship in this whole land. My soul is hers, my gifts are hers, my crown is hers that she may rule the Two Lands and she shall command all the living.'

In this way the texts and scenes of the mortuary temple illustrate and justify the entire life of the pharaoh from the very moment of his or her conception and sustain the king even in death. Thus, the temple served as biographical template. It was also seen as a living entity; the first breath of creation. It pulsated with hidden powers and magical forces that seeped quietly into the shadows of the innermost chambers. This was the domain of the priesthood whose task it was to harness the celestial energy and mediate between the land of men and the gods.

The temple of Hatshepsut was the embodiment of ancient Egyptian elegance, luxury and grandeur. It was approached by an avenue of sphinxes, trees and artificial ponds. On the southern end of the first terrace there was a small sanctuary dedicated to Hathor, to the north a second was reserved for the worship of the funerary god Anubis. On the second terrace there was a row of statues that show Hatshepsut in the Osiride form. Behind these there was an open court and altar that was dedicated to the service of the sun god Re.

Built during the 19th Dynasty, the Ramesseum [Fig. 69] is a fine example of late New Kingdom architecture. Its most famous remnant is a colossal granite statue, one of a pair, that had toppled to the floor [Fig. 70]. The statue, probably one of the largest surviving statues of the ancient world, inspired Shelley's poem 'Ozymandias'.

I met a traveller from an antique land
Who said: Two vast and trunkless legs of stone
Stand in the desert. Near them, on the sand,
Half sunk, a shatter'd visage lies, whose frown
And wrinkled lip and sneer of cold command,
Tell that its sculptor well those passions read
Which yet survive, stamp'd on these lifeless things,
The hand that mock'd them, and the heart that fed;
And on the pedestal these words appear:
'My name is Ozymandias, king of kings,
Look on my works, ye Mighty, and despair!'
Nothing beside remains. Round the decay
Of that colossal wreck, boundless and bare,
The lone and level sands stretch far away.

The temple is designed with two forecourts, a hyperstyle hall and antechambers. The first and second pylons of the temple are decorated with the battle scenes of Ramesses II to whom the temple is dedicated. Ramesses II was among Egypt's greatest warrior kings and fought one of the first recorded military engagements in history, the battle of Kadesh. His military scenes include battle camps, the torture of enemy spies and the trampling of the Hittite foe. Other images depict siege warfare and show Egyptian soldiers breaking down the doors of an enemy fortress and rampaging over its battlements.

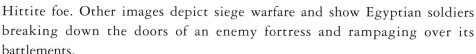

Medinet Habu is one of Egypt's finest mortuary temples [Fig. 71]. Its modern name is derived from another temple, dedicated to Amenhotep son of Habu the deified architect of Amenhotep III, which stood a few hundred metres to the north. The land upon which it was built had important mythological associations; it was connected to the Ogdoad, a group recognised collectively as the first gods of creation, who were believed to have originated in this area.

The temple was dedicated to Ramesses III. This 20th Dynasty king emulated Ramesses II in many ways, even adopting many of his titles, and the design of his mortuary temple is clearly based on that of the Ramesseum. The temple was originally linked to the Nile by means of a canal and a landing quay that was built at the eastern entrance. The Egyptians built an innovative gatehouse here,

Fig. 69: The Ramesseum, the mortuary temple of Ramesses II, with the colossal figures of the king, holding the crook and flail and dressed in the regalia of Osiris, principal god of the dead. (Photograph: Bridget McDermott)

Fig. 70: A colossal statue, now lying in the dust at the Ramesseum. It may have been appropriated by Ramesses II from a previous ruler, Amenhotep III, and is one of the largest statues known in Egypt. (Photograph: Bridget McDermott)

Fig. 71: A large ceremonial pylon, decorated with scenes of the king smiting his enemies, on the entrance gate to Medinet Habu, looking down the central axis of the temple. (Photograph: Bridget McDermott)

its design influenced by the Asiatic *migdol* or fortress, and decorated it with images of the king trampling the enemies of Egypt. The upper rooms of the gatehouse are particularly interesting – they are known as the harem, for they show the king relaxing with the women of the court. To the left of the gatehouse there are the remains of several mortuary chapels; these belonged to Divine Adoratrices of Amun who were buried here during the 26th Dynasty.

Today the temple is well preserved and the wall inscriptions accompany what are Egypt's last surviving grandiose military images depicting Egyptian soldiers in battle against the Libyans, Asiatics and the Sea Peoples. The main temple was known as 'The Temple of User-Maat-Re Meriamun, United with Eternity in the Possession of Amun in Western Thebes'. Its pylons are decorated with elaborate carvings depicting the king smiting his enemies – indeed, the building has over 7,000 square metres of decorated surfaces. Many of the themes shown are military: here the soldiers of pharaoh's army cut off the hands and penises of their enemies – the victors then string these grisly trophies on ropes which they wear around their waists and breasts.

On the north side of the court stand a series of large statues that represent the king in his Osiride form. Similar statues also appeared in the second court, but were destroyed by zealous Christian Copts who converted the temple into a church. However, the coloured pigments have survived in certain areas in the court and fine images of the king and his children can still be seen. The hyperstyle hall and beyond are largely destroyed. However, a group of side rooms dedicated to various gods including the deified Ramesses II contain some well-preserved scenes. The shrine of the Theban Triad, Amun, Mut and Khonsu, was placed at the rear of the temple and is equipped with a false door that allowed the king's Ka to pass in and out of the building. A magnificent brick-built palace was found in the southern area of the temple and the visitor can still see the 'window of appearances' in the first courtyard where the king would stand to present awards and gifts during festivals and official ceremonies.

The temple's architectural design was clearly influenced by the solar cycle. While the entrance pylons imitated the sacred space where the sun god was reborn each morning, the main processional route represented the sun's path on its daily journey. Finally, the sacred shrine was placed in the west. The temple itself was timeless; it functioned between the worlds. However, the prescribed rituals were necessary to sustain this order and so groups of priests were employed to perform daily ceremonies at the temple on behalf of the king.

EIGHT

Equipping the Dead

An offering which the king gives Osiris, Lord of Busiris, foremost of westerners, lord of Abydos in all his realms; a thousand loaves of bread and jugs of beer, a thousand unguent jars and fine cloth, a thousand of all good and pure things for the offering table from which the spirit loves to eat.

Inscription, stele of Tjeti, Thebes

A great deal of our knowledge of ancient Egypt is derived from tombs. In them, the ancient Egyptians placed their finest, most valuable and elaborate equipment. They then closed the door of the tomb and committed these prized and treasured objects to eternal darkness. Ironically, the objects we view today, from the delicate ornate beads of an Egyptian necklace to the gold mask of Tutankhamun, were never meant to be seen by the eyes of the living. The exquisite craftsmanship and elaborate designs were placed with or upon the dead to be used or worn in the afterlife. The planning and preparation for burial was an astonishing feat. While large objects were transported and placed in the tomb, others had important practical or spiritual functions. Although we may wonder at the array of objects found, seemingly haphazardly deposited in a tomb, each was carefully considered. The Egyptians employed many types of funerary goods and we shall look at them in detail in the following sections.

FUNERARY STATUES

The importance of the preservation of the body is evident from Early Periods of Egyptian history when plaster masks were often used on corpses so that some at least of their likeness was retained. During the Old Kingdom the Egyptians began to place substitute statues or heads in their tombs so as to afford extra protection to the king should his body become damaged. Sculptured heads, now known as reserve heads, were made of white limestone or clay. They have been found in the north at Giza, Abusir, Saqqara and Dahshur. The heads, plain, featureless and damaged in antiquity, were discovered in passageways just outside the burial chambers of the 4th Dynasty mastaba tombs.

During the Old Kingdom the Egyptians also used funerary statues as substitutes for the body if it was damaged or neglected, for they were aware that an individual's funerary cult would eventually become defunct. The statues were placed in the Serdab area of the mastaba tomb. Old Kingdom statuary had formal and simple classical lines and most were made of stone or wood. Firstly women were shown in plain dresses and simple wigs, their arms and hands placed at the sides of the body. The male was shown striding forwards, usually carrying a stick. Many of these statues are strengthened by a back panel that was often inscribed. Group statues were common. Judging by the numbers found, another popular piece comprised the figures of a man and woman sitting on

Fig. 72: A beautiful pair statue of Rahotep and his wife Nofret dated to the 4th Dynasty. Eyes of quartz and rock crystal outlined with black paint give their expressions a deeply powerful resonance. Old Kingdom figures. *(Eygptian Museum, Cairo/Photograph: Bridget McDermott)*

Fig. 73: Copper statue of Pepi I from the temple of Horus at Heirakonpolis. The eyes are inlaid with limestone and obsidian. *(Egyptian Museum, Cairo/Photograph: Bridget McDermott)*

blocks, their hands placed on their thighs. Single men are shown seated cross-legged on the ground with scrolls unrolled across their lap. Many statues depict husband and wife [Fig. 72]. Some individuals are shown with short, bobbed wigs that terminate at the shoulders, while some men are shown with cropped hair. They wear long or short kilts with triangular aprons while the women adopt a long linen dress. Many such statues include the couple's children. Triad statues, carved from single blocks of stone, show the king accompanied by a pair of voluptuous female deities. While wooden statues are noticeably smaller than statues made of stone, they too are carefully carved with inlaid eyes. Their arms are constructed separately and attached by tenons. Both stone and wooden statues were painted. The male was covered in a wash of red while a pale yellow was the preferred tone for women. The hair was painted black as were the rims of the eyes. Rare statues from the late Old Kingdom are made of copper [Fig. 73]. The statues were decorated with jewellery, namely collars, bracelets and anklets.

Some of these statues bear real portraiture – while they exhibit obviously individual features, they are also forced to conform to the Egyptian ideals of youth, beauty and vigour. Piety also plays an important role in the design of statuary, for many individuals chose to adopt the physical features of the king.

Although Middle Kingdom art is highly regarded only a few examples of large-scale stone and wooden statuary have survived. Large statues portray males who are shown seated on blocks with their hands placed on their knees. Offering texts are inscribed on the front of the block. Some men are shown wearing a long fringed cloak, a device that enabled the sculptor to create an elegant image without having to carve the complicated lines of the body. The men wear shoulder-length wigs and are shown with their hands placed against their hearts. Large standing figures were crafted from a single block of cedar or cypress wood while the arms were sculpted separately and attached by dowels. The statue was fixed to a wooden base on which religious inscriptions were placed. Another type of Middle Kingdom funerary statue shows a man seated on the ground with his legs folded back under his body. Again, he wears a long woollen cloak and his hand is placed across the breast, a position in which women can also be seen. This type of statue inspired the block statue, which remained popular during the New Kingdom and shows a cloaked figure with its knees drawn up to the chin. The flat panel created at the front of the statue provided a perfect palette for religious inscriptions. Another popular New Kingdom statue, a kneeling male in the act of presenting offering jars to the gods, also originated during this time.

Private tomb sculpture reached its peak during the New Kingdom. During the reign of Tuthmosis III the popularity of the pair statue flourished. It depicted a man and his wife seated side by side, their arms placed around each other's shoulders. During this time women were shown equal in height to their husbands – previously they had often been rendered on a smaller scale. The offering formulae (so important to the cult of the deceased) were carved on the back of the seat or on a narrow panel that supported the back of the statue [Fig. 74]; sometimes they were shown below a pair of Wadjet eyes. Some texts call upon the god Amun to provide 'bread and water, the breath of incense on the fire, jugs of wine and milk, geese and choice cuts of meat'. Following earlier practice, the flesh of the male is painted a dark red while his wife is depicted in pale yellow. Sometimes a child is shown seated between the parents. During this period the statues of individuals are shown praying to a solar deity. These elegant effigies have the tomb owner kneeling with arms raised, before him a large stele inscribed with a hymn to the sun god, a text influenced by the Book

Fig. 74: The New Kingdom nobleman Yunni offering an enshrined statue of Osiris. The back panel of the statue is inscribed with religious texts. *(Metropolitan Museum, New York/Photograph: Bridget McDermott)*

Fig. 75: The crocodile god Sobek and the king Amenhotep III. The magnificent calcite pair statue is of such delicate soft stone that it often seems to glow. *(Luxor Museum/ Photograph: Bridget McDermott)*

of the Dead. Wood was still used for small statues, while expensive stone was employed for royal commissions [Fig. 75]. During the 18th and 19th Dynasties some Egyptians still chose to have themselves portrayed as seated scribes while others chose single or pair statues where men and women embraced. Now they were dressed in elaborate wigs with beautiful and accentuated pleated clothing [Fig. 76].

Fig. 76: Amenhotep son of Hapu and favoured courtier of Amenhotep III. Considered by his contemporaries as a wise man and a trusted aide, he is shown in this beautiful sculpture as a learned scribe, a roll of papyrus on his knee. *(Luxor Museum/Photograph: Bridget McDermott)*

TOMB GOODS

From the Predynastic Period onwards the dead were buried with objects that were associated with daily life. During the Early Period even simple burials included domestic items such as pots and slate palettes while women were buried with jewellery, combs and fecundity figures. To secure their comfort in the afterlife the upper classes of ancient Egypt filled their tombs with a multitude of objects: funerary scenes depict large processions of men carrying boxes that contain furniture, weapons, clothes and everything possible a person might need in his or her house of eternity [Fig. 77]. Many beautiful models [Fig. 78] have been recovered from the ancient Egyptian tombs; some show the traditional crafts of the period while models of houses, complete with verandas and gardens, provide us with a clear impression of ancient Egyptian dwellings. Military life is also represented with some models depicting soldiers marching in rows [Fig. 79]. Although these objects are less grand than the treasures found in the royal tombs they are an invaluable source of material for scholarly research. Indeed, so much information is provided by these finds that

Fig. 77: Funerary goods were transported to the tomb in boxes. Here we see items such as jewellery, jars, chairs and archery equipment being taken to the place in the west. Reproduction from a Theban tomb from the Metropolitan Museum of Art. *(Reproduction from the Metropolitan Museum of Art, New York/Photograph: Bridget McDermott)*

Fig. 78: A model of a butcher's workshop, where cattle are being bound and slaughtered, from the tomb of Meketre at Thebes. *(Metropolitan Museum of Art, New York/ Photograph: Bridget McDermott)*

Fig. 79: This sumptuous 11th-Dynasty wooden model of armed soldiers marching in rows was found in the tomb of Meserheti at Asyut. *(Egyptian Museum, Cairo/Photograph: Bridget McDermott)*

Egyptology students who enrol on doctoral programmes can spend up to six years studying research topics as diverse as ancient Egyptian household furniture, Egyptian textiles or food production. To such students these smaller objects, that provide so much detail about everyday life in Egypt, are manna from heaven.

The tomb of Meketre at Thebes, excavated in 1920 by Harry Burton and Herbert E. Winlock who were working for the Metropolitan Museum of Art, New York has yielded a large number of impressive models. The collection is now on display in the museum. The tomb dates to the 12th Dynasty and the reign of Ammenemes I (1991–1962 BC). At first Burton and Winlock were disappointed with their commission. The burial had been robbed in antiquity and had been previously excavated. They found little to excite them. However, one night Burton was working late in the tomb when he came across an intact chamber which was literally bursting with wooden objects. Once opened, the chamber revealed a large collection of brightly painted funerary models – the pristine condition of these objects makes them unique. Here we see a model of the house of the tomb owner, brightly painted and equipped with a garden, columns and traditional decor. Even more breathtaking is a magnificent model that shows Meketre and his officials seated in the shade beneath a columned podium while they inspect a herd of brown, black and cream cattle. Among the collection we see butchers' shops, a granary, bakery and brewery. Not only are these models beautiful, they are also functional [Fig. 78]. They provide us with unique information about agricultural practices. Some models show women as offering bearers dressed in long black wigs and plain linen dresses. In one hand they carry a duck, while the other is raised to support a basket of bread which they balance on their head. A pair of green and ochre fishing boats share a single net. The oarsmen sit at the prow guiding the boat while fishermen busy themselves on deck. These men, of course, are supplying food for the afterlife.

One cannot describe such a rich find without calling to mind what is surely the world's greatest archaeological discovery. The Tomb of Tutankhamun was discovered by Howard Carter in November 1922. Beside the grand golden coffins and prized elegant furniture the personal effects of the king often seem the more poignant. Among the tomb equipment Howard Carter found a mannequin [Fig. 80]. It was no ordinary object. Although it was designed as a clothes hanger the object was fashioned in the form of the king, its head a portrait of the pharaoh, and it bore a crown decorated with royal insignia. The eyes, wide and almond shaped, are rimmed with kohl. It caused Harry Burton to make the irreverent suggestion that Tutankhamun was a latter-day dandy. The

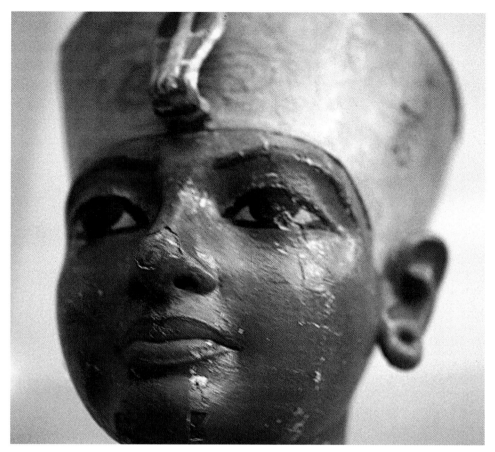

Fig. 80: A painted wooden mannequin from the tomb of Tutankhamun. It bears the typical features of the king, a royal headdress protected by an uraeus serpent. The mannequin, comprised of the upper body and without arms, may have been designed to hold the king's jewellery. *(Egyptian Museum, Cairo/Photograph: Bridget McDermott)*

ancient Egyptians, of course, loved fine clothes; for them cleanliness and order were very close to godliness and one didn't get much closer to god than the young pharaoh. Sadly, the abundant remains of textiles found in the tomb were badly recorded and much was lost. The condition of the material was often fragile and Carter commented, 'the condition of textiles varies. Cloth in cases is so strong that it might have come fresh from the loom, whereas in others it has been reduced by damp almost to the consistency of soot.' A number of Tutankhamun's clothes did survive, the majority made of fine linen. They consisted of underwear, shirts, sashes, kilts, headdresses and some fine dyed gloves that had just become fashionable among military men of his time.

Tutankhamun was also buried with his baby and childhood clothes. Many pieces of footwear were discovered in the tomb – one pair of sandals had the enemies of Egypt painted on the soles so that the king could symbolically crush them underfoot. Golden sandals were found on the mummy. Other sandals were made of papyrus or leather which were overlaid with gold or sewn with beads. One of the most fabulous textiles found in the tomb was an embroidered tunic made from a single piece of linen. It had an embroidered neck-line designed in the shape of an ankh, the symbol of life. In a box now labelled '54', Carter also found an amazing military garment, its collar joined to an armoured breast panel by golden braces that fitted around the shoulders. The collar itself was connected to the armoured breast panel by a large gold pectoral that was balanced by a second pectoral at the back. The scaled armour panels were inlaid with gold and carnelian. Ritual apparel, worn by the king in his role as a priest, was also found. Carter describes these as 'an imitation leopard-skin cloak in cloth, with gilt head, and spots and claws of silver; while two of the others were head-dresses, made in the semblance of hawks with outstretched wings'.

Many objects, including clothes, jewellery and even his grandfather's archery equipment, had been inscribed with the name of Tutankhamun's family and were termed heirlooms by Howard Carter. The finds suggest that the Egyptians placed sentimental value on such objects and that family members had a strong, loving relationship, a theory that is lent weight by the fact that personal items were found in the tomb. For example, there is an exhibit which Carter labelled 'The King's side-lock as a boy' and a sample of hair that had belonged to the young king's grandmother that was discovered in a pendant. More personal items were found in the tomb, among them a bed, shaving box and mirror cases that were designed in the shape of an ankh. Carter also found cosmetic spoons and kohl tubes used during the application of the king's eye make-up. An ointment box designed in the shape of a double cartouche had been decorated with two inlaid plumes, symbols of Amun. This beautiful object, delicately carved with the king's titles, still retained its original salve. Baskets and pottery filled with food were also found in the tomb. Clearly, the Ka of this king would never go hungry. The king was supplied with numerous loaves of bread, the staple diet of the ancient Egyptian, along with a small bunch of garlic cloves that had been perfectly preserved. Wheat and grinders were also supplied so that a virtual granary was placed at his disposal. Meat, including beef and goat, had been placed in boxes alongside nine ducks and two geese. Pulses such as lentils and chick peas were included as were a large number of herbs such as fenugreek, coriander and cumin. The king had been provided with the sweet things of the ancient Egyptian world such as jars of honey and baskets of fruit.

SHABTIS

> Hail shabti, you who have been given to me, if I be called to do any work which must be done in the realm of the dead; if hindrances are placed before you or I, as with a man who is at his work, you shall work for me on every occasion of cultivating the fields, of inundating the land or of carrying sand from east to west. 'Here I am!' you shall say.

The realm of Osiris, the Egyptian world of the dead, was also known as the Fields of Reeds. This heavenly domain was seen as a garden of paradise that produced abundant fields of crops. Gardens were important to the ancient Egyptians who saw the desert as a vile and dangerous landscape to which their cultivated fields and gardens acted as a sharp contrast, symbolising order over chaos. The Egyptians went to great lengths to irrigate and preserve their plants, trees and crops. Illustrations that show the Fields of Reeds reveal acres of land that required tending. Here, enormous fields of wheat and barley were ploughed and sewn by Egyptians dressed in their finest garments, jewellery and wigs. However, in reality the upper classes of Egyptian society were leisure-loving people who had no intention of spending their time in the afterlife ploughing fields. For this reason they designed model figures known as shabtis to do this, and other manual work, for them.

Fig. 81: A blue faïence shabti typical of the 18th Dynasty period. The inscriptions on the body tell of the shabti's intention to work for its owner. Probably from the tomb of Sety I. *(Louvre Collection, Paris/Photograph: Bridget McDermott)*

Fig. 82: A collection of elaborate gold shabtis from the tomb of Tutankhamun. *(Egyptian Museum, Cairo/Photograph: Bridget McDermott)*

Shabtis, which were fashioned in the shape of humans, were made of various materials such as bronze, wood or clay. The most popular figures were fashioned from faïence [Fig. 81]. Others were made of hardwood or limestone and were overlaid with gold. They were often shaped like mummies, their faces carved in exquisitely fine detail so producing appealing and endearing expressions [Fig. 82]. Inscriptions, carved or painted onto the lower body of the shabti, highlight its responsibilities as a manual worker: when called, the shabti – with great enthusiasm – is seen to reply: 'I will do it. Here I am!'

shabtis first appear during the Middle Kingdom and were used until the Ptolemaic Period. Although shabtis are commonly fashioned in the form of human servant statues they were also placed among animal burials. For commoners they were made to order or mass produced; shabtis of the upper classes often carry royal insignia. Some have their hands crossed over the chest while others are pivoted so that they could hold tiny hoes, baskets or copper tools. Some bear water carriers upon their backs. shabtis vary in quality and height, the average being about 12½ centimetres tall. During the New

Kingdom a great number of large shabtis were produced. As these models increased in popularity the Egyptians included supersized boxes of them in their tombs, the sets accompanied by special figures known as overseers. During the New Kingdom period large numbers of shabtis were placed in the tombs of the upper classes – the pharaoh Sety I possessed over 700.

STELAE

> I am an excellent official on earth, and will be an excellent spirit in the necropolis – for I gave bread to the hungry, clothes to the naked, have fed my fellow man. I have not begged. I looked after the estate of my parents, they are buried and made to live.
>
> *From an inscription on the 12th Dynasty stele of the priest Horemkhauf, from his*
> *tomb at Hierakonpolis*

A stele is a block of stone or wood that was painted or carved with commemorative images and used for funerary purposes by the Persians, Egyptians and Greeks. The ancient Egyptians employed funerary stelae from the Predynastic Period onwards. The stele served many functions and could be placed in domestic quarters or in personal shrines. As we have seen, the ancient Egyptians painted the walls of their tombs with the things that they would need in the afterlife. They also stored tomb goods. The stele provided extra security for it was a written text that could be read or used magically to activate important resources. They were not only placed in the tomb but could also be commissioned and erected at cult centres such as Abydos, situated in Middle Egypt, where they were left as personal donations to the gods.

During the Predynastic Period stelae were crafted as small oval-topped slabs of stone that were carved with a few symbols. However, these objects are important to language students as they tell us a great deal about the evolution of hieroglyphic writing. An early limestone stele belonging to an individual called Sen-Ba was found in a small chamber in the funerary complex of King Djer at Abydos dating to the 1st Dynasty. The tablet is carved with the crude image of a seated man and his name is spelt out in three hieroglyphs. By the Old Kingdom period the Egyptians had come to favour a rectangular-shaped stele. These objects were much more elaborate than their predecessors and show the tomb owner seated at a table spread with a feast of bread, onions, meat and vegetables. During the Middle Kingdom the ancient Egyptians continued to use this rectangular-shaped stele and carved hieroglyphs over the image of the

Fig. 83: Soldier armed with bow and stave and accompanied by a hound. During a long period of civil unrest it was fashionable for Egyptian men to be portrayed as soldiers for eternity. Middle Kingdom stele. *(Museo Archeologico, Florence/Photograph: Bridget McDermott)*

tomb owner which scholars translate as offering prayers. Although the deceased is often shown alone, he can also be seen with his wife and children poised before a table of beer, leeks and joints of meat.

The Middle Kingdom was a time of civil unrest and many males chose to be shown with archery equipment or staves [Fig. 83]. On the stele of Dedu (11th Dynasty) now housed in the Metropolitan Museum of Art, New York, Dedu is accompanied by his wife Sit-Sobek. Dedu grasps a military stave in one hand

and a tall stick in the other. His wife, who places her arm protectively around his shoulders, is depicted with a mirror. Women could establish their own stele. Indeed, a single stele could belong to several women, each represented in fine detail among the painted scenes. The styles of stele varied from brightly coloured panels crowned by a cavetto cornice to plain round stopped blocks carved in sunk relief [Fig. 84]. By the New Kingdom period, inscribed stelae were being commissioned for official declarations, erected at important monuments and used as boundary markers that defined the limits of the territory affiliated to the king. Stelae were commonly used as funerary objects and were inscribed and painted with the biographies and images of their owners.

Fig. 84: Funerary offerings are placed on a table before the tomb owner and his wife Ihi. Between them is their son Antef. The bright colours on this Middle Kingdom stele of Amenemhetare are still evident. It is one of the best preserved examples of these ancient Egyptian objects. *(Egyptian Museum, Cairo/Photograph: Bridget McDermott)*

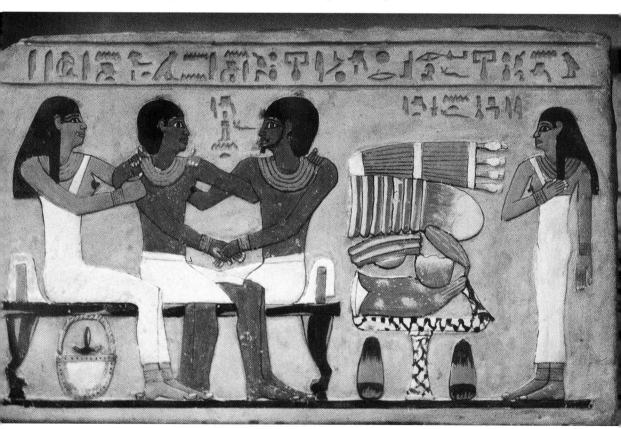

During the New Kingdom the paintings and inscriptions found on funerary stelae became increasingly ornate. They could carry inscriptions of prayers or hymns in praise of the sun god. During this period, too, miniature stelae were commissioned, some of which were less than 11 centimetres in height. They were decorated with a portrait of the deceased, his hands raised in praise of a table piled with offerings. During the 19th Dynasty stelae were often decorated with the tall mummiform figure of Osiris who is often accompanied by his wife Isis. The deceased, his wife and, in some cases, his children, kneel before Osiris or are shown before him in attitudes of worship. Sometimes, their cupped hands are blessed by a stream of water poured by a beneficent goddess.

JEWELLERY

Jewellery was highly regarded both for its value and for its spiritual significance. In life, the Egyptians loved fashion and cosmetics – they delighted in the wearing of fine ornaments and many of these items were transported with their body to the tomb. In addition, the Egyptians commissioned special rings, necklaces, bracelets and diadems that were designed especially for funerary purposes. Because of the enduring nature of the materials used in the manufacture of their jewellery, personal adornments are the most durable components of their grave goods. Stone beads and gold and silver amulets were found in the earliest graves. The arm of Djer – the earliest example of an embalmed human limb – was decorated with jewellery. The Egyptians draped their dead in ornaments, each piece having a specific role in the magical protection of the dead – indeed, certain spells in the Book of the Dead detail the correct ways that jewellery should be arranged on the corpse. The body itself was covered with protective amulets, into many of which precious stones were incorporated. During the Amarna Period, earrings became fashionable and men and women wore large gold ornaments in their ears. A mask of papier-mâché and painted plaster was placed on the face of the mummy; the mask was often overlaid with gold. The Egyptians also wore elaborate collars. These came in many styles and were often made of a series of beads and panels. It is this type of collar, examples of which are often designed in the style of a vulture with outstretched wings, that was found on the body of Tutankhamun. Spell 157 in the Book of the Dead is a part of a collection of incantations specifically intended to ensure that the correct jewels were placed on the mummy; the recitation was: 'to be spoken over a golden vulture with this spell inscribed upon it; it is to be fixed as a protection for this goodly soul on the day of burial, may it a million times be true'.

Necklaces of gold, precious stones or faïence beads and pendants were fastened with ornamental clasps. Pectorals were commonly placed on the breast of the mummy for which the most common design was that of a winged scarab beetle that represented regeneration. Decorated at left and right with the figures of Isis and Nepthys, the pectoral was inscribed with an invocation to the heart: 'Oh my heart, heart of my mother, hear me, do not rise up and speak against me; speak not against me in the presence of the judges.' Heavy bracelets were worn on the arms and ankles while elaborate guards were worn on the fingers and toes. Jewellery also appears on the outer panels of the coffin where it is painted on the face, hands and ankles of the deceased. The neck is painted with brightly panelled collars, the folded hands bear rings and in some instances large elaborate earrings can be seen beneath the cascading wigs of both men and women.

The many materials from which Egyptian jewellery was fashioned include electrum, silver and iron while semi-precious stones such as carnelian, lapis lazuli and turquoise were popular. Many funeral adornments were inscribed with hieroglyphs that spelt out the name of the deceased or their favoured gods and there are exquisite examples of ancient jewellery designed in the shape of hieroglyphic signs that fitted together to spell out important religious phrases. The colour of the jewels was also important. While green and blue faïence represent fertility, precious metals such as gold or silver represent the power of the sun and moon.

Pectorals, too, had funerary functions. Eight examples alone were found in the tomb of Tutankhamun. They show the vulture goddess Nekhbet and the cobra goddess Wadjet resting on inlaid baskets, their wings shrouding the mummiform image of Osiris. The Osirian triad, Isis, Osiris and Horus, are commonly depicted on popular pendants while the heart scarab, which is often inscribed with Chapter 30b of the Book of the Dead, the title of which is 'A spell for not letting the heart rise in opposition', is also common as a funerary object. The most popular scarabs were made from a dark green schist or a flame-coloured jasper and were often overlaid with gold.

Both in daily life and as accompaniment in death, the less wealthy too wore jewellery. Simple jewellery included disk- and barrel-shaped rings. Beads strung on one or a series of cords were popular. Egyptian men and women also wore chokers made of beads that were crafted in different sizes and shapes: some were round, some oval and some lozenge shaped. Valuable pieces were designed in the form of flowers, leaves and fruits made of precious metals and inlaid with vibrant coloured stones. Gold pendants were fashioned in the style of flies –

these were often awarded to or worn by military men as they represented persistence and bravery in the face of the enemy. The necklaces, ornaments and girdles placed on Egyptian mummies were believed to possess protective powers. Figures of divinities represented included Osiris, Thoth, Horus, Maat and Bes and were worn along with animal amulets in the form of fish, birds and insects. The major deity of the New Kingdom, Amun, was known as the hidden one and as such is rarely represented. However, many items of jewellery were crafted with hollow barrels that were designed to hold spells or invocations many of which petitioned Amun. The Egyptians often used sceptre symbols to represent divinity while the Wadjet Eye, or Eye of Horus, was crafted into plaques that were thought to have healing qualities. The Wadjet Eye was believed to be the left eye of Horus which was stolen by Set, the god of chaos. Later, it was returned and the eye was healed by Thoth, the god of wisdom. Therefore, the eyes became a symbol of light and healing and were often employed as protective amulets. From the late Old Kingdom eyes were painted on the doors of tombs and placed on coffins and sarcophagi. While the Ankh symbol (still worn as a popular amulet today) represented life, the Djed Pillar was believed to promote strength and stability.

COFFINS AND SARCOPHAGI

I begged from his majesty, the god, that there be brought for me a white stone sarcophagus from Tura. His majesty has his officials and a company of soldiers under his command to bring this sarcophagus from Tura. It came in a great boat of the court, together with a lid, a doorway lintel and two doorjambs and a libation table. Never had the like been done before for a servant, for I was fine in his majesty's heart.

The autobiography of Weni from his tomb chapel at Abydos, 6th Dynasty

In the sarcophagus chamber of the Pyramid of Unas the sky goddess Nut, who is often shown painted on coffins or sarcophagi, is represented to give protection to the king:

O Osiris
Nut your mother, spreads herself above you,
She conceals you from every evil,
She protects you from every evil
You, the finest of her children.

Fig. 85: A pair of eyes is often found on Middle Kingdom coffins to enable the deceased to survey his surroundings in the tomb. Coffin of Senebtisi. *(Metropolitan Museum of Art, New York/Photograph: Bridget McDermott)*

There is some evidence to suggest that the tomb was gradually stocked with funerary equipment over a number of years. This was certainly the case with the tomb of Merneptah during the 19th Dynasty. Preparation for burial was of the utmost importance and coffins were pre-ordered from workshops by individuals during their lifetimes. They would choose specific and fashionable designs for their coffins and sarcophagi while the royal family and some of their high officials would send great expeditions to secure stone for their funerary equipment. An inscription from the rock-cut stele of Mentuhotpe IV describes an expedition that was sent to Wadi Hammamat to quarry granite for the sarcophagus of the king. The inscription tells how a slab of stone was chosen for the lid of the sarcophagus when a gazelle was seen to give birth on it: 'Day 27, the lowering of the lid of this sarcophagus, a stone of four by eight by two cubits. Calves were slaughtered, goats sacrificed, and incense lit. Three thousand soldiers from lower Egypt transported it to Egypt.' From the middle of the 18th Dynasty the mummified body of the king was placed in a series of coffins that were designed like Russian dolls so that they fitted one inside the other. The coffins were then placed in a sarcophagus which was protected by a number of shrines, some of which were made of precious metal.

During the Early Periods the ancient Egyptians wrapped the body in reed mats, skins or furs. The dead were sometimes placed in pots. The king, his family and the upper classes were placed in coffins. The Egyptians looked on the coffin as an object from which they would be reborn. This principle of regeneration is evident in the use of the word 'suhet' to describe the inner coffin, a word that can be translated as 'egg', the symbol of emerging.

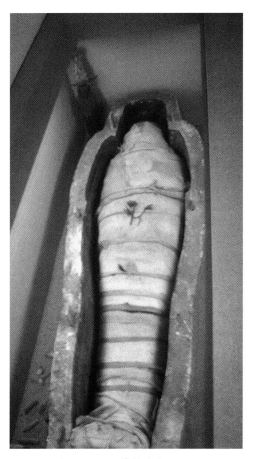

Fig. 86: An anthropoid coffin probably dating to the early 18th Dynasty. *(Bristol University Museum/Photograph: Bridget McDermott)*

The first elaborate royal sarcophagi date to the 3rd Dynasty. These were made of stone and were often equipped with vaulted lids. While many remained plain, the images of false doors began to appear on sarcophagi of this period. During the Middle Kingdom coffins were crafted from wood, which were then painted and decorated with a large pair of eyes intended to enable the deceased to look out and survey his tomb [Fig. 85]. Bands of hieroglyphs were painted on the outer and inner panels of the coffin, along with false doors, jewellery, clothing and weapons. The early coffins were designed in the shape of large rectangular boxes and this style remained common throughout the Middle Kingdom. During this period, too, the anthropoid coffin became fashionable and was used as an inner container. Furthermore, the name of Osiris now starts to appear among the offering spells that decorate the outer panels of the chest. Human figures also feature. Finally, the 'court style' coffin, adorned with bands of hieroglyphs and embellished with gold leaf, was reserved for members of the royal family.

The anthropoid coffin [Fig. 86] became standard during the Second Intermediate Period, acquiring a more lifelike appearance. The lids were adorned with fabulous images of the vulture goddess protecting the dead with her outstretched wings, a decorative element that has led to such coffins becoming known as 'rishi' after the Arabic word for feather. The coffins were painted or plastered and many show signs of gilding.

New Kingdom coffins were made of stucco, gilded wood or precious metal. The sarcophagus was made of stone; the finest were crafted from granite and carved with sacred images and hieroglyphs. Isis and Nephthys were shown guarding the head and foot of the sarcophagus while other deities connected to Osiris were painted on the surface to create a ring of eternal protection around the deceased. Osiris appears frequently on New Kingdom caskets and his emblems influence their decor. For example, the king is shown with a false beard or with his hands crossed over his breast, features that are considered typically Osirian. The body is shown protected by the wings of deities that fold protectively around the heart.

Sarcophagi is a Greek word that means 'flesh eater'; in ancient Egyptian they are known as the 'neb ankh' which means 'vessel of life'. Designed to hold a single or series of coffins, during the New Kingdom they were used for royal burials from the reign of Hatshepsut onwards. During the 18th Dynasty the corners of the sarcophagi were rounded to form the shape of a cartouche and Anubis and the four sons of Horus were carved on the sides [Fig. 87]. From the reign of Amenhotep III the favoured material for the construction of sarcophagi was red granite and some were decorated with beautiful cavetto cornices. Later, during the 19th Dynasty when tombs were widened and access became easier, the Egyptians used enormous red granite sarcophagi that weighed many tons.

During the New Kingdom the lower classes were buried in shrouds or in coffins made from cheap materials such as pottery or reed. The upper classes would buy a sarcophagus, casket and inner coffin. The Egyptians used sycamore, acacia or cedar for their coffins while gold and silver caskets were reserved for the pharaoh [Fig. 88].

Pieces of funerary equipment were made in a specialist workshop, where standard issue coffins were mass produced and personal names would be added

Fig. 87: Anubis with two of the four sons of Horus on an early 18th Dynasty coffin. *(Museo Archeologico, Florence/Photograph: Bridget McDermott)*

Fig. 88: A magnificent coffin of wood, gold, lapis and glass which belonged belonging to Egypt's 'heretic' king Akhenaten, recognised by many as the father of Tutankhamun. The face and names depicted on the coffin have been destroyed in an attempt to kill the 'soul' of the king. *(Egyptian Museum, Cairo/ Photograph: Bridget McDermott)*

to outer panels at the time of purchase. The upper classes might visit the workshops on several occasions to view their 'designer' caskets being crafted. By the middle of the 18th Dynasty, while non-royal coffins were often covered in pitch, the finest coffins had gilded faces and the bands were made of gold leaf. During the New Kingdom members of the upper classes were also able to buy multiple coffins for their burials, along with magnificent sarcophagi to hold them. The sarcophagi were designed with a 'roof' that imitated the shrines of the Archaic Period. Large wooden sledges were needed to transport this type of funerary equipment from the boat to the tomb [Fig. 89].

During the Ramesside period coffins were brightly painted with images of the gods and covered with vignettes that carried excerpts from the Book of the Dead. The dark resinous coffins of the 18th Dynasty were replaced during the 19th and 20th Dynasties by yellow-ochre caskets, the new colour a symbol of fertility and rebirth. On this background the Egyptians painted vivid representations of the gods in tones of reds and blues. The anthropoid coffins show the arms crossed at the breast. Males are shown with clenched hands that often grip amulets while women are depicted with their arms lying flat on the breast. Often, the mummy was covered with a false lid or mummy board which was made in two pieces. One part composed the face, collar and arms, while the second piece revealed the lower part of the body, its bandaging and inscriptions. During the early 19th Dynasty a new type of mummy board and lid was employed which portrayed the dead in a more lifelike manner and lavished a great deal of attention on the garments and hair. The hands of the males were now placed on the thighs while those of the women were pressed to the breast and held a flower or plant.

Fig. 89: A small model funerary boat carrying a coffin and mourner to the west. The canopy is painted with a cheetah skin, probably an imitation of a shield designed to protect the deceased. Location unknown. *(Photograph: Bridget McDermott)*

Throughout the 21st Dynasty only anthropomorphic coffins are known. During the Late Period Ramesses XI popularised solar themes and cosmological images with Geb, god of the earth, and Nut, the sky goddess, taking primary roles. While offering scenes were painted on the coffins, scenes dominate of the sun god's journey through the underworld and his triumph over death and the forces of chaos. Osirian themes were also popular. By the end of the 21st Dynasty coffins were painted in bright colours and were often varnished and fitted with a foot pedestal so that the mummy could be stood upright. In many cases the backs of the coffins were decorated with a Djed Pillar, the symbol of the backbone of Osiris and the hieroglyphic sign for stability. In what is a marked departure from earlier customs, during the later periods the family often kept the deceased in their coffins in the family home, a practice that became common during the Roman period when the casket was placed in a special room so that the deceased could participate in family gatherings.

CANOPIC JARS

Canopus is identified as a famous helmsman who served under the Greek ruler Menelaeus. Legend has it that when Canopus and Menelaeus were sailing to Greece a storm hit their ship and they were forced to land in Egypt. Canopus died and was buried in a city that bore his name. Here he was worshipped in the form of a human-headed jar. Early Egyptologists made a connection between the story and the small jars that contained the visceral remains of the Egyptian dead so the term is now generally used to describe these varied and interesting containers.

As we have seen, the earliest example of visceral remains come from the tomb of Hetepheres, the wife of Sneferu. They were kept in a calcite chest that was divided into four compartments each of which contained the remains of her internal organs. By the 4th Dynasty such remains came to be placed in jars of stone or clay. The Egyptians went on to establish their viscera in elaborate chests or in cavities in the walls of their tomb; however, having been interred in pits in the floor, during the later periods they were discovered in close proximity to the sarcophagus.

During the First Intermediate Period the lids were fashioned in the shape of human heads. Until this phase the inscriptions on the jars were limited to the name and titles of the deceased. During the Middle Kingdom small mummy masks adorned the linen packages that contained the viscera. Later, jars were placed in wooden chests each bearing an inscription that corresponded to the

Fig. 90: Calcite canopic chest of Tutankhamun set into an ornate sledge, a piece of unsurpassed craftsmanship. Each of its four compartments is designed with a lid that terminates in a bust of Tutankhamun. His eyes are painted with rims of kohl and his head is adorned with the traditional nemes headdress of an Egyptian king. It is surmounted by a cobra and a vulture which represent two goddesses who rule the north and south of Egypt. The compartments house four golden coffins that contained the viscera of the king. *(Egyptian Museum Cairo/Photograph: Bridget McDermott)*

coffin texts. These chests were often decorated with the recumbent figure of Anubis who is shown guarding the contents in his jackal form. During the early 18th Dynasty canopic chests became more ornate – they were meant to imitate a religious shrine and were often placed on a sledge. The jars had separate identities and functions. For example, one jar would hold the liver and was thought to be protected by the deities Imsety and Isis. The jar stopper terminated in the shape of a human head. In another jar the lungs were protected by Hapy and guarded by Nepthys – it was capped with the head of a baboon. The stomach, under the guardianship of Duamutef, was protected by the goddess Neith. This container had a dog-headed stopper. Finally, the intestines were associated with Qebsenuef and the goddess Selket. This jar is adorned with the head of a falcon. The inscriptions that invoked the protection of these goddesses were written on the inner part of the chest.

The four sons of Horus who guard the canopic jars first appear in the ancient Egyptian Pyramid Texts and later in the Book of the Dead where they help Re to overthrow the demon Apophis and act as guardians of the dead. The four sons of Horus were believed to protect the mummified corpse or coffin and often appear in paintings as four small jars, each of their stoppers being fashioned in the shape of a human head. In Spell 151 each of the guardians speaks; for example, Hapi says:

'I have come to protect you. I will knit together your limbs and head. I will smite your enemies.' Imsety declares, 'I have come to protect you. I will make your house flourish as is commanded by Ptah and as is commanded by Re.'

During the New Kingdom canopic jars were made from various materials such as calcite, limestone, pottery, wood cartonage and alabaster [Fig. 90]. From the reign of Amenhotep III we find lids designed to resemble the features of the king himself while the canopic chest of Tutankhamun matched other items of his funerary equipment such as the coffin and sarcophagus. The gilded wooden goddesses that guard the corners of his sarcophagus are the same deities who embrace his canopic chest with outstretched arms. This chest is made of gold and had four compartments that contained a miniature gold coffin that held the viscera of the king [Fig. 90]. During the 21st Dynasty the viscera were replaced into the body cavity along with effigies of the four sons of Horus. However, 'dummy', that is empty canopic jars, were still included in burials. During the 25th Dynasty canopic jars became rounder and less elaborate; they were replaced during the Ptolemaic Period by tall chests resembling brightly coloured shrines.

NINE

Mummification, Ritual and the Royal Ancestors

So Joseph died, being an hundred and ten years old; and they embalmed him, and he was put into a coffin in Egypt.

Genesis 50:26

The usual definition of to mummify is described as to preserve the corpse of a person or animal for burial by embalming it and wrapping it in cloth. However, this definition seems limited when we consider the complexities that surround the subject of mummification. There are, in fact, several types: deliberate mummification occurs when a body is placed in a specific position or location that aids dehydration or preservation; accidental mummification can occur when external conditions aid the preservation of the soft tissue.

Although mummification is closely associated with Egyptian archaeology the practice did not originate in the Nile Valley. The Chinchorro who inhabited northern Chile and southern Peru were the first human beings artificially to mummify their dead. They lived in the Atacama Desert, the most arid landscape known to man. Like the Egyptians they observed the way that human flesh dried in the sand and then tried to induce the process artificially. They used several procedures. The heads were removed from the corpses and the limbs were separated. The skin was removed from the body and later re-used. The internal organs were eviscerated, the bones cleaned and dried. Then the body parts were reassembled, and even the hair was carefully replaced. The features of the face were painted and the body clothed. The Inca sacrificed members of their communities on the highest mountain peaks of the Andes and the frozen remains of Inca mummies are startlingly well preserved. Many of the bodies were discovered by mountaineers. In 1964, Eric Grogh located a mummy near the summit of El Toro mountain in north-west Argentina while the Ampato Maiden was discovered on another peak by the American anthropologist Johan Reinhard. The bodies had been placed in a pit lined with stone. The Inca, whose

175

empire extended through Ecuador, Peru, Chile and north-west Argentina, believed that the mountains were inhabited by the gods. The people built shrines and made sacrifices on the summits in order to appease the gods. The humans whom the Inca sacrificed may have been abandoned to freeze to death; however, many were struck on the head with a blunt instrument. Some evidence suggests that the victims were killed by strangulation.

Ritual murder was also practised among the European Iron Age peoples who sacrificed members of their communities and threw their bodies into bogs. Two hundred of these bodies have been recovered from the British Isles alone. The Bog Bodies were naturally preserved and their skin, hair, flesh and internal organs show a remarkable degree of preservation. The sacrificial ritual was clearly of great importance to the community, for magnificent processional walkways have been excavated that were designed as an approach to the bogs. We still know little of the victims, except that they seem to have been treated well before death and that a high percentage had physical deformities. The bog bodies are regarded as 'votive dispositions' and it is unclear whether their communities were aware of the preservative qualities of the bog, which was viewed as a gateway between the world of the living and that of the gods. In her book *The Mummy Congress* Heather Pringle tells of an American businessman who tried to buy a bog in order to manufacture its properties as an anti-ageing cream. The attempt to preserve one's youth and beauty is a concept of which the Egyptians would certainly have approved.

The Inuit of Qilakitsoq, Greenland, also mummified their dead. Covered in sealskin, the mummified remains of six tattooed women and two children were found by a hunting party in 1972. In northern Australia, Aboriginal peoples preserved their dead through smoking and drying techniques, while other Australian cultures left corpses exposed to the elements on platforms in trees. The partially eviscerated body was placed in a sitting position, the knees pulled up towards the chest. When dry the epidermis was peeled off and the corpse covered with red ochre. Religious images were painted on the face and chest. Body hair was pulled out and used to make waistbands or ornaments.

As humans we are deeply attached to the living image of the people we admire and love, and so seek to preserve our memories of the dead, in some cases by inscribing names and setting photographs on their tombstones or graves. It is through this trait that we identify with the people of ancient civilisations and with the Egyptians in particular. As humans we are also primed to be repelled by death and disease – the image of a rotten corpse is abhorrent to most people. In modern times we find it increasingly necessary to sanitise death; we hand over the bodies of relatives to professional morticians who often keep them from view. For the Egyptians time was of the essence – the corpse, as in modern Egypt, was dealt with swiftly before the heat started to cause putrefaction.

What happens to the body when the heart stops beating? Although the brain dies quickly, activity in the body does not immediately cease, but declines at varying rates. The cells and tissues die off slowly, while the hair and nails continue to grow. The muscles begin to contract, and rigor first occurs in the jaw, mouth and fingers. The eyes sink into the sockets. After thirty-six hours the body is cold. Coliforms and clostridia spread into the body from the intestines – the Egyptians knew at an early date that this is the first organ to putrefy. Autolysis, the breakdown of the body, begins. The pancreas starts to digest itself. Gas is released from the tissues and the abdomen swells. Sores appear on the skin and the tongue swells; fluid leaks from the mouth and nose. If the corpse was left untreated, the hair, nails and teeth would break away from the body and the tissues would eventually liquefy and the body cavities erupt.

In a hot country an untreated cadaver will reach the first stages of putrefaction in a matter of days. Such a corpse will produce a vile odour – the smell is derived from hydrogen sulphide and methane escaping from the body. In Egypt if the body was left out in the sun and protected from scavengers it would probably mummify naturally. However, if the body were kept in the house or cellar the decomposition process would speed up. In a hot climate insects could rapidly deflesh a corpse. A variety of organisms feed on the body, including dogs, birds, beetles, flies and ants. The carrion flies are actually known as sarcophagus flies. The blowfly, *Calliphora erythrocephala*, lays up to 2,000 eggs in clusters of 70 to 100. In a hot country, therefore, the corpse can be completely infiltrated by maggots in a single day. The Egyptians knew about this process for they wrote with horror about corpse-eating worms in some of their religious texts. In Spell 154 of the Book of the Dead, 'A Spell for Not Letting the Corpse Perish', it is said of an untreated corpse: 'He who is decayed. All his bones are weakened, his flesh is defeated, his bones are soft, his flesh is now foul water, his decaying body smells and he turns into many worms.' It is surprising that as Egyptologists we often ask why the Egyptians felt inspired to preserve their loved ones. We sometimes forget there are simple answers. As humans we have a natural aversion to physical decay. Most of us connect to the physical image of the people we love and place great emphasis on the face and body; and we like to remember them in images that are both familiar and comfortable.

EGYPTIAN MUMMIES

Egyptian mummification is mentioned in the Bible. Genesis 50:2–3 reads: 'And Joseph commanded his servants and physicians to embalm his father . . . and forty days were fulfilled for him, for so are fulfilled the days of those which are embalmed; and the Egyptians mourned for him for three score and ten days.'

Mummification is now synonymous with ancient Egyptian culture. However, the practice did not reach its peak until the New Kingdom period, having evolved slowly throughout many centuries of trial and error. For a long time Egyptologists believed that there were no attempts to preserve the body during the Archaic Period. However, new evidence is emerging to suggest that we may have been wrong. Early remains dating to the Naqada II phase have been found at Hierakonpolis. The incision marks found on the bones of these early Egyptians have led to suggestions that the bodies were defleshed before being wrapped in bandages. Some scholars have even speculated that these early communities were practising cannibalism. Although we cannot ascertain this practice as fact, many early societies have been shown to practise ritual cannibalism during early transition periods. It is interesting to note, too, that cannibalism was a predominant theme in the Old Kingdom Pyramid Texts.

During the Archaic Period, when corpses were placed in pit burials wrapped in reeds or mats, the remains were often disturbed and exposed. At this time the Egyptians would have observed that the physical features of

Fig. 91: A mummy from a pit in the temple enclosure at Deir el Medina. The Theban necropolis was once littered with corpses. Even as late as the end of the twentieth century guards at various sites would earn extra money by taking tourists to see a hidden corpse or two.
(Photograph: Jason Semmens)

some of the bodies had been exceptionally well preserved – to them, it must have seemed miraculous. Soon, the preservation of physical features became a prerequisite for the survival of the spirit in the afterlife. Furthermore, as tombs became more complex, the corpse was transferred to a subterranean level. Ironically, these bodies were more likely to decay once removed from the sand. The Egyptians then had to find artificial ways of desiccating the body [Fig. 91]. With their long history of dry-curing fish and meat the Egyptians knew that the removal of body fluids was essential to the preservation of tissue. However, we know very little of their early mummification techniques; equally, there are no representations of the embalming process. Furthermore, no mummification texts have been found from Egypt and although texts known as the 'Ritual of Embalming' have survived, they concentrate on the prayers and religious rites conducted at the funeral.

Mummification is described in two sources, Herodotus and Diodorus. Herodotus says of the process:

There are a set of men in Egypt who practise the art of embalming, and make it their proper business. When a body is brought to them these persons show the bearers various models of corpses, made in wood, and painted so as to resemble nature. The most perfect is said to be after the manner in him whom I do not think it religious to name in connection with such a matter; the second sort is inferior to the first, and less costly; the third is the cheapest of all. All this the embalmers explain, and then ask in which way it is wished that the corpse should be prepared. The bearers tell them, and having concluded the bargain, take their departure, while the embalmers, left to themselves, proceed to their task. The mode of embalming, according the most perfect process, is the following: they take first a crooked piece of iron, and with it draw out the brain through the nostrils, thus getting rid of a portion, while the skull is cleared of the rest by rinsing with drugs; next they make a cut along the flank with a sharp Ethiopian stone, and take out the whole contents of the abdomen, which they then cleanse, washing it thoroughly with palm-wine, and again frequently with an infusion of pounded aromatics. After this, they fill the cavity with the purest bruised myrrh, with cassia, and every other sort of spicery except frankincense, and sew up the opening. Then, the body is placed in natrum for seventy days, and covered entirely over. After the expiration of that space of time, which must not be exceeded, the body is washed, and wrapped round, from head to foot, with bandages of fine linen cloth, smeared over with gum, which is used generally by the Egyptians in the place of glue, and in this state it is given back to the relations, who enclose it in a wooden case which they have had made for the purpose, shaped into the figure of a man. Then, fastening the case, they place it in a sepulchral chamber, upright against the wall. Such is the most costly way of embalming the dead.

Herodotus, Histories, Book II:§ 86

If persons wish to avoid expense, and choose the second process, the following is the method pursued: syringes are filled with oil made from the cedar-tree, which is then, without any incision or disembowelling injected into the bowel. The passage is stopped, and the body laid in natrum the prescribed number of days. At the end of the time the cedar-oil is allowed to make its escape; and such is its power that it brings with it the whole stomach and intestines in a liquid state. The natrum meanwhile has dissolved the flesh, and so nothing is left of the dead body but the skin and the bones. It is returned in this condition to the relative without any further trouble being bestowed upon it.

Herodotus, Histories, Book II:§ 87

The third method of embalming, which is practised in the case of the poorer classes, is to clear out the intestines with a purge, and let the body lie in natrum the seventy days, after which it is at once given to those who come to fetch it away.

Herodotus, Histories, Book II:§ 88

Modern scholars take the accounts of Herodotus with a pinch of salt. Herodotus wrote during the later periods of Egyptian history and relied heavily on stories when compiling his records. However, he makes several important points that are generally accepted by Egyptologists, one being that the Egyptians employed professional morticians or embalmers. Herodotus also states that the body was dried with natron. For a long time, Egyptologists thought the body was soaked in a bath of natron solution; however, it now seems more likely that dry natron was piled over the body.

An inscription from the doorjamb of the tomb of Meresankh III, the great-granddaughter of King Sneferu states: 'The King's daughter Meresankh, Year I, month I of the third season, day 21, her Ka went to rest, and she proceeded to the Wabet [house of mummification].' The recorded date of her interment suggests that there was a gap of 272 days between her death and her burial. This means that the Egyptians of the Old Kingdom required a longer period of dehydration than that practised during the New Kingdom.

Herodotus states that the bodies of high-ranking women were kept from the embalmers for a short period of time. This meant that the morticians would be less tempted to use the corpses for sexual intercourse. He states: 'Now the wives of important men, when they die, are not handed over to be embalmed at once, not women who are especially beautiful or famous. Not until the end of the third or fourth day has elapsed are they given to the embalmers. They do this to prevent the embalmers violating the corpse.'

Although the writings of the Sicilian, Diodorus Siculus, mirrored much of the information found in the works of Herodotus, he also provides details about the cost of embalming and gives the prices of three types of treatment. He also states that the person who made the first incision in the side of the body was considered to have defiled the corpse. He was therefore thought to be 'unclean' and was chased and abused as a scapegoat by the other mortuary workers.

OLD KINGDOM MUMMIFICATION

The first example of mummified remains was discovered by Flinders Petrie during his excavations of the royal tombs of Abydos. Here he found the arm bone of an important individual that had been wrapped in linen and decorated with jewellery. James Quibell (1867–1935) also found the remains of a female at Saqqara that are dated to the 2nd Dynasty. Inside its wooden coffin the body was found contracted and surrounded by linen wrappings. Because there is little evidence regarding mummification during this time, Egyptologists believe that embalming skills were still at a primitive stage. The remains of King Djoser, ruler of the 3rd Dynasty, were discovered by Jean Phillipe Lauer in 1934. They were found in a granite sarcophagus in the burial chamber of the Step Pyramid at Saqqara. These remains consisted of the upper half of the right humerus. Skin samples still covered the shoulder. Although only a number of ribs and vertebrae had survived, the left foot and toes, still wrapped in resin-soaked linen, were also recovered. It is during the 4th Dynasty period that more evidence comes to light. The American Egyptologist George Reisner (1867–1942) discovered the tomb of Queen Hetepheres in 1925. Hetepheres was the wife of Sneferu and the mother of Khufu (Cheops) the builder of the Great Pyramid. Although her stone sarcophagus was empty, excavators found a small alabaster box designed to hold her viscera. The internal organs were wrapped in packages that had been soaked in natron. This was a very important find. It proved that the Old Kingdom embalmers knew it was necessary to remove the internal organs in order to preserve the corpse, a discovery that heralded the beginning of true mummification. The use of natron as a drying agent was also important. Found in Wadi Natron 64km north-west of modern-day Cairo, natron is a substance that absorbs water and has antiseptic properties, so was used during all periods of mummification. Furthermore, the Egyptians revered natron as a sacred substance – they called it 'neteryt' which can be translated as 'of the god'. It was thought to be a cleansing agent and priests chewed pellets of natron to cleanse their mouths before uttering the holy words in the temple.

> O rise up Teti
> Take your head,
> Gather your bones and limbs,
> Shake the earth from your flesh,
> Take your bread that does not decay,
> Your beer that fails to sour,
> Stand at the gates that are closed to the commoners.
> The gatekeeper comes out to you, he takes your hand
> Leads you to heaven, to your father Geb.
>
> Inscription from the Old Kingdom Pyramid of Unas

A number of preserved bodies can be dated to the 4th Dynasty. William Flinders-Petrie (1853–1942) found one now well-known example in 1891 at Meidum. The mummy was described as follows: 'The body was shrunk, wrapped in linen cloth, then modelled all over with resin, into the natural form and plumpness of the living figure.' Grafton Elliot Smith (1871–1937) and Warren Dawson (1888–1968) examined this mummy at the Royal College of Surgeons in London, but it was later destroyed in an air raid during the Second World War.

During the 5th Dynasty mummification practices evolved further. The mummy of Setka was found by the German Egyptologist Hermann Junker (1877–1962) in an excavation dated to 1925/6. It revealed that the Egyptians were attempting to preserve the genitals and improve the shape of the body through bandaging. The abdominal and thoracic organs had been removed and linen had been introduced into the cavities. The mummy of an Old Kingdom court singer found in the tomb of Nefer was discovered at Saqqara in 1966 by Ahmed Moussa. The body had been carefully embalmed. The eyes, brows and moustache are outlined on the linen wrappings in paint. In fact, it was so well preserved that even a callous on the sole of one foot was still visible. The mummy of a woman dated to the 6th Dynasty was found in 1933 at Giza. The face, which was moulded in linen, had painted eyes and brows. She was dressed in the typical fashion of the day, namely a long linen dress with a V-shaped split between the breasts. The intestines had been left in the abdominal cavity and had leaked into the surrounding matter. The heart and lungs had been left in the body. The royal mummy, Merenre I, had been the fourth king of the 6th Dynasty. His body, which was buried in a black granite sarcophagus in his pyramid at Saqqara, was found in 1881. The mummy had suffered much damage. The upper front teeth and lower mandible were missing and the head had been torn from the body by ancient tomb robbers. In their attempts to steal valuable items of jewellery from the remains, they had smashed the thoracic wall. The mummy was examined by Maurice Bucaille. In his book, *Mummies of the Pharaohs: Modern Medical Investigations*, he reported that the decayed remains retained their vile smell.

MIDDLE KINGDOM MUMMIES

The first known royal mummies of the Middle Kingdom are dated to the 11th Dynasty and were found in the tombs of the mortuary temple of Mentuhotpe II at Deir el Bahri. The bodies were examined by Dr Douglas Derry in 1942. These mummies belonged to the royal women of Mentuhotpe, namely Ashayet, Amonet, Mayet and their sisters. The female mummies of the Middle Kingdom often show signs of tattooing and the abdomen of the mummy of Amonet, now in Cairo Museum, is adorned with tattoos while others had decorated limbs.

Ancient Egyptian women wore tattoos for religious purposes. Many chose a pattern that decorated the abdomen like a belt. It was worn as a form of magical protection against the loss of children. Others bore the image of the household god Bes on their thighs.

Mummification techniques sometimes show that evisceration incisions were made on the left side of the abdomen – however, the ethmoid bone had not yet been broken, and the cranial cavity still contained brain tissue.

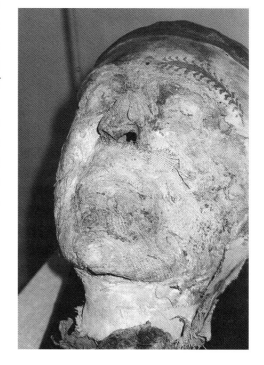

Fig. 92: A mummy of the soldier Djeuty-Nakht. The features of Middle Kingdom mummies were often painted over the bandages. Here a thick, black-painted eyebrow is still visible. *(Museum of Fine Arts, Boston/Photograph: Bridget McDermott)*

The body was carefully bandaged, each limb being individually tended. The embalming materials were thought to contain magical properties and were safely buried in special jars. Senebtisi, a Middle Kingdom female, was examined by Elliot Smith who found signs of careful evisceration; the body cavities were packed with sawdust and linen soaked in resin. Although some Middle Kingdom mummies were dried through natural means, most mummies of the period were in an advanced state of preservation, indicating that the Egyptians were working successfully with natron [Fig. 92]. The physical features were well preserved and the Egyptians no longer relied on linen moulding to retain a physical likeness. Mummy masks of linen or cartonage became popular during this period. In some cases the viscera was removed from the abdomen, but this was not a general practice. The Egyptian embalmers inserted resin into the rectum to dissolve the internal organs, a process that was used on the royal princesses found in the temple of Mentuhotpe II. It is described by Herodotus as a second-class method of mummification.

NEW KINGDOM MUMMIES

While peasants continued to be buried in pits in the sand [Fig. 93] New Kingdom rulers and nobles were brought to the 'wbu', probably a purification tent located near the river. The corpse was rinsed with water and natron. This ritual was depicted on the walls of Egyptian tombs and shows the blackened form of the deceased as he or she kneels on the floor or lies on a bier. The gods are shown pouring water over the body in order to regenerate it. The embalming took place in the house of mummification, which was known as the 'per-nefer' or the 'House of Beauty', where

Fig. 93 *Left and pages 185 and 186:* In the 1940s British soldiers posted to Egypt often came across open mummy pits. The location of these pits is unknown. *(Photograph: Courtesy of Guy Rothwell, Ancient Relics)*

the body was placed on a sloping bed so that the body fluids would drain efficiently [Fig. 94]. The embalmers removed the brain by passing a sharp instrument through the ethmoid bone into the cranial cavity, the brain was mashed and the residue passed down the nose. Some embalmers used another method of brain removal, draining the remains through the base of the skull. The empty skull cavity was then packed with sawdust and linen soaked in resin. A long incision was made on the left side of the abdomen and all the contents, except the kidneys, were removed. The Egyptians knew it was important to remove the stomach and intestines as these are the first organs to decompose. (If left untreated these organs would begin to ferment – a process that forms a gas that would enhance putrefaction and cause the abdomen to bloat.) The diaphragm was then cut and the thoracic contents taken out. The heart, revered by the Egyptians as the seat of conduct, was left in place. If the heart was accidentally removed it was sewn back into the body. Several spells in the Book of the Dead were designed to prevent the heart from being removed from the

Fig. 94: Anubis tending the dead, from the funeral sledge of Khonsu, the tomb of Sennedjem, Thebes. Ancient Egyptian embalmers were expected to wear the jackal mask while tending to the dead. Here an embalmer treats the body of Khonsu which lies on a lionheaded bed overlaid with a canopy. *(Photograph: Jason Semmens)*

body, Spell 29 being entitled 'A Spell to Prevent the Heart from Being Taken away from a Vindicated Man in the Necropolis'; it states: 'My heart is with me and it shall not be taken away, for I am a possessor of hearts who unites hearts. I live by truth, in which I exist.'

The thoracic and abdominal cavities were washed with palm wine and spices. The viscera were dried in natron and treated with resin and afterwards placed in canopic jars. During the later periods, the viscera were placed in packages and returned to the body, a practice that continued until the 26th Dynasty when canopic jars were reintroduced. The body cavities were packed with materials.

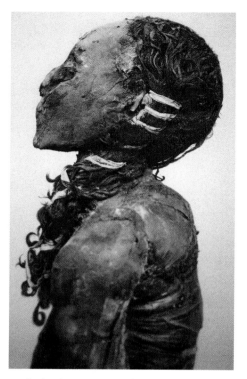

Fig. 95: The noblewoman Nsikhonsu with long braided tresses. Hair is often the best preserved feature of an Egyptian mummy. (*Reproduction from* The Royal Mummies, *G. Elliot Smith. (Photograph: Bridget McDermott)*

Dry natron powder in linen packages was used to prevent the collapse of the abdominal walls while the head, thoracic and abdominal cavities were stuffed with resin-soaked linen, myrrh, cassia, cloth, sawdust, dry lichen and even onions. The hair was often perfectly preserved [Fig. 95]. After dehydration, the body was taken from the natron bed and the temporary packing materials were removed. Since embalming materials were magically charged, they could not be destroyed. After use they were buried in funerary deposits near the tomb of the deceased.

Traditionally, Egyptologists have suggested that the mummification process took seventy days. This seventy-day period also had a deep religious significance as it was considered a phase of stability and corresponded with the time when the decons remained below the horizon. As the spirit of the deceased descends to the underworld it spends seventy days in the house of Geb, the earth god. Sacred texts describe this as a time of purification when the stars regenerated themselves. At this time the body was not only dried in natron but anointed, bandaged and censed. The seventy-day mummification period also covered the many important rituals that were conducted over the body and included the burial itself.

BANDAGING

It took fifteen days to bandage the body [Fig. 96]. The bandages were made of linens of different quality – only the upper classes were able to choose the most elaborate type of material which is simply described as 'fine linen'. The mortuary workshops had a large supply of bandages and the upper classes would

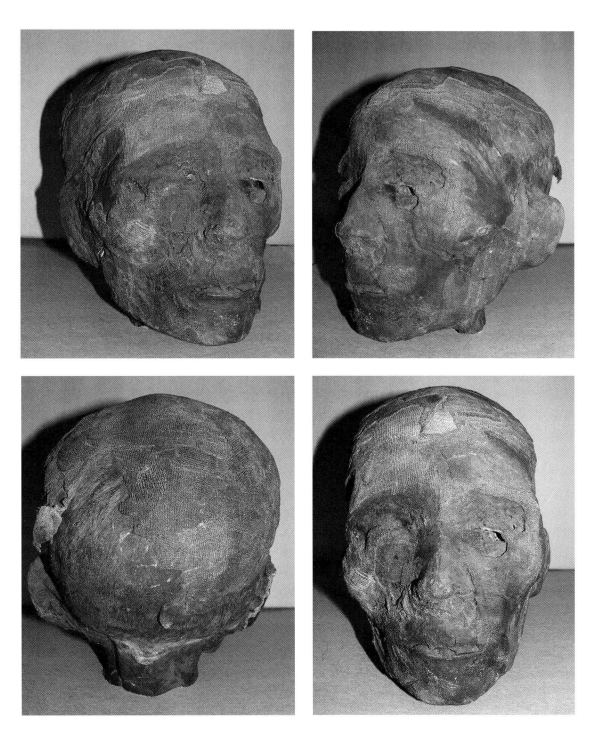

Fig. 96: A severed head, probably that of a young boy, bandaged in the typical style with resin-soaked linen. *(Photograph: Cyfarthfa Castle Museum and Art Gallery)*

wrap their dead in the finest materials. Yards of textiles could be used on an individual body – a single strip could be 12 metres long and several shrouds could be used to wrap an individual corpse.

The toes and fingers were capped with ornamental shields. Then the mortuary workers bandaged the fingers until each digit had been individually wrapped. A wide strip of linen was placed at the shoulder, stretched to the head and criss-crossed along the torso. The mortuary attendants then transferred the wrapping around the legs. Each layer was soaked in molten resin. If the body had been damaged in the mortuary – either by animals or humans – artificial arms, legs and feet might be used to replace missing limbs.

Every movement was carefully choreographed and had a strong religious significance. Healing amulets were placed above the embalming wound. Designed to protect the dead in the underworld, a complex array of magical emblems was placed on the body and between the bandages. The ceremony of embalming and the placing of amulets were sacred tasks. During this period, experienced mortuary priests would recite prayers and magical texts over the body.

THIRD INTERMEDIATE PERIOD MUMMIES

In ancient Egypt the practice of mummification reached its peak during the 21st Dynasty. The body was then made to look more lifelike and was stuffed with subcutaneous packing. Sand and sawdust were used to mould the face and body. This process often went too far and the bodies burst open, the faces bloated and the features were destroyed. The bodies of men were painted in red ochre while women were decorated with yellow pigments. Their eyes were replaced by glass and stone. They were wrapped in a shroud painted with the image of Osiris. Although the tomb was still equipped with dummy canopic jars the viscera were now placed in packages that were found between the legs. The wonderful mummy of Queen Nojmet is now on display among the royal mummies at the Egyptian Museum, Cairo. She was partially unwrapped by the Egyptologist Jean Maspero (1885–1915) on 13 September 1906. A fine example of a 21st Dynasty mummy, she reveals the new techniques employed by embalmers of this period. Nojmet had been treated with linen wads that were designed to pad out the cheeks and neck and make the features more lifelike. The body was decorated with red or yellow ochre and artificial eyes were added.

PTOLEMAIC PERIOD AND EARLY ROMAN MUMMIES

During this period mummification fell into a steep decline. Although the viscera were still removed from the body and placed in packages between the legs, the bodies were never fully treated. Emphasis was placed on the outer part of the mummy and elaborate wrappings were common. Multicoloured bandages were wrapped around the mummy to form lozenge shapes that were studded with gold disks. The bodies were then covered with shrouds that were decorated with images of Isis and Nepthys, the traditional protectors of the dead. The upper part of the mummy was covered with a beautiful portrait panel that had been executed during the lifetime of the deceased. These portraits, now known as the Fayoum Portrait Panels [Fig. 97], were popular from the middle of the first century AD. While many portraits are strikingly poignant others are surprisingly gaudy and incorporate features such as inlaid eyes, eyebrows and jewellery.

Fig. 97: A young woman dressed in earrings and necklaces; these were often included on the figures of women on ancient Egyptian coffins. The portrait, tempera on wood, would be placed at the head of the mummy and sealed into the elaborate bandaging. Roman period Fayoum portrait panel, Hawara. *(Egyptian Museum, Cairo/Photograph: Jason Semmens)*

THE FUNERAL

The funeral of officials and royal persons was a ritualistic spectacle. Members of the family would follow funerary goods [Fig. 77] and coffin as they were carried and dragged by a sledge to the burial site. Here they would weep and gesticulate, expressing their grief by throwing their arms in the air, a role sometimes adopted by professional male and female mourners who were hired by the family. The mourners would rip their clothes and throw dust on their hair. The women smeared their faces with dirt; leaving the upper part of their bodies exposed, they would strike at their heads and breasts. It is likely that they would have given voice to similar cathartic wailing sounds as those produced by modern-day women mourners at funerals in Egypt. A primeval sound that seems to echo the call of carrion birds, it captures keenly the terrible sense of loss one feels at the death of a loved one. The Egyptologist Maspero likened the funeral procession to a home removal – it is a keen observation. Paintings show rows of servants transporting food, pottery, vases, figurines and tools. Others carry boxes which contained clothes and wigs. A further procession bore furniture, chariot parts, weapons, staves, sceptres and sunshades. These tomb goods may have been used during the lifetime of the deceased or they may have been gifts from the mourners and family. It is likely that they were a combination of both.

The sarcophagus itself was hidden beneath a catafalque that was drawn by oxen. It was taken to the river and placed on a boat flanked by statues of Isis and Nepthys in their traditional role as protectors of the dead. The procession was met by a number of small sailing boats. The funeral barge was equipped with a cabin that was decorated with elaborate leather canopies. Here, priests dressed in fine linen kilts, jewellery and cheetah skins would burn incense to appease the gods. The boat would then cross the river that divided the world of the living and the dead. As they gathered at the western bank, the mourners would wait in the shade as the coffin was unloaded and placed on its sledge. They would then travel in procession to the tomb.

The party was welcomed at the tomb by the Mu. Described by scholars as the 'agents of the beyond', like Hathor the Mu were believed to receive and guide the deceased to the underworld. The Mu are shown in human form with papyrus stalk headdresses that have a strong similarity to those worn by the whirling dervishes of Old Cairo. Thought to have appeared first during the Old Kingdom, the Mu remained an important feature of funerary iconography until the New Kingdom period. They appear at the funeral as a troupe of dancers.

Fig. 98: The Mu dance to welcome the dead.
(Drawing: Bridget McDermott)

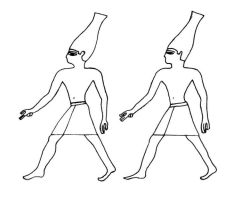

In funerary scenes from the tomb of Renni and Paheri at el-Kab, the Mu are shown greeting the funeral procession of the tomb owner. In the tomb of Nebamun, the goddess of the west watches over the entire funeral procession as they are saluted by the Mu [Fig. 98]. Aside from the Mu other enigmatic and mysterious figures are to be seen in funeral scenes. These are the Tekenu, who are depicted as human bodies bound in sacks and placed on sledges. Very little is understood about the meaning of these figures, although they may have some connection with the sacrificial victims of earlier periods. There are few references to the Tekenu, but an inscription in the tomb of Rekhmire states: 'Causing to come to the god Re as a resting Tekenu, to calm the lake of Khephri.'

At the entrance to the tomb the coffin was placed upright and the women would kneel and wail [Fig. 99 and plate 3]. Bowmen, who escorted the party, would fire arrows to the four corners of the land in order to define the

Fig. 99: Mourners before the tomb door. Fragment. *(Brooklyn Museum, New York/Bridget McDermott)*

boundaries affiliated to the dead. The mummy was placed against the chapel wall on a platform of sand that was meant to represent the first mound of creation while the eldest son of the deceased would then perform the ceremony of the opening of the mouth. In a highly ritualistic act he would take a special fishtail-shaped instrument and hold it to the mouth and nose of the mummy, a gesture that brought breath to the dead and freed his or her spirit. During this time animals were sacrificed and offerings were made to the gods. A leg was severed from a calf and, while its tendons still pulsed, it was offered to the mouth of the deceased (see plate 3). Before the coffin was interred mourners placed garlands of flowers around its neck.

The remaining funerary objects were then placed in the tomb. Themes of regeneration were exemplified by many of these objects, the strangest being the Osiris bed, which was a wooden frame carved in the shape of the god of the dead. Inside there was a bed of soil that was planted with seeds. After the door of the tomb was finally shut, the seeds would germinate and grow in the dark realms of the burial chamber, symbolising the triumph of life over death. When the vault had been censed and ritually activated, the priests and their assistants would close and seal the doors. They would then brush their footsteps away as they retreated. As the funeral laments of the harpists began, friends and relations gathered in the courtyard where they would feast and remember the dead.

The importance of funerary music is stressed on an inscription from a Middle Kingdom stele. The stele of Intef II records:

> You who rejoice at the arrival of Hathor, who love to see her beauty
> I rejoice in her, sacred music for Hathor, music a million times,
> Because you love music, music a million times
> For your Ka wherever it may be
> I am he who makes the singer bring the music for Hathor.

THE MORTUARY CULT

The eldest son was held responsible for provisioning the tomb for his father. This was discussed frequently in the ancient Egyptian wisdom texts and considered a matter of morality and honour. Once the tomb was closed the deceased would require daily rituals where food, oil and clothing were presented and prayers recited on behalf of the family. Upper-class families would hire priests to conduct these rites. The celebrants were known as 'the Servants of the

Ka' and were rewarded with agricultural produce or land endowments. Naturally they kept the offerings they presented at the tomb. The family would also visit the tomb to pay their respects in person. On festival days they would bring a feast to share with the dead. Offerings such as bread and beer were placed on tables in front of the false door of the chapel while traditional chants and the recitation from biographical stelae would be conducted in the courtyard. During the later periods strangers were asked to recite a prayer as they passed the tomb; they were promised heavenly rewards for reading the tomb inscriptions aloud and keeping the tomb owner's name alive. Some stelae even issue threats to those who would ignore this petition.

The Egyptians set up statues in the Serdab or funerary chapel. These effigies acted as substitutes for the dead, whose body could become damaged; they therefore safeguarded and ensured the survival of the soul. Subsequently, votive statues of the deceased were set up in the temple precincts so that the dead could also co-exist with the gods in all their holy places.

THE ROYAL MUMMIES: THE DEIR EL BAHRI CACHE

One of ancient Egypt's most important discoveries took place at Deir el Bahri in 1881. Here, excavators located a tomb containing the mummies of Egypt's great pharaohs. The story is now legendary. A local villager, Ahmed Abd el-Rassul, discovered the cache when one of his goats fell down a tomb shaft. After clambering down to the bottom of the passage el-Rassul lit a candle. As his eyes grew accustomed to the dark, he found himself among an amazing array of dusty wooden coffins that had been piled up one against the other. Unknown to el-Rassul, some of the coffins still bore their royal insignia. For several years the Abd el-Rassul family managed to keep the find secret, during which time they decided to trade off many of the burial goods on the antiquities market. This gradual filtering of archaeological treasure was bound to arouse suspicion and eventually the appearance of shabtis, papyri and bronze vessels was brought to the attention of the authorities. Rassul and his brother Hussein were arrested. After several months the first brother was released from custody having refused to talk. However, he soon realised that the family business was finished; encouraged by a large sum of money, he began to sing like a canary and the location of the tomb was a secret no longer.

We can imagine the excitement of the crowd as they gathered around the entrance to the tomb shaft. Expectantly, they stood and watched as the Egyptologist Emile Brugsch was lowered down into the crumbling shaft. In an interview for *Century Illustrated* monthly magazine in 1887 he was reported to have been amazed by what he saw: 'Soon we came upon cases of porcelain funerary offerings, metal and alabaster vessels, draperies and trinkets, until, reaching the turn in the passage, a cluster of mummy-cases came into view in such number as to stagger me. Collecting my senses, I made the best examination of them I could by the light of my torch, and at once saw that they contained the mummies of royal personages of both sexes. . . . I took in the situation quickly, with a gasp.' He continued, 'Their gold coverings and their polished surfaces so plainly reflected my own excited visage that it seemed as though I was looking into the faces of my own ancestors.' Realising what lay before him, Brugsch decided that the contents needed immediate attention and protection. He said that he had to empty the tomb quickly due to tensions that had arisen among the local villagers. The contents were hauled up and carried to the government steamer waiting to transport them to Cairo. An exquisite film, *The Night of the Counting of the Years* (1969) successfully reconstructs the unique atmosphere of those days. It contains a spine-tingling scene that captures the moment when the women of the village climbed the Theban hill to watch their dead ancestors being transported to the river. As the drumming began, the slow and steady sound of the Egyptian funerary lament could be heard. It was a fitting tribute to the pharaohs as they were removed forever from their ancient resting places. Cynical Egyptologists have said that the villagers were merely mourning their lost income. However, these people, who have always remained fiercely independent of the wider community of Luxor, truly adhere to the belief that they are the direct descendants of the ancient Egyptian tomb builders.

How had the royal mummies arrived in this solitary tomb? Tomb robbery had been known in Egypt from early times. In an early inscription from the tomb chapel of Hetepherakhet (5th Dynasty) the tomb owner says: 'I made for myself a tomb in the west side in the pure place in which there is no other tomb in order to protect the possessions of one who has gone to the Ka. As for anyone who would enter the tomb, impure and aiming to do evil – the great god will bring a judgement against them. I was endowed with this tomb, honoured by the king who brought me a sarcophagus.' During the later period of Egyptian history and throughout the reign of Ramesses XI the lure of tombs and their treasure became irresistible. The Theban area was under the control of the High Priests of Amun who did their best to secure and protect the Valley of the Kings. However, they were fighting a loosing battle. Thebes was often attacked by foreigners disrupting activities at the site of the tomb-workers' village, and the transport of rations to the village was often affected. This led to strikes and protests by hungry workmen.

The Theban cemeteries, too, had been plundered for years. Reports dated to this period show that many of the tombs had been inspected for damage. It was a time of unrest and political intrigue. People accused of tomb robbery were able to avoid arrest by bribing officials. They then went back to their lucrative practice. The tomb robbers were familiar with the terrain and highly organised. They worked in gangs that included stone masons and miners. Discreet boatmen were also required to ferry the treasure from the Theban area. Once inside the tomb the robbers would hack, tear and set fire to the royal corpses and retrieve precious jewels from the debris. During lean times, it is not surprising that the workmen themselves could fall under suspicion. By the end of the first decade of the reign of Ramesses IX, robbery had reached an unprecedented level.

Records of tomb robbery dated to the 20th Dynasty can be found in important ancient documents such as Papyri Leopold II, Amherst and Harris A. Fascinating details are included in these texts. A tomb robber confesses: 'We opened their sarcophagi and their coffins in which they were, and found the noble mummy of this king adorned with the khepesh [sword] many amulets and jewels that were upon his neck. His mask of god was upon him. The great mummy of the king was adorned by gold and his coffins with gold and silver, inside and outside – and inlaid with may precious stones.' The robbers, who went on to burn the mummy, were dealt with in the severest fashion. This hideous crime was punished by dismemberment and impalement.

The priests of Amun decided to move the royal mummies to a secure position in a higher tomb now known as DB 320 where they rested in peace for many centuries until they were discovered by the el-Rassul family. The occupants of the tomb had numbered over fifty mummies of kings, queens and royal officials. Among the royal cache were the magisterial icons of the New Kingdom: Ramesses I, Sety I and Ramesses II, the military giants of their day. Other famous occupants included Tuthmosis III, the explorer and soldier, Ramesses III, the last great temple builder, and Sequenre Tao who bore a series of terrible wounds that indicate this ruler was a victim of a bloody assassination. The coffins of these men and women were surprisingly crude. Dockets showed that several mummies had been removed from their resting places and stored for safety in various locations. They had been moved around from tomb to tomb for over 200 years. Their final resting place was a tomb that belonged to the High Priest Pinudjem II whose own relations were found at rest among the illustrious royal dead. There is still some confusion among Egyptologists about the identity of the royal mummies, who, during their restoration, were placed in various assorted coffins that often bore the name of other rulers. For example, the body of Ramesses II was found within a coffin that dated to the Amarna Period. The great warrior king Tuthmosis III was originally identified by Maspero as Pinudjem because he had been placed in a coffin that had been usurped by the latter. When Smith examined the royal mummies he noticed that the body of Sety II bore no actual physical resemblance to the later kings of the 19th Dynasty and this led him to question the fact that many mummies looked younger than their recorded age at death. There was further confusion when excavators realised that the mummy of Amenhotep II had been removed from his tomb to be rewrapped in a workshop at the mortuary temple of Medinet Habu. Today the identification of the royal mummies still causes much debate.

It became clear that it had taken several years for the priests of Amun to examine and repair the damage incurred by the mummies. Many had been plundered. Many had been hacked with axes and daggers and the bandages torn from their bodies. In some cases the limbs of the deceased were severed. The tomb robbers had little respect for their royal ancestors, being chiefly concerned with the gold or precious stones that had been placed upon the dead. Desperate to get at the treasure, they had set fire to the mummies recovering only precious metal from the debris.

AN EXAMINATION OF THE BODIES OF THE ROYAL MUMMIES

The body of Sequenre Tao, a 17th Dynasty ruler [Fig. 100], was among those discovered at Deir el Bahri in 1881. However, little is known of his reign except for a fragmentary letter sent to him by the Hyksos king Apophis I. The usurper complained that he was unable to sleep because of the barking of the ruler's hippopotami some 800km away at Thebes! The Hyksos were foreign invaders who ruled northern Egypt between 1674 BC and 1578 BC. At the same time Sequenre Tao was one of a new group of rulers rising to power at Thebes in the south whose line would eventually bring Egypt back to independence.

Sequenre Tao's body was examined by Maspero on 9 June 1886. Maspero describes the mummy as badly damaged and still possessing a spicy fragrance. The brain remained in the cranium and the New Kingdom embalmers had packed the abdominal cavity with linen. Sequenre Tao had suffered terrible wounds. His nasal bone had been smashed, while another blow had fractured the skull. The blow, inflicted by an axe, was so severe that the scalp had peeled from

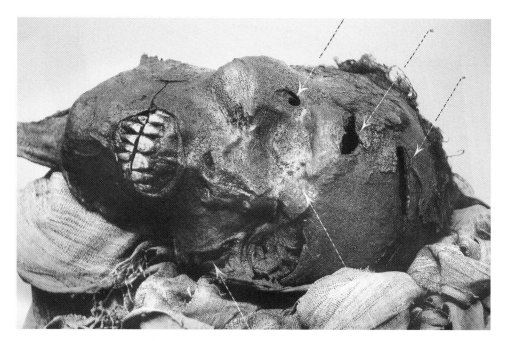

Fig. 100: The mummy of Sequenre Tao. The arrows indicate the wounds that brought about his death. *(Reproduced from* The Royal Mummies, *G. Elliot Smith/Photograph: Bridget McDermott)*

the bone and the hair was matted with blood. The second blow, which had smashed the frontal bone, had been executed with a blunt instrument. A spear or stave had been driven into the left side of the head, just below the ear. The fatal wounds, five in total, were administered by men wielding axes and short swords.

For Egyptologists trying to reconstruct the attack, there are two possible scenarios. Sequenre Tao may have been felled on the battlefield by a single blow and then have been finished off by enemy soldiers who administered several strikes. However, there is a problem with this theory. It is highly unlikely that an Egyptian ruler could be killed on the battlefield in this manner. In reality, the ruler was heavily protected during conflict, being considered more valuable as a figurehead than as a warrior. Secondly, the wounds are so terrible that one can almost sense the malice behind them. A battlefield attack would have produced one or two injuries, but not five – spaced evenly around the skull. These wounds are so well placed as to suggest that the insurgents carefully planned their position of attack and administered the blows with malicious intent when the king was sleeping or restrained. It is most probable that the king was assassinated – and that several persons inflicted the wounds so that no individual could feel or be held responsible for the murder.

Sety I [Fig. 101] was a warrior king and a skilled diplomat, his foreign policies are considered to be the most astute of any New Kingdom ruler. Sety I also had a great passion for building. On his accession he began construction of a magnificent cenotaph at Abydos, the cult centre of Osiris. He then started to construct his tomb in the Valley of the Kings at Thebes; it was to be one of the finest examples of funerary architecture that Egypt had ever known.

Tuy was the Great Royal Wife of Sety I. Her family had important connections to the military, her father being a revered officer in the most prestigious branch of the army, the Chariot Corps. They had many children, of whom the most important was their son and heir Ramesses II, who would later be known as Ramesses the Great. Sety I emphasised his links with the north of Egypt and established a palace at Qantir in the Delta. During the first year of his reign he went to war, leading his army into Sinai. The army travelled along desert roads that were lined with forts and wells. However, after years of neglect, the forts were occupied by natives. As Sety reached Tjel, a fort station in Syria, he encountered serious trouble. After quashing the rebellions there, Sety marched towards Megiddo, following in the footsteps of his ancestor, the great warrior king Tuthmosis III. He arrived at Beth-Shan, and then led his army into northern Palestine and from here marched into Lebanon. During the next few years of his reign he reached as far as the Orontes and Kadesh – the gateway to Syria. There, Sety battled with the Hittites. His victory led to the establishment of firm territorial boundaries between the two states.

Sety I died after fifteen years on the throne, leaving his empire in the hands of his son, Ramesses II. He was buried in tomb No. 17 in the Valley of the Kings. The tomb is, without doubt, one of the finest and well preserved of the ancient Egyptian burial sites, and reveals many innovative features. It is decorated with many magnificent and finely detailed religious paintings and several important funerary texts such as the Litany of Re. The most impressive feature of the tomb is the burial chamber which is decorated with a fabulous astrological ceiling. Sety also built monuments at Abydos, which had been a holy site since the Predynastic Period. In an attempt to link his family forever with the cult of Osiris, Sety erected an L-shaped mortuary temple together with an Osireion, a replica tomb of Osiris, which he built to the south-east side of the village. The temple was left unfinished at his death and was later completed by Ramesses II.

The tomb of Sety I was discovered by Belzoni on 16 October 1817. His mummy, restored in ancient times by the high priests of Amun at Thebes, was

Fig. 101: The mummy of Sety I. *(Reproduced from The Royal Mummies,* G. Elliot Smith/*Photograph: Bridget McDermott)*

discovered among the royal mummy cache. The body was housed in a wooden coffin and had been wrapped in a linen shroud. Many scholars believe that the embalming techniques used on this mummy are among the most sophisticated found during the New Kingdom. The mummy is certainly among the best preserved of the royal rulers – to look upon the face of Sety I is a spine-tingling experience. His austere countenance and the firm set of his lips are balanced by a sensitive jaw and high cheekbones. Elliot Smith described the mummy as having 'manly dignity'. The body was unwrapped on 9 June 1886 by Maspero. He found that the head had been broken off the trunk and the abdomen plundered. The body and its bandages were covered in resin and Maspero suggested that the skin would have become darker as time progressed. The king's hands were placed in front of the chest. The remains of the heart were visible as a dark mass on the front of the body and the abdomen was filled with black masses of cloth. While the eyebrows remain and the eyelids are closed no hair is visible.

The son of Sety, Ramesses II [Fig. 102] was a glamorous and iconic ruler. He came to the throne in 1279 BC and went on to rule Egypt for an astounding sixty-seven years. Today Ramesses the Great is remembered for his magnificent building programme and his famed military prowess. The visitor to modern Egypt cannot fail to be astonished by the numerous grandiose buildings that mark his reign. As with his prisoners of war, Ramesses branded numerous religious buildings and statuary with his cartouche – even those that didn't strictly belong to him! While he built his own private funerary monuments such as the Ramesseum and Abu Simbel, he also added features and enlarged the domain of temples such as Luxor and Karnak.

In the fourth year of his reign Ramesses led his army into Tjel and extended Egypt's borders as far as Canaan, Tyre, Byblos and Amurru. After the allies of

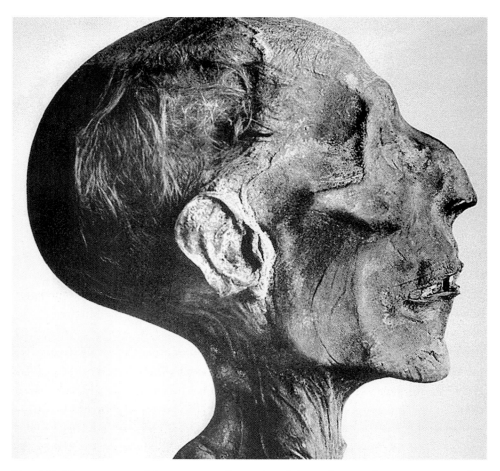

Fig. 102: The mummy of Ramesses II. *(Reproduced from* The Royal Mummies, *G. Elliot Smith/Photograph: Bridget McDermott)*

the Hittites surrendered to Ramesses, he returned to Egypt via Phoenicia. Later he marched towards Syria. He set out from his capital Piramesse, in the Delta, and marched through Canaan, towards the River Jordan. The army passed the Beqqa Valley and finally reached Kadesh, an important strategic location because of its position between Lebanon and Antilebanon. On their way to Kadesh, the Egyptians captured a group of spies. They told the delighted pharaoh that the enemy was still far away from Kadesh. His heart gladdened, Ramesses pressed on – little knowing that he was heading into a trap. As the king's division arrived at Kadesh the Hittites mounted a surprise attack. In the manifold accounts of the battle that Ramesses placed on the walls of his temples, he tells of how he and his shield bearer Menna were caught right in the centre of the oncoming enemy chariots. The king called for help, but there was none to be had. He was forced to stand alone before the terrifying waves of enemy soldiers. There was only one thing left to do. He prayed to his father Amun. Ramesses says:

> He [Amun] gave me his hand and I celebrated
> He called
> Forward, I am with you
> I, your father, my hand is with you,
> I prevail over a hundred thousand men
> I am lord of Victory, who loves valour.

The king boasts of the manner in which he contained the enemy until his reinforcements arrived and forced the Hittites to retreat. The Hittite king Mutwatallis requested a truce, and Ramesses accepted. In official rhetoric, however, the king would always claim a great victory against the Hittites.

Ramesses, who never forgot his experience at Kadesh, was determined to portray his hour of triumph on every important monument he built. Images of the battlefield were accompanied by a form of poem which describes the events. However, Ramesses II was also concerned with his image as a family man. More than any other king, he promoted the cult of the family through representations and writings on the walls of his temples. Here we see the delicate and rounded features of his mother Tuy together with those of his chief wife, Nefertari, whose wondrous beauty was celebrated on temple walls and with a series of official statues – albeit on a smaller scale than those belonging to her husband. Although Nefertari had many children, her first-born son, Prince Amunherkhopeshef, did not survive his father. Another well-known son was Prince Khamwase, who was born to the Lady Istnofret, a secondary wife of Ramesses II. He is often referred to as the world's first archaeologist as he excavated many sites in Egypt that were, by the 19th Dynasty, already ancient. Ramesses II also contracted numerous diplomatic marriages with the daughters of foreign rulers, and the king profited from the magnificent dowries he demanded from their exasperated fathers – ancient letters that were sent to the king are littered with complaints about his greed. Despite this, the gifts were plentiful, and foreign women were bundled off to the Egyptian court with presents of gold, silver, copper, slaves and horses without limit. However, this was not enough for Ramesses II who went on to demand cattle, goats and sheep in their thousands. Ramesses II had many children, their number has been calculated at ninety. Recent excavations have revealed that Ramesses II built a large tomb, KV5, for his sons. It has now proved to be the largest tomb in the Valley of the Kings.

Ramesses II, with his finely chiselled face and large aquiline nose, inherited his mother's features. He too was found in the Deir el Bahri cache in a coffin that clearly dates to the reign of Tutankhamun. He has several interesting features, including dyed finger and toe nails that were slightly overgrown. His hair too had a reddish tint. The skin of the royal mummies did not darken under the thick resins used during this period and the features seem more resolute. The mummy was packed with linen. Material was even placed in the nostrils in order to preserve the shape of the face. The upper lip of Ramesses II is prominent and still has the remains of greying facial hair. Both his ears show signs of piercing. The Egyptians suffered a great deal from dental problems, for the desert sand was absorbed in their food and quickly ground the enamel of their teeth. However, for a man of his great age, Ramesses had surprisingly fine teeth.

The reign of Ramesses II was a long one. His successor, Merneptah [Fig. 104], came to the throne at a very late age. By this stage, Egypt was no longer as wealthy as she had been during the reign of Ramesses II and the country faced internal struggles. The Libyans who came from the western desert were infiltrating Egypt in a desperate search for land. The aged king was forced to repel the tribes from the Delta region. Records suggest that 25,000 of these enemy soldiers travelled with their families and possessions in ox-drawn carts. During his reign Merneptah would successfully deal with periodic waves of Libyan invaders – they had no hope of overpowering the Egyptians who possessed superior weaponry, armour and chariots. Merneptah's rule was brief, no more than ten years, and a group of short-lived kings succeeded him. The mummy of Merneptah was unwrapped on 8 July 1907 in the Cairo Museum. It was wrapped in a long piece of linen. The head was bald except for a few strands of white hair and the body much damaged. Plunderers had slashed at the throat, chest and abdomen with hatchets.

Ramesses III [Fig. 103] was the last of ancient Egypt's great warrior kings. He ruled during the 20th Dynasty when Egypt no longer enjoyed the wealth and economic superiority that had sustained the magnificent building programmes of the 18th and early 19th Dynasties. Inspired by his hero Ramesses II, Ramesses III attempted to emulate the architectural style of his renowned ancestor and established his mortuary temple, Medinet Habu, at Thebes. Here he depicted the battles he fought against the Libyans who were

Fig. 103: The mummy of Ramesses III.
(*Reproduced from* The Royal Mummies,
*G. Elliot Smith/Photograph: Bridget
McDermott*)

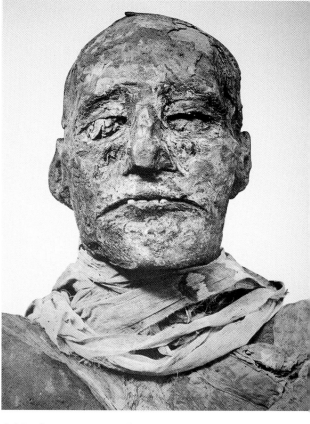

still periodically infiltrating the Delta. The king was assured of success. He had a magnificent army that fought under the banner of the great god Amun.

After the enemy had fled the king would count his captives. The soldiers would be paraded before the king and bound in shackles. While their leaders were executed, the prisoners of war were regarded as cattle and ritually branded with the cartouche of the king. Prisoners would include women and children who would be taken into the temple or used in domestic service.

Ramesses III was to face a more formidable foe than the Libyans. We know little about the Sea Peoples, who may have originated from the Mediterranean, other than that they arrived by sea via Crete and travelled by land from Anatolia. They made their journey with their families in carts yoked to oxen. Later, they would settle in Palestine which took its name from one of their group, the Peleset. The Sea Peoples had invaded the city states of Syria and had set their sights on Egypt. Ramesses III led his army against the Sea Peoples fighting a great land and sea battle. Fighting on land the Sea Peoples mobilised their chariots, archers and infantry; on water, they used ships equipped with elaborate sails. The Egyptians met them at the mouth of the Delta where they engaged in hand-to-hand fighting. Lookouts were positioned on the masts of Egyptian battleships, while slingmen were positioned in crow's-nests ready to hurl stones upon the heads of the enemy. The Egyptians rammed their boats into the narrow channels of the Delta, while archers attacked the enemy from the shore.

The mummy of Ramesses III was unwrapped on 1 June 1886. He was bandaged with resin-soaked linen, his hands fully extended with the palms

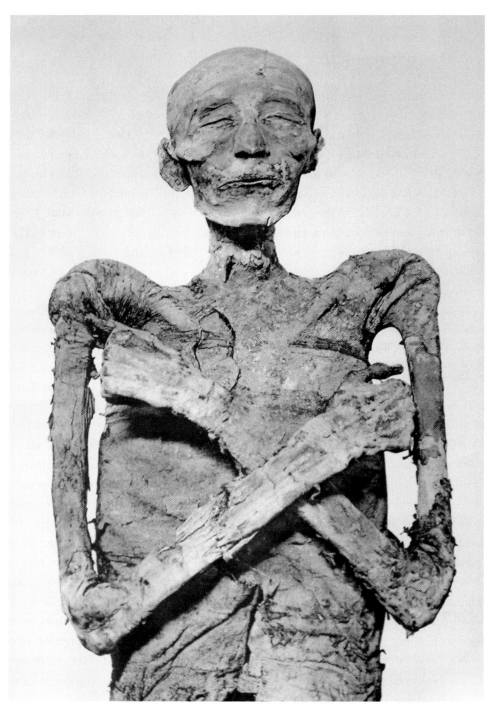

Fig. 104: The mummy of Merneptah. *(Reproduced from* The Royal Mummies, *G. Elliot Smith/Photograph: Bridget McDermott)*

carefully placed on his shoulders – a position repeated with many of the 20th Dynasty mummies. The face was adorned with artificial eyes. Modern examinations of the mummy suggest that vascular calcification had taken place in the mummy.

Most of the royal mummies show evidence of post-mortem trauma. Damage to the remains was incurred when the bodies were handled by grave robbers or restorers – in fact, only the bodies of Ramesses III and Amenhotep II were found in good condition. Most damage was done by tomb robbers who ripped at the bodies in their attempts to secure jewellery. In many instances there is evidence of the amputation of hands as noted in the cases of Tuthmosis I and Queen Ahmes-Nefertary. The right forearm of Sety II is also missing. Merneptah [Fig. 104] has a deep axe cut from the shoulder to the chest, severing the inner end of the clavicle and ribs; his right arm was broken midway between the elbow and wrist and was held together only by the tendons and muscles. The lower body had been hacked by axes.

Lesser known mummies found in the royal cache are also of interest. Queen Nodjmet [Fig. 105] and the Lady Rai [Fig. 106] are two of the finest surviving female mummies. The Lady Rai, identified as a mummy of the 18th Dynasty, was wrapped in a great number of bandages and shrouds. While her youthful body was perfectly embalmed her skin was stained in dark ochre resin revealing features that are both vibrant and proud. Her hair was dressed in a fashionable array of individual plaits that were then separated to form two long sections. Her hands were left to rest upon the thighs. Nodjmet, who is now included in the exhibition of the royal mummies in the Egyptian Museum, Cairo, was first unwrapped in 1886. She died during the 21st Dynasty and her body is of particular interest. Her remains reveal that embalmers were now placing stone eyes under the eyelids. During this time external packing was used to shape the limbs – the buttocks, legs and abdomen were treated in this manner. Her greying hair had been covered with an elaborate wig of luxurious brown plaits. Most orifices such as ears, mouth and nose were packed with sawdust and linen. Likewise, the cheeks were tightly packed, as were the gums and lips. The body was greatly damaged having been slashed on the forehead and chest; one arm and both wrists were broken. The resin still on the arm held an impression of a stolen bracelet, although many fragments of jewellery remained. Her name and titles, Nodjmet, High Priestess of Amun, were found in hieroglyphics on the bandages that covered her feet.

As the Romans fashioned Egypt into a lucrative province between 332BC and AD 395 the art of embalming had already fallen into decline and the practice was

Fig. 105: The mummy of
Notmejet. *(Reproduced from* The
Royal Mummies, *G. Elliot Smith/
Photograph: Bridget McDermott)*

Fig. 106: The mummy of the
Lady Rai. *(Reproduced from* The
Royal Mummies, *G. Elliot Smith/
Photograph: Bridget McDermott)*

soon discontinued. However, as we have seen, ancient Egyptian mummies continued to fascinate the people of conquering countries and few were destined to rest in peace.

MUMMIES – THE MAGIC INGREDIENT

Mummified tissue, or 'mummia', a Persian name meaning pitch or asphalt, was used in classical times for medical purposes. It was prescribed as early as AD 1100 as a cure for the sick of Alexandria, while Abd el-Latif, a twelfth-century scientist, believed that mummia, when mixed with water and inhaled or swallowed as a tincture, would cure all ills. Demand increased. Tombs were defiled and mummies were ripped apart as thieves sought this precious commodity. Mummia was also exported, being shipped across the Mediterranean and sold in the apothecary shops of Europe. Several recipes were used. Paracelsus (AD 1492–1541) developed a popular remedy that included treacle and a balsam of mummy which he purchased on his trips in Alexandria. Here, Syrian visitors swore that Egyptian mummy was a cure for all ailments. As locals began to export fake mummies one can only wonder at the type of crimes that were committed in order to meet demand. Mummia was used to treat many disorders including skin diseases, paralysis and abscesses. During the sixteenth and seventeenth centuries mummia was so popular in Britain and Europe that the ingredient was mentioned by Shakespeare in *Romeo and Juliet*. James Shirley (1596–1666) in *Bird in a Cage* laments, 'Make Mummy of my flesh and sell me to the apothecaries'. When used it was rubbed on the body or consumed orally – the patient mixed what must have been a foul-tasting substance with herbs. The trade flourished until the early nineteenth century when the Egyptians finally outlawed this practice. However, Egyptian mummies held other fascinations.

VICTORIAN MUMMIES

During the Victorian period wealth generated by her thriving industries and trade propelled Britain into an elaborate consumer culture. It became fashionable to explore certain aspects of spiritualism and the occult. During this fascinating period scientific developments clashed with established spiritual beliefs and new scientific discoveries were changing traditional worldviews. The Victorians were inspired by the concept of travel, their imaginations fired by novels and newspapers that were crammed with stories of exotic places.

Antiquities and curios became highly fashionable along with oriental pottery and exotic plants. Empire building led to a notable interest in civilisations associated with grandeur, longevity and power. Mummy mania had arrived. It is not surprising, therefore, that the Egyptian mummy became a highly sought after souvenir. Their popularity is even reflected in contemporary literature, for Egyptian mummies feature in more than a dozen popular narratives published between 1880 and 1914. The fashion reached the royal household, for we know that in the latter part of the nineteenth century the king of Persia sent Queen Victoria mummia for her health. Tourists took Nile trips and interest in Egypt blossomed. Museums that invested in excavations in Egypt were rewarded with mummies and these exhibits fuelled the excitement of the public. Moreover, the unwrapping of authentic Egyptian mummies became commonplace at parties and small gatherings across London. This sort of spectacle was organised by Belzoni at the opening of his London exhibition in 1821. It was a type of parlour game that had little scientific value until Dr Thomas Pettigrew, who had 'unrolled' several mummies under the scrutiny of scientific audiences, published his book *A History of Egyptian Mummies* in 1834. Pettigrew (1791–1865) was a member of the Royal College of Surgeons and well known for his interest in philosophy and ancient history. As the treasurer of the British Archaeology Society Dr Pettigrew may have influenced the Duke of Hamilton, who is believed to have offered his body for research in the mummification process. Hamilton died in 1852 and was duly wrapped and placed in an Egyptian coffin. He was buried in a sarcophagus that had once belonged to an Egyptian princess and was placed in a mausoleum.

PRESERVING HUMAN BODIES IN ANCIENT AND MODERN TIMES

People have always been fascinated with the preservation of human remains. Some made an art of it. In the Zymoglyphic Museum in San Mateo, California there are engravings of the work of Frederik Ruysch (1638–1731), a Dutch anatomist who was a pioneer in the preservation of human tissue. He made a series of dioramas. His sculptures show the remains of human skeletal embryos which are placed in various poses: one plays a violin whose strings are made of human arteries. It sings 'Ah fate, ah better fate'. An eighteenth-century anatomist and painter Jean-Honoré Fragonard also created a series of exhibits based on human remains. His work, which involved the deliberate preservation of human organs, can be seen at the Musée Nationale d'Anatomie Humaine, Paris. This museum has a fine collection of anatomical wonders that includes the modern mummified bodies of a Parisian couple and their child which are displayed in a Victorian curio cabinet. Curiosities and grotesques that include collections of embryos, anatomical exhibits (including the skulls of the guillotined) and human taxidermy highlight the interest that people have always shown in the preservation of human flesh. In the king's Capuchins' Catacombs of Palermo, Italy, there are a large number of mummified remains that span the period from 1599 to 1920. The first mummy interred in the catacombs was that of a revered monk. When local people saw his mummy many decided that they wanted to be interred there in the same way. Over the years human bodies were crammed into niches, corridors and passageways. Corpses were hung on walls and children were posed in rocking chairs. A visit to the catacombs is a startling if not macabre experience. However, the body of a child, Rosalia Lombardo, is so well preserved one cannot help but marvel at the mysterious techniques used to preserve her. Although many of the inhabitants are now skeletal, many have been perfectly mummified retaining clothes, hair, flesh and eyes. It is believed that the bodies were dipped in arsenic or lime. Some were placed in cells or pits where they were dried for eight months. They were then washed in vinegar.

Deliberate self-mummification was practised among some religious communities until the late nineteenth century. Mummies of Buddhist priests have been discovered in temples in the north-western mountains of Japan. The mummies were highly revered and had been placed in special cases by the temple priests. The process, regarded as a form of self-discipline, was undertaken when death seemed near. At this point monks would change their diet consuming only bark, nuts and tree resins. They then fasted until they died. Some are to be found in a crossed-legged position while others were buried alive in wooden coffins.

More recently, in the early summer of 1994, scientists from the University of Maryland and the Long Island University mummified the human corpse of an elderly man from Baltimore who had died of heart failure. Ronn Wade, Director of Anatomical Services at University of Maryland Medical School in Baltimore and Bob Brier, an Egyptologist associated with Long Island University, named the mummy Mumab. During the process they removed the brain of the cadaver and rinsed both the abdominal and thoracic cavities with palm wine, frankincense, cedar and myrrh, keeping the temperature in the room consistent with that of an Egyptian embalming tent. They used replica embalming tools and linen. They dried the body in 600lb of natron imported from the Wadi Natron in Egypt. While the scientists found that it took thirty-five days to dry the mummy, in ancient Egypt, the entire process is known to have taken seventy days.

An organisation based in Utah, in the United States, and known as Summum, has developed a method of mummification that can be used on humans and their pets and involves a thirty-day dehydration process. The body is taken to a pyramid where the organs are removed and rites of transference are conducted. It is then placed in a mummiform coffin. Robert Lenkiewicz, a Cornish artist, is famous for both his interest in the macabre and for faking his own death. Fascinated by Egyptian embalming techniques he decided to make his own mummy. He befriended a tramp, Edwin McKenzie, who lived in a barrel near Lenkiewicz's home. He called him Diogenes after the Greek philosopher. 'Diogenes' left his body to Robert in order that he could mummify his remains. After the embalming had taken place the authorities were alerted; a cat-and-mouse game then ensued between Robert and the Department of Health, who wanted to reclaim the body. He was forced to hide the remains in a bottom drawer in his library, which contained a fine collection of antiquarian books, skulls and funeral objects.

The international exhibition *Body Worlds*, held in London in 2002, raised many questions with regards to the public display of human cadavers. The plastination technique, used to preserve human organs with reactive polymers and employed on animal and human remains, was discovered by Gunther von Hagens in 1977 at the Department of Anatomy at Heidelberg University. During this process water and fat are removed from the tissues and replaced with acetone and polymers. Experiments conducted by von Hagens showed that various materials could be useful in preserving different parts of the body. For example, sliced body parts were successfully treated with Epoxide resins while silicone rubber cures enable the body parts to retain a more lifelike appearance. Another technique, Cryonics, avoids freezing the body but employs Cryo-protectants to cool tissue at a very low temperature below 120 degrees. To its detractors the technique is questionable. However, its proponents point to the fact that the use of frozen embryos would once have been considered a medical impossibility. Finally an American religious organisation, the Kemetic Orthodox Faith, has revived ancient Egyptian funeral rituals including the ancient ancestor cult which entails worshippers leaving offerings for the dead and proferring ceremonial devotion to the Akhu (the dead).

THE MUMMIFICATION OF ANIMALS AND BIRDS

The cult worship of animals and birds was fully established by the ancient Egyptians from the Predynastic Period. Archaic art reveals a reverential attitude towards the natural world and shows that the veneration of a wide variety of species was already very widespread. This led to the crafting of totem images of bulls, cattle, birds, lions and various exotic creatures that may have had mythical origins. From an early date the titles of Egyptian rulers were inextricably linked to fierce animals, namely lions and bulls, which were often carved on slate palettes that acted as metaphorical images of kingship. As the early settlers began to cultivate tracts of land around the Nile they became dependent on animals such as oxen that enhanced their livelihoods; some, such as crocodiles, acted as possible threats to it. This meant that many of the early gods had cattle features and early forms of a bovine goddess, Hathor, rose to prominence. It also meant that animal sacrifice was performed to appease the gods and ensure stability between the community and the natural environment.

During the Predynastic Period the Egyptians buried animals wrapped in linen or matting. In some cases cows, dogs and sheep were placed in human graves. During the Early Period the gods were gradually anthropomorphised and came to be shown with human bodies and animal heads. Although the images of Egyptian gods are sometimes considered exotic or startling, they affect our subconscious in subtle ways. From the very beginning of history men and women have been fascinated by hybrid images and have felt compelled to bestow human characteristics on animal forms. Many cultures believe that man has an animal energy-body. Even in modern times we create endless animated images of endearing or frightening animals that speak and possess human characteristics. The Egyptians were fond of this type of satirical imagery, painting animals in human roles. In some papyri, cats and mice are shown as soldiers breaking down enemy fortresses while others are depicted as farmers herding animals into pens.

Although the ancient Egyptians deliberately embalmed animals, many were preserved by accident. Lizards, insects, beetles and mice have been conserved within the wrappings of Egyptian mummies. Feasting on the corpse they were almost certainly caught up in the embalmers' resins. The Egyptians were fond of their animals and artistic representations often show children with monkeys, cats and ducklings. Soldiers and hunters were depicted with their dogs for which they made collars and provided names. Animals were mummified as beloved pets. A baboon that was buried with Maatkare, the daughter of Pinudjem I, once caused confusion for Egyptologists as it was thought to be the body of the young girl's baby. In other examples of animal burials a monkey and a mummified horse were found near the New Kingdom tomb of the official Senmut. The horse had been placed in a sarcophagus while the monkey had been provided with food offerings.

Various birds and animals were viewed as manifestations of Egyptian deities and many had specific associations with Egyptian townships. A particular species of animal and bird would be bred and sacrificed purely for ritual purposes: X-rays of sacrificed animals show that many had had their necks broken or skulls crushed. During the Late Period animal mummification increased dramatically and massive cemeteries were created to accommodate their mummies. Excavations have produced a surplus of mummified animals; in one noted instance during the twentieth century, tons of mummified cats were transported to Liverpool to be used as fertiliser.

The practice of animal mummification served various purposes. As we have seen, some animals were preserved as beloved pets, others as food supplies. Individually wrapped joints of beef and poultry were simply preserved as sustenance for the dead. Mummified animals were also left in sacred shrines where they were dedicated to the gods to whom the animals were believed to be sacred. Several animals could be presented. For example, many crocodiles were embalmed in family groups, a practice that reached the height of its popularity during the Graeco-Roman Period. Animals were bred, killed and mummified at cult centres where they were purchased by visiting pilgrims, who would then leave them in shrines or catacombs as offerings to the gods. Well-known catacombs, such as those at Tuna el Gebel, were sacred to Thoth the god of wisdom. The ibis and baboon were presented as mummies to this deity. Live ibis are thought to have been held by the feet and plunged into a vat of liquid resin before being wrapped in linen bandages. They would be placed, three or four at a time, in ceramic jars that would be stored in the catacombs. Every year at Saqqara, over 10,000 birds are believed to have been offered. In the same way, dogs and jackals were buried at Abydos. At Bubastis the Egyptians worshipped the feline goddess Bast. Here there were a number of cat cemeteries. Fish too were mummified and placed in graves ranging from the very small to 2-metre long mummies. During the Late Period every imaginable creature was embalmed. While a Greek text describes a sacred lion necropolis at Saqqara, the mummies of cows, bulls, cats, dogs, baboons, jackals, scorpions and snakes were commonplace.

Many ancient animal cemeteries have been discovered in Egypt, most of which were divided into sections that contained various individual species. For example, one cemetery was divided into three areas that contained oxen, goats and fish respectively. The oxen and goats were buried in irregular shallow pits varying in depth from about 45 to 60 centimetres. The fish, which had been treated with ash and wrapped in linen, were buried in single graves. Late cemeteries were found near the holy city of Abydos. They contained falcons and rodents: large pottery jars held great numbers of birds while groups of mummified rats had been placed in eight gilded and painted limestone coffins.

During an excavation conducted during the 1960s the Egyptologist Walter Emery examined a number of animal burials that were dated to the 26th Dynasty. Among the remains of the animal cemetery at Saqqara he found two sacrificed bulls. He also examined a number of sacred ibis mummies that may have been worshipped as part of the cult of Imhotep, the builder of the Step Pyramid. Emery found two catacombs overflowing with mummified ibis – their number was estimated at over a million. Furthermore, while examining the

Fig. 107: Priests lead the Apis Bull in procession. Detail from Medinet Habu. (Photograph: Jason Semmens)

temple area, he came across a number of baboons, sacred falcons and a catacomb containing the remains of the mothers of the Apis Bulls. Another ibis gallery was found at Abusir in the north in an area surrounded by marsh land that may have acted as a breeding ground for the birds. The extraordinary assortment of animals found at the cemeteries of Saqqara included rams, cats, dogs and lions.

BULL CULTS

The ancient Egyptian bull cults were established from the Early Period onwards. The bull was seen as a symbol of power and sexual vigour. During the Archaic Period the king identified himself as a bull and is often seen in this form on ceremonial slate palettes.

The bull cults were served by priests who worshipped these animals as living gods. They were stabled in magnificent surroundings, supplied with fine food and provided with a harem of cows. The Egyptians believed that the bull was connected to Ptah, a creator god who was thought to have fashioned the human race. Later the bull came to be associated with the cult of Osiris. In *Roman Lives* Plutarch states: 'The Apis Bull was a fair and beautiful image of the soul of Osiris.' This divine status belonged to only one bull at a time. In his *Histories* Herodotus writes, 'The Apis Bull is the calf of a cow that is never afterwards to have another. The Egyptians believed that a flash of light descends upon the cow from heaven, and this causes her to conceive the Apis. The Apis calf has distinctive marks; it is black with a white square on its forehead, the image of an eagle on its back, the hair on its tail double and a scarab under its tongue [3.28].' On its succession the newly appointed Apis Bull was taken to visit various sites in Egypt before being brought to its cult centre at Memphis. Its arrival occasioned a seven-day festival. Furthermore, the annual appearance of the Apis Bull drew many pilgrims. Here they watched as the priests led the animal through the city at the head of a magnificent procession [Fig. 107]. During the display it was thought to bless the land. The bull was also regarded as an oracle and it was petitioned with questions that could be answered by positive or negative responses.

When the bull died it was embalmed and entombed with the kind of ceremony reserved for royalty. It was cleansed and mummified. Artificial eyes were inserted while priests placed gilding on its horns. It was then wrapped in a shroud and placed in a massive stone sarcophagus often weighing more than 50 tonnes. The Apis mummy was then transported to the Serapeum, a tomb designed for a large number of Apis Bulls and located in the north of Egypt.

It has the dark and strangely disturbing atmosphere unique to Egyptian monuments.

Aware that the Greek author Strabo, writing in the first century BC, had identified an avenue of sphinxes leading to the burial place of the sacred Apis Bulls, in the middle of the nineteenth century Egyptologists began to look for the bull burials. It was the French Egyptologist Mariette who uncovered more than one hundred of these sphinxes that lined a great processional way. He then found that the avenue came to a halt in front of a buried temple courtyard. Below the temple, dedicated to Osiris-Apis, the archaeologist found a sacred catacomb. Mariette describes the site: 'the walls are covered with stelae, you walk on statuettes of all colours, on vases, on fragments of wooden sarcophagi. All this is in dreadful disorder, such disorder that at first sight I despaired of ever recognising anything.' The subterranean sections of the catacomb, known today as the Serapeum, consisted of a long gallery lined with a series of stelae and sealed by a huge sandstone door. The chambers contained twenty-four magnificent granite sarcophagi each weighing up to 66 tonnes. They are dated to the 26th Dynasty. During the spring of 1852 further galleries were found; these were hewn in a similar fashion and contained bull burials that dated to the 19th and 22nd Dynasties. During the 19th Dynasty Prince Khamewase, a much celebrated son of Ramesses II, made several attempts to restore this monument and was even thought to have been buried here. Mariette's work at the Serapeum continued throughout 1852 during which time he discovered several smaller bull burials. He found decorated chambers that contained two huge painted rectangular coffins embellished with gold leaf; they were accompanied by four enormous canopic jars that contained the viscera of the bulls. The alabaster containers were sealed by human-headed stoppers and were guarded by a statue of Osiris. Here, the excavator found two shrines dated to the reign of Ramesses the Great. They show the king and his son making offerings before the sacred Apis. Two large painted sandstone shabtis belonging to Khamewase were set into a niche in the south wall. In another niche there was a Djed amulet and fragments of gold leaf. Two hundred and forty-seven hard stone, calcite and faïence shabti figures were found; the footprints of the ancient priests could still be seen on the floor.

When the bull mummies were examined it was found that each carcass had been broken. The reasons for this are unclear. It has been suggested that in an attempt to consume the power of the animal the Egyptians had eaten parts of the bull before it was embalmed. Eventually the remains had been coated with resin and placed in rectangular coffins while their heads had been overlaid with gilded masks.

Another cult, dedicated to the Buchis Bull, was established at the city of Armant. It was connected to the cults of Re and Osiris but was also associated with the war god Montu. The bulls were specifically chosen for their markings, namely a black face with a white body. Many of the bulls and their mothers were buried in a cemetery called the Bucheum. When embalming these animals the Egyptians used similar techniques to those conducted on human corpses. During the mummification process the entrails of the Buchis Bulls were removed through the anus. The bull was bandaged while it lay on a mummy table, its legs folded beneath its body. The animals were provided with inlaid eyes and gilded masks that were adorned with ostrich plumes.

Another centre associated with the worship of bulls was the site of Heliopolis where the Minervis cult was established. The bulls were connected to both the sun god Re and the fertility deity Min of Coptos.

MUMMIES ALIVE!

The discovery of the tomb of Tutankhamun in 1922 generated the world's first major media hype. New technology, and media deals between Carter and the London newspapers, meant that reports could be efficiently transmitted from Egypt to England. Egyptian themes dominated fashion, literature, home decoration and cinema. The Art Deco movement was heavily indebted to Egyptian paintings, jewellery and furniture. Cinemas, dance-halls and even the outer walls and gate of a Sheffield cemetery were designed with Egyptian features and simulated temple facades. In the world of fashion women chose to wear shoes, shawls, blouses and dresses woven and beaded with Egyptian motifs. Luxury and opulence reigned. Women started wearing their hair in short bobs, a trend influenced by the images of women in ancient Egyptian tomb scenes. It is not surprising that cosmetics were marketed by promoting the benefits of ancient ingredients or by having a picture of Cleopatra gracing the box. In the dance halls they composed music that celebrated the discovery of the tomb and even the dance steps – like the Tutankhamun or Anubis Trot – reflected the excitement generated by the contemporary finds.

The first 'mummy revival' actually began in the early nineteenth century, and it was then that they first began to appear in literature. In 1818 Mary Shelley has Victor Frankenstein saying of his creature: 'Oh! No mortal could support the horror of that countenance. A mummy again endued with animation could not be so hideous as that wretch!' In her three-volume novel *The Mummy! A Tale of the Twenty-Second Century* (1827) Jane Webb was one of a number of authors who continued to use electricity as a way of reviving corpses; this time King Cheops is the mummy who, once reanimated, uses a hot air balloon to evade a group of archaeologists. *Some Words with a Mummy* by Edgar Allan Poe was published in 1850. In it, a mummy is revived by a voltaic battery. Louisa May Alcott, author of *Little Women*, also penned a mummy short story in 1869 called 'Lost in a Pyramid' or 'The Mummy's Curse'. In 1880 Grant Allan wrote a short story entitled 'My New Year's Eve among the Mummies' in which the narrator discovers that mummies are revived every thousand years to partake of tomb feasts and make merry. It was followed in 1892 by a short story, the rip-roaring mummy yarn 'Lot 249' by Sir Arthur Conan Doyle. The mummy books continued into the twentieth century – two years after the discovery of the tomb of Tutankhamun, H.P. Lovecraft ghost-wrote the book *Under the Pyramids* (1924) for Harry Houdini while Agatha Christie, herself a keen amateur Egyptologist, wrote *The Adventure of the Egyptian Tomb*. In 1927 a sixteen-year-old Tennessee Williams wrote the novel *The Vengeance of Nitocris*; and in 1938 Henry Bloch produced his novel *The Eyes of the Mummy*. That same year Edgar Allan Poe penned 'Ligeia', a tale centred on the untimely death of the narrator's two wives, for the second of whom he plans an Egyptian-style burial. Finally, there are the modern classics: Edgar Rice Burroughs's *The City of Mummies* (1948), Joe Lansdale's *Bubba Ho-Tep* (1994) and *Seven Stars* (2000) by Kim Newman. Anne Rice is the author of the stunning *Vampire Chronicles*. While her books are brimming with images of Egypt and the gorgeous un-dead, it is *The Mummy or Ramses the Damned* (1989) that takes her readers on a gruesome journey into the dark realms of the Egyptian tomb.

Computer games designers have incorporated mummies and their tombs into their programs in various delightful ways. Egyptologists and mummies appear in the PC game *The Mummy Maze*, while *Amenophis-Resurrection*, and *Sherlock Holmes, The Mystery of the Mummy* entertain the more serious. The Tomb of Ramesses III, Hatshepsut's mortuary temple and the Giza Pyramid provide sublime battle sites in the unsurpassed First-Person Shooter, *Serious Sam*. Figures and models of mummies abound, among them the spin-off toys from *Mummies Alive!* and the McFarlane's monster series that continue to produce mean and gruesome fiends from hell. Mummies also feature in children's games. While *The Mummy, The Altar Electronic Re-Animation Playset* provides a dungeon, secret doors, creepy sound effects and a corpse with glowing eyes, the cryogenic lab kit enables you to freeze an Ice Mummy that you can later dissect at leisure. A deck of cards is designed in the shape of Egyptian mummies while the game Old Maid is renamed by one manufacturer as Old Mummy. Two board games supposedly based on objects found in ancient tombs are *Senet* – the instructions more difficult to follow than a hieroglyphic text, and *Ancient Egyptian Mehen – The Game of the Forbidden Snake* – untested by the author. Many strange and miscellaneous products are named after the Egyptian dead. In the 1920s Huntley & Palmer designed their biscuit tins in the shape of an Egyptian funeral jar while a brand of condom was named after Ramesses II, reputedly the father of a vast brood of children. The truly delicious Yummy Mummies were invented as a range of monster breakfast cereal of the late 1980s along with Fruit Brute and Count Chocula. Urban legends and folklore stories continue to circulate on the Internet, the author's favourite being the 'Honey Mummy'. The story goes that one night a group of travellers arrived at the pyramids where they stumbled upon a jar of honey. Sticking a hand in the jar to scoop up the honey one of them suddenly felt hair underneath his fingers. As he reached deeper into the jar he found it contained the body of a mummified child.

MUMMIES ON FILM

Until the early 1930s the horror genre had focused its attention on traditional monsters such as Mary Shelley's Frankenstein. In 1931 when Boris Karloff revived yet another tired old *Frankenstein* fiend, Universal Studios began to search for a different demon to unleash on the cinema-going public. What was more topical than a mummy? Advertised as 'It Comes to Life!', *The Mummy* (1932) starred Karloff, the master of horror, and was directed by Karl Freund. In it, an expedition from the British Museum discovers the mummy of the Egyptian prince Imhotep. It goes on to find a scroll belonging to the Egyptian god of wisdom Thoth, its ancient hieroglyphs endowed with the power to raise the dead. A member of the team reads the scroll and activates the mummy. The mummy must recover the scroll in order to revive his lost love, an Egyptian princess, whose soul is to be reborn through the archaeologist's daughter. This film was followed by *The Mummy's Hand* (1940) which was promoted as the 'Tomb of a thousand terrors!' While searching for the tomb of Princess Anakara a group of unfortunate archaeologists accidentally stumbles upon the resting place of Kharis, her guardian, who vows to kill each member of the expedition. The film borrows heavily from *The Mummy* (1932). Kharis goes on to appear in several more films including *The Mummy's Tomb* (1942), *The Mummy's Curse* (1944) and *The Mummy's Ghost* (1944).

Although Universal Studios were the first to bring Boris Karloff and his definitive Egyptian mummy to the big screen, the early films relied on visual magnetism rather than imaginative plots. Some attempt was made to establish historical accuracy when Hammer included several realistic scenes in their films showing the coffin of Princess Ananka being dragged by a sledge pulled by oxen. Their films also attempted to recreate scenes of Egyptian mourners, and some speeches uttered by Kharis were taken from the Book of the Dead. In *The Mummy's Shroud* (1976) there is at least an attempt to recapture the appearance of the mummy, his facial features being depicted on the outer layers of his bandages. These were drawn onto the linen wrappings around the mummy's face and had been clearly influenced by those of a Roman mummy in the British Museum collection.

Themes of reincarnation dominated the early films along with repetitive plots that centred on love lost. So synonymous is this theme with the mummy genre that is was still being used in the 1999 version of *The Mummy* when Arnold Vosloo casts aside his wrappings and is revealed in all his glory as the vigorous and diabolical High Priest Imhotep. (Incidentally, in *Egyptian Darkness Lit by Blood Red Incandescent Lamps: The Influence of Ancient Egypt on Cinema*, Keith R. Amery points out the strange resemblance between Arnold Vosloo and the sculpture of an Egyptian priest known as the Berlin Green Head.) The film was followed by *The Mummy Returns* (2001) in which classic scenes include a group of Egyptian soldier mummies chasing a London bus.

Love-struck corpses appear in the earliest mummy films. In *The Romance of the Mummy* (1910), based on a story by Theophile Gautier, an archaeologist falls asleep in a tomb and dreams of a romantic affair with an ancient queen. On waking he finds a girl who bears a strange resemblance to his lover. Reincarnation, often involving an Egyptian queen or princess, is also frequently addressed in mummy films. In the fifteen-minute silent film *When Soul Meets Soul* (1912) an Egyptian princess is recovered by her reincarnated love and in *The Mummy* (1959) British archaeologists played by Christopher Lee and Peter Cushing discover the body of yet another Princess Ananka, this time played by the exotic actress Dolores Cassinelli. When they open the tomb they activate an ancient curse and waken the mighty guardian Kharis who is sworn to protect her. The evocative film *She* (1965), based on the novel by Rider Haggard, also deals with themes of loss and regeneration as does *Blood from the Mummies Tomb* (1972) based on the fabulous tale *Jewel of the Seven Stars* by Bram Stoker. This last book also inspired *The Curse of the Mummy* (1970), *The Awakening* (1980) and *Legend of the Mummy* ('the terror begins') (1998).

For an Egyptian mummy nothing tastes sweeter than revenge. In *The Dust of Egypt* (1915) the mummy of a vicious Egyptian princess comes to life in a New

York Museum. In *The Wrath of the Tomb* (1915) another irritable royal beauty figures, this time haunting the streets of London in a search for her dismembered hand. The latter is the first British full-length horror film. In *The Vengeance of Egypt* (1912) an Egyptian tomb is excavated by Napoleon. Here a foolhardy soldier steals a scarab ring from a mummy. Subsequently, everyone who comes to possess the ring meets a gruesome end. In *The Curse of the Mummy's Tomb* (1964) an angry mummy, 'Half bone, half bandage . . . all blood-curdling terror!' goes on the rampage in foggy London after the violation of his tomb. In *I Was a Teenage Mummy* (1962) Professor Petrie and his assistant Peaches LaVerne unearth a 3,000-year-old mummy which they take back to America. The mummy, again, is far from pleased.

Aside from the horror genre, mummies also figure in lighter roles. They act as the subject of comedy in *Mercy, the Mummy Mumbled* (1918) and in *We Want Our Mummy* (1939) when the three stooges visit Egypt hoping to win a $5,000 reward. Their aim is to find the mummy of King Rootin-Tootin; the mummy turns out to be a midget. High jinx abound in *Abbot and Costello Meet the Mummy* (1955). An actor dressed as a mummy must rush to the birth of his child in Steven Spielberg's *Amazing Stories – 'Mummy/Daddy'* (1985). An American TV comedy, *Under Wraps* (1997) reveals three children trying to reanimate a 3,000-year-old mummy on Halloween – if the mummy fails to return to his resting place by midnight he will lose for ever his long-lost love. In the *All New Adventures of Laurel and Hardy: For Love or Mummy* (1998) a professor's daughter needs protection from a reincarnated mummy, while *The Mummy Parody* (2001) is an MTV skit on the mummy films of the late 1990s and stars Snoop Doggy Dogg.

More serious and thoughtful films dealing with the subject of death and regeneration include the awesome animation *Ra, Path of the Sun God* (1990) which focuses with unparalleled intelligence on the mythical cycle of the sun god. In *The Night of the Counting of the Years* or *El Mumia* (1969) Shadi Abdel Salam directs a deeply atmospheric dramatisation of the story of the discovery of the royal mummy cache at Deir el Bahri.

Live humans take on the role of mummies in the silent film *Wanted – A Mummy* (1910) and in *The Mummy* (1912) a man poses as a revived corpse in order to fool his sweetheart! The popularisation of Mary Shelley's novel *Frankenstein* in literature and film can be identified in very early mummy films such as *The Mummy* (1911) in which an unfortunate girl is mummified by electricity. Mummies also appear in special features and can be seen in the Superman animation *The Mummy Strikes* (1943) in which an Egyptologist is found dead and his assistant is convicted of the murder. Reporter Clark Kent has growing suspicions regarding 'the curse of King Tush'. A TV animation *Mummies Alive!* aired in 1977 highlights the plight of the Egyptian dead reborn into San Francisco. A battle of good versus evil ensues. A mummy also features in *Hercules: the Legendary Journeys* (1994–9, Season 3). *The Magic Mummy* (1933) was a short animation for RKO Radio Pictures while *Tales from the Darkside – 'The Grave Robber'* (1986, Season 4), has a mummy challenging an archaeologist to a game of strip poker. The archaeologist loses, and as the challenger's wrappings are discarded he finds himself being transformed into the mummy.

Mummies have also featured in erotic films, notably in *El Secreto de la Momia Egipcia* or *Love Brides of the Blood Mummy* (1974) in which the mummy, who figures as a living man, sucks blood, tortures his victims and sexually molests women. Mummies also appear in pornographic films. As the narrator of a rather bizarre film, *Secrets of Sex* (1969), a mummy invites us to view topless safecracking and go-go dancers being pelted with vegetables. The pornographic film *Mummy Raider* (2000) features Misty Mundae, a rather dubious alternative to Lara Croft, and was followed by a sequel, *Lust in the Mummy's Tomb*, in which Misty and her un-dead lover I-Hop-Shank (the mummy) are united in many and varied ways.

Appendix I

FURTHER SOURCES FOR TRANSLATIONS

'Admonitions of Ipuwer', Faulkner, R.O., *Journal of Egyptian Archaeology*, 51 (1965), 53–62

'Battle of Kadesh Inscriptions', Lichtheim, M., *Ancient Egyptian Literature*, II, *The New Kingdom*, Berkeley, CA,1976, 57–71

'Book of the Dead', Faulkner, R.O., *The Ancient Egyptian Book of the Dead*, London, 1985

'Coffin Texts', de Buck, A., *The Egyptian Coffin Texts*, Chicago, 1935–61

'Declaration by Ramesses II at Medinet Habu', Breasted, J.H., *Ancient Records of Egypt*, IV, Chicago, 1988, 39

'Inscription from the Tomb Chapel of Hetepherakhet', Breasted, J.H., *Ancient Records of Egypt*, I, Chicago, 1906–7, 253

'Papyrus Anastasi', Gardiner, A.H., *Egyptian Hieratic Texts: Literary Texts of the New Kingdom*, Hildersheim, 1964

'Rock-Cut Stele of Mentuhotep IV', Lichtheim, M., *Ancient Egyptian Literature*, I, *The Old and Middle Kingdoms*, Berkeley, CA, 1975, 113–15; Breasted, J.H., *Ancient Records*, I, Chicago, 1906–7, 439–43 & 452–3

'Royal Harem Conspiracy', Breasted, J.H., *Ancient Records of Egypt*, IV, Chicago, 1988, 208–21

'Spell for the Protection of a Child', Borghouts, J.F., *Ancient Egyptian Magical Texts*, Leiden, 1978, 42–3

'Autobiography of Weni, The', Breasted, J.H., *Ancient Records of Egypt*, I, Chicago, 1906–7, 292–4; Lichtheim, M., *Ancient Egyptian Literature*, I, *The Old and Middle Kingdoms*, Berkeley, CA, 1975, 18–22

'Conception and Birth of Hatshepsut, The', Breasted, J.H., *Ancient Records of Egypt*, II, Chicago, 1988, 80–5

'Dispute Between a Man and his Ba, The', Lichtheim, M., *Ancient Egyptian Literature*, I, *The Old and Middle Kingdoms*, Berkeley, CA, 1975, 163–9

'Doomed Prince, The', Peet, T.E., *Journal of Egyptian Archaeology*, 11 (1925), 227–9; Lichtheim, M., *Ancient Egyptian Literature*, II, *The New Kingdoms*, Berkeley, CA, 1976, 200–3

'Famine Stele, The', Lichtheim, M., *Ancient Egyptian Literature*, III, University of California, 1980, 94

'Instruction Addressed to King Merikare, The', Lichtheim, M., *Ancient Egyptian Literature*, I, *The Old and Middle Kingdoms*, Berkeley, CA, 1975, 97–109; Gardiner, A.H., *Journal of Egyptian Archaeology* (1914), Vol. 1 20–36; Erman, A., *The Literature of the Ancient Egyptians*, London, 1927, 75–84

'Instruction (Maxims) of Ptah-Hotep, The', Erman, A., *The Literature of the Ancient Egyptians*, London, 1927, 54–67

'Instruction of Any, The', Lichtheim, M., *Ancient Egyptian Literature*, II, *The New Kingdoms*, Berkeley, CA, 1976, 135–45; Erman, A., *The Literature of the Ancient Egyptians*, London, 1927, 234–42

'Instruction of Prince Hardjedef, The', Lichtheim, M., *Ancient Egyptian Literature*, I, *The Old and Middle Kingdoms*, Berkeley, CA, 1975, 58–9; Brunner-Traut, E., *Zeitschrift für ägyptische Sprache und Altertumskunde*, 76 (1940), 3–9, pl. 1

'Litany of Re, The', Piankoff, A., *The Litany of Re*, New York, 1964

'Prayer from the Tomb of Nisedjerkai', Lichtheim, M., *Ancient Egyptian Literature*, I, *The Old and Middle Kingdoms*, Berkeley, CA, 1975, 15

'Prophecies of Neferti, The', Lichtheim, M., *Ancient Egyptian Literature*, I, *The Old and Middle Kingdoms*, Berkeley, CA, 1975, 139–45; Gardiner, A.H., *Journal of Egyptian Archaeology*, 1 (1914), 100–6

'Pyramid Texts, The', Faulkner, R.O., *The Ancient Egyptian Pyramid Texts*, Oxford, 1998; Lichtheim, M., *Ancient Egyptian Literature*, I,, *The Old and Middle Kingdoms*, Berkeley, CA, 1975, 29–44

'Report of Wenamun, The', Erman, A., *Zeitschrift für ägyptische Sprache und Alterumskunde*, 38 (1900), 1–14

'Satire of the Trades, The', Lichtheim, M., *Ancient Egyptian Literature*, I, , *The Old and Middle Kingdoms*, Berkeley, CA, 1975, 184–92; Van de Walle, B., *Chronique d'Égypte* (1949), 244–56

'Shipwrecked Sailor, The', Lichtheim, M., *Ancient Egyptian Literature*, I, *The Old and Middle Kingdoms*, Berkeley, CA, 1975, 211–15; Erman. A., *The Literature of the Ancient Egyptians*, London, 1927, 29–35

'Story of Sinuhe, The', Gardiner, A.H., *Notes on the Story of Sinuhe*, Paris, 1916; Lichtheim, M., *Ancient Egyptian Literature*, I, *The Old and Middle Kingdoms*, Berkeley, CA, 1975, 222–33

'Three Tales of Wonder', Brunner-Traut, E., *Altägyptische Märchen*, Dusseldorf-Cologne, 11–24; Lichtheim, M., *Ancient Egyptian Literature*, I, *The Old and Middle Kingdoms*, Berkeley, CA, 1975, 215–22

Appendix II

CHRONOLOGY OF RULERS OF ANCIENT EGYPT
(AFTER GRIMAL, 1992)

**4500–3150 BC: Archaic-Predynastic
Period**
4500–4000 BC: Badarian
4000–3500 BC: Naqada I (Amration)
3500–3300 BC: Naqada II (Gerzean A)
3300–3150 BC: Naqada III (Gerzean B)

3150–2700 BC: Early Dynastic Period
3150–2925 BC: 1st Dynasty
   3150–3125 BC: Narmer-Menes
   3125–3100 BC: Aha
   3100–3055 BC: Djer
   3055–3050 BC: Djet
   3050–2995 BC: Den
   2995–2950 BC: Anedjeb-Semerkhet
   2960–2926 BC: Kaa

2925–2700 BC: 2nd Dynasty
   Hetepsekhemwy
   Reneb
   Nynetjer
   Weneg
   Sened
   Peribsen
   Sekhemib
   Khasekhemwy

2700–2190 BC: Old Kingdom
2700–2625 BC: 3rd Dynasty
   Nebka
   Djoser
   Sekhemket
   Khaba
   Neferkare
   Huni

2625–2510 BC: 4th Dynasty
   Snoferu
   Cheops (Khufu)
   Djedefre
   Chephren
   Baefre (?)
   Mycerinus
   Shepsekaf

2510–2460 BC: 5th Dynasty
   Userkaf
   Sahure
   Neferkare-Kakai
   Shepseskare
   Neferefre
   Neiserre
   Menkauhor
   Djedkare-Isesi
   Wenis

2460–2200 BC: 6th Dynasty
  Teti
  Userkare
  Pepy I
  Merenre I
  Pepy II
  Merenre II
  Nitocris

2200–2040 BC: First Intermediate
  Period
2200–c. 2160 BC: 7th and 8th
  Dynasties
  Many short-lived kings

2160–c. 2040 BC: 9th and 10th
  Dynasties (Herakleopolis)
  Meribre Khety I
  Neferkare
  Nebkaure Khety II
  Neferkare Meribre
  Wahkare Khety III
  Merikare

2160–2040 BC: 11th Dynasty (Thebes)
  Mentuhotpe I
  Inyotef I
  2118–2069 BC: Inyotef II
  2069–2061 BC: Inyotef III
  2061–2040 BC: Mentuhotpe II

2040–1674 BC: Middle Kingdom
2040–1991 BC: 11th Dynasty (Unified
  Egypt)
2040–2009 BC: Nebhepetre Mentuhotpe
  II
2009–1997 BC: S'ankhkare
  Mentuhotpe III
1997–1991 BC: Nebtawyre Mentuhotpe
  IV

1991–1785 BC: 12th Dynasty
1991–1962 BC: Ammenemes I
1962–1928 BC: Sesostris I
1928–1895 BC: Ammenemes II
1895–1878 BC: Sesostris II
1878–1842 BC: Sesostris III
1842–1797 BC: Ammenemes III
1797–1790 BC: Ammenemes IV
1790–1785 BC: Sobekneferu

1785–1633 BC: 13th and 14th
  Dynasties
  Sekhemre-Khutawy
  Ammenemes V
  Sehetepibre II
  Ammenemes VI (Ameny the Asiatic)
  Hornedjheritef 'The Asiatic'
  c. 1750 BC: Sobekhotep I
  Reniseneb
  Hor I
  Ammenemes VII
  Ugaf
  Sesostris IV
  Khendjer
  Smenkhkare
  Sobekemsaf I
  c. 1745 BC: Sobekhotep III
  c. 1741–1730 BC: Neferhotep I
  Sahathor
  Sobekhotep IV
  1720–1715 BC: Sobekhotep V
  Neferhotep II
  Neferhotep III
  Iaib
  c. 1704–1690 BC: Iy
  Iny

1674–1553 BC: Second Intermediate
  Period

1674–1553 BC: 15th–16th–17th
   Dynasties
1674 BC: Dedumesiu I
Dedumesiu II
Senebmiu
Djedkare
Monthuemsaf

15th and 16th Dynasties – Hyksos
Salitis
1650 BC: Yaqub-Har
Khyan

17th Dynasty – Thebes
Rahotep
Inyotef V
Sobekemsaf II
Djehuty

1633 BC: End of 14th Dynasty –
   Thebes
Mentuhotpe VII
Nebiryau I
Inyotef VII
Sequenre I
Sequenre II
Kamose

1633 BC: End of 14th Dynasty –
   Hyksos
Apophis I
Apophis II

1552–1069 BC: New Kingdom
1552–1314 or 1295 BC: 18th Dynasty
1552–1526 BC: Ahmose
1526–1506 BC: Amenophis I
1506–1493 BC: Tuthmosis I
1493–1479 BC: Tuthmosis II

1479–1425 BC: Tuthmosis III
1478–1458 BC: Hatshepsut
1425–1401 BC: Amenophis II
1401–1390 BC: Tuthmosis IV
1390–1352 BC: Amenophis III
1352–1348 BC: Amenophis IV
1348–1338 BC: Akhenaten
1338–1336 BC: Smenkhare
1336–1327 BC: Tutankhaten –
   Tutankhamun
1327–1323 BC: Ay
1323–1295 BC: Horemheb

1295–1188 BC: 19th Dynasty
1295–1294 BC: Ramesses I
1294–1279 BC: Sety I
1279–1212 BC: Ramesses II
1212–1202 BC: Merneptah
1202–1199 BC: Amenmesse
1202–1196 BC: Sety II
1196–1190 BC: Siptah
1196–1188 BC: Twosre

1188–1069 BC: 20th Dynasty
1188–1186 BC: Setnakht
1186–1154 BC: Ramesses III
1154–1148 BC: Ramesses IV
1148–1144 BC: Ramesses V
1144–1136 BC: Ramesses VI
1136–1128 BC: Ramesses VII
1128–1125 BC: Ramesses VIII
1125–1107 BC: Ramesses IX
1107–1098 BC: Ramesses X
1098–1069 BC: Ramesses XI

1069–702 BC: Third Intermediate
   Period
1069–945 BC: 21st Dynasty Theban
   Chief Priests

1070–1055 BC: Pinudjem I as High
  Priest
1069–1043 BC: Smendes
1054–1032 BC: Pinudjem I as King
1054–1046 BC: Masaharta
1045–992 BC: Menkheperre
1043–1039 BC: Amenemnisu
1039–993 BC: Psusennes I
993–984 BC: Amenmope
992–990 BC: Smendes
990–969 BC: Pinudjem II
984–978 BC: Osorkon
978–959 BC: Siamun
969–945 BC: Psusennes
959–945 BC: Psusennes II

945–715 BC: **22nd Dynasty** Theban
  High Priest
945–924 BC: Sheshonq I Iuput
924–889 BC: Osorkon I Shoshenq
890–889 BC: Sheshonq II Smendes
889–874 BC: Takelot I Iuwelot Harsiese
870–860 BC: Harsiese
874–850 BC: Osorkon II Nimlot
850–825 BC: Takelot II Osorkon

23rd Dynasty
825–773 BC: Shoshenq III Pedubastis I
787–759 BC: Osorkon III
773–767 BC: Pimay
764–757 BC: Takelot III
767–730 BC: Shoshenq V
757–754 BC: Rudamon
754–715 BC: Iuput II

747–525 BC: **Late Period**
747–656 BC: 24th Dynasty/
  25th Dynasty
747–716 BC: Piankhy
727–716 BC: Tefnakht
716–715 BC: Bocchoris
716–702 BC: Shabaka
690–664 BC: Taharqa

26th Dynasty
672–664 BC: Necho I
664 BC Tantamani
610–595 BC: Necho II
595–589 BC: Psammetichus II
589–570 BC: Apries
570–526 BC: Amasis
526–525 BC: Psammetichus III

Bibliography

Adams, B. *Ancient Hierakonpolis*, Warminster, 1974

———. *Egyptian Mummies*, Warminster, 1984

Aldred, C. 'Hair Styles and History', *Bulletin of the Metropolitan Museum of Art* 15 (1957), 141–7

———. *Egypt to the End of the Old Kingdom*, London, 1965

———. *Egyptian Art*, London, 1980

———. *Akhenaten: King of Egypt*, London, 1988

Amin, A. 'Ancient Trade Routes between Egypt and the Sudan', *Sudan Notes and Records* 51 (1970), 23

Andrews, C. *Egyptian Mummies*, London, 1984

———. *Ancient Egyptian Jewellery*, London, 1990

Arkell, A.J. 'The Prehistory of the Nile Valley', *Handbuch der Orientalistik* (Leiden) VII (1975), 1.2

Arnold, D. 'Der Tempel des Königs Mentuhotep von Deir el-Bahari', Band III, *Archäologische Veröffentlichungen des Deutschen Archäologischen Instituts, Abteilung Kairo*, Cairo

Baer, K. *Rank and Title in the Old Kingdom. The Structure of Egyptian Administration in the Fifth and Sixth Dynasties*, Chicago, IL, 1960

Bahn, P.G. (ed.). *Tombs, Graves and Mummies: 50 Discoveries in World Archaeology*, London, 1996

Baines, J. and Malek, J. *Atlas of Ancient Egypt*, Oxford, 1986

Bakry, H.S. *A Brief Study of Mummies and Mummification*, Cairo, 1965

Balout, L., Robert, C. and Desroches-Noblecourt, C. *La Momie de Ramses II*, Paris, 1985

Bass, W. and Jefferson, J. *Death's Acre. Inside the Legendary 'Body Farm'*, London, 2003

Baumgartel, E.J. *The Cultures of Prehistoric Egypt I*, Oxford, 1955

———. *The Cultures of Prehistoric Egypt II*, Oxford, 1960

Belzoni, G. *Narrative of the Operations and Recent Discoveries within the Pyramids, Temples, Tombs, and Excavations in Egypt and Nubia*, London, 1820

Bendann, E. *Death Customs: an Analytical Study of Burial Rites*, London, 1930

Bierbrier, M.L. *The Tomb-Builders of the Pharaohs*, London, 1984

Blacking, J. (ed.). *The Anthropology of the Body*, London, 1977

Blackman, A.M. *The Rock Tombs of Meir*, Vol. 1, London, 1914

——. *The Edwin Smith Surgical Papyrus II*, Chicago, IL, 1930

——. *Medinet Habu*, 8 vols, Chicago, IL, 1930–2

——. *The Rock Tombs of Meir*, Vol. 5, London, 1953

——. *Ancient Records of Egypt*, 5 vols, Chicago, IL, 1988

Borchardt, L. *Catalogue général des Antiquités égyptiennes du Musée du Caire. Nos. 1–1294. Statuen und Statuetten von Königen und Privatleuten im Museum von Kairo*, Berlin, 1911

Breasted, J.H. *The Edwin Smith Surgical Papyrus*, Chicago, IL, 1930

Brothwell, D. and Sandison, A. (eds). *Diseases in Antiquity*, Chicago, IL, 1967

Brown, P. and Tuzins, D. (eds). *The Ethnography of Cannibalism*, Washington, DC, 1983

Brunton, G. *Qua and Badari*, Vol. 2, London, 1928

——. *Qua and Badari*, Vol. 3, London, 1930

Brunton, G. and Caton-Thompson, G. *The Badarian Civilisation*, London, 1928

Brunton, G. and Morant, G.M. *Mostagedda and the Tasian Culture*, London, 1937

Bruyère, B. *Rapport sur les Fouilles de Deir el Medineh*, Cairo, 1924–7

Calverley, A.M., Broome, M. and Gardiner, A.H. *The Temple of King Seti I at Abydos*, Vol. 4, *The Second Hypostyle Hall*, Chicago, IL, 1933–58

Caminos, R.A. *Late-Egyptian Miscellanies*, Oxford, 1954

Caminos, R.A. and Fischer, H.G. *Ancient Egyptian Epigraphy and Paleography. The Recording of Inscriptions and Scenes in Tombs and Temples*, New York, 1976

Capart, J. *Les Debuts de l'Art en Égypte*, Brussels, 1904

——. *Primitive Art in Egypt*, London, 1905

Carter, H. *The Tomb of Tut'ankh'Amen*, 3 vols, 1927–33

——. *The Tomb of Tutankamun*, London, 1972

Case, H. and Payne, J.C. 'Tomb 100: The Decorated Tomb at Hierakonpolis', *Journal of Egyptian Archaeology* 48 (1962), 5–18

Chamberlain, A.T. *Human Remains*, London, 1994

Citola, B. 'Ramses III and the Sea Peoples: A Structural Analysis of the Medinet Habu Inscriptions', *Orientalia* 57 (1988), 275–306

Cockburn, A.E. (ed.). *Mummies, Disease and Ancient Cultures*, Cambridge, 1980

Collins, L. 'The Private Tombs of Thebes: Excavations by Sir Robert Mond.1905–1906', *Journal of Egyptian Archaeology* 62 (1976), 18–40

Daressy, M.G. *Catalogue général des Antiquités égyptiennes du Musée du Caire. Nos. 24001–24990. Fouilles de la Vallée des Rois*, Cairo, 1902

D'Auria, S., Lacovara, P. and Roehrig, C. *Mummies and Magic: The Funerary Arts of Ancient Egypt*, Musuem of Fine Arts, Boston, 1998

David, A.R. *Mysteries of the Mummies*, Manchester, 1978

——— (ed.). *The Ancient Egyptians, Religious Beliefs and Practices*, London, 1982

———. *Science in Egyptology*, Manchester, 1988

Davies, N. *Human Sacrifice: in History and Today*, New York, 1981

Davies, N. de G. *The Rock Tombs of el Amarna*, 6 vols, London, 1903–8

———. *The Tomb of Kenamun at Thebes*, New York, 1930

———. *The Tombs of Menkheperrasonb Amenmose and Another*, London, 1933

———. *Ancient Egyptian Paintings*, Vol. 1, Chicago, IL, 1936

———. 'Research in the Theban Necropolis: 1938–1939', *Bulletin of the Metropolitan Museum of Art (New York)*, Vol. 34 (1939), 280–4

———. *Tomb of Rekh-mi-Re' at Thebes*, Vol. 2, New York, 1943

Davies, V.W. and Friedman, R. *Egypt*, London, 1998

Dawson, W.R. *A Bibliography of Works Relating to Mummification in Egypt*, Le Caire, IFAO, 1929

Dawson, W.R. and Gray, P.M.K. *Catalogue of Egyptian Antiquities in the British Museum, 1: Mummies and Human Remains*, London, 1968

Debono, F. and Mortensen, B. 'The Predynastic Cemetery at Heliopolis', *Archäologische Veröffentlichungen des Deutschen Archäologischen Instituts, Abteilung Kairo*, Cairo, 1988

De Buck, A. and Gardiner, A.H. *The Egyptian Coffin Texts. IV. Texts of Spells 268–354*, Chicago, IL, 1951

Derry, D.E. 'Mummification', *Annales du Service des Antiquités de l'Égypte* (1942), 235–65

Diodorus Siculus, *History*, trans. C. Oldfield, Cambridge, Mass., 1935; London, 1968

Dodson, A.M. 'The Tombs of the Kings of the Early Eighteenth Dynasty at Thebes', *Zeitschrift für Ägyptische Sprache und Altertumskunde* 115 (1988)

Downes, J. and Pollard, T. (eds). *The Loved Body's Corruption: Archaeological Contributions to the Study of Human Mortality*, Glasgow, 1999

Drioton, E. and Lauer, J.P. *Sakkara, the Monuments of Zozer*, IFAO, 1939

Duell, P. *The Mastaba of Mereruka*, Chicago, IL, 1938

Ebell, E. *The Papyrus Ebers, the Greatest Egyptian Medical Document*, Copenhagen, 1937

Edgerton, W.F. and Wilson, J.A. *Historical Records of Ramses III*, Chicago, IL, 1936

Edwards, I.E.S. and Shorter, A. *A Handbook to the Egyptian Mummies and Coffins Exhibited in the British Museum, London*, London, 1938

Emery W.B. *The Tomb of Hemaka*, Cairo, 1938

———. *Excavations at Saqqara 1937–1938. Hor-Aha*, Cairo, 1939

———. *Great Tombs of the 1st Dynasty*, Cairo, 1949

Epigraphic Survey. 'The Tomb of Kheruef', *Archaeology*, 27 (1980; Chicago), 12–18

——. *The Egyptian Coffin Texts*, Warminster, 1973

——. *The Ancient Egyptian Book of the Dead*, London, 1985

Faulkner, R.O. *The Ancient Egyptian Pyramid Texts*, Oxford, 1998

Filer, J. *Disease*, London, 1995

Fleming, S., Fishman, B., O'Connor, D. and Silverman, D. *The Egyptian Mummy, Secrets and Science*, Philadelphia, PA, 1980

Fletcher, A.J. 'Ancient Egyptian Hair: A study in style, form and function', Ph.D. thesis, University of Manchester, 1995

Frankfort, H. *The Birth of Civilization in the Near East*, London, 1951

Frankfort, H. and Pendlebury, J.D.S. *The City of Akhenaten II. The North Suburb and the Desert Altars*, London, 1933

Furneaux, R. *Primitive Peoples*, London, 1975

Gardiner, A.H. *The Tomb of Huy, Viceroy of Nubia In The Reign of Tut'ankhamun*, No. 40. Theban Tombs Series 4, London, 1915

——. *The Attitude of Ancient Egyptians to Death and the Dead*, Cambridge, 1935

Garstang, J. *The Burial Customs of Ancient Egypt*, London, 1907

Ghaliounghi, P. *Magic and Medical Science in Ancient Egypt*, Amsterdam, 1973

Ghaliounghi, P. and Dawakhly, Z. *Health and Healing in Ancient Egypt*, Cairo, 1965

Goedicke, H. *Perspectives on the Battle of Kadesh*, Baltimore, MD, 1985

Griffiths, J.G. 'The Interpretation of the Horus-Myth of Edfu', *Journal of Egyptian Archaeology* 44 (1958), 75–85

——. *The Conflict of Horus and Seth from Egyptian and Classical Sources*, Liverpool, 1960

Grimal, N. *A History of Ancient Egypt*, Oxford, 1992

Groenewegen-Frankfort, H.A. *Arrest and Movement. Space and Time in the Art of the Ancient Near East*, Cambridge, Mass., 1987

Gwyn-Griffiths, J. 'Human Sacrifices in Egypt: The Classical Evidence', *Annales du Service des Antiquités de l'Égypte* 48 (1948)

Hamilton-Patterson, J. and Andrews, C. *Mummies: Death and Life in Ancient Egypt*, London, 1978

Hanke, R. *Amarna-Reliefs aus Hermopolis*, Hildesheim, 1969

Harris, J.E. and Weeks, K. *X-Raying the Pharaohs*, New York, 1973

Harris, J.E. and Wente, E.F. (eds). *X-Ray Atlas of the Royal Mummies*, Chicago, IL, 1980

Hassan, S. *Excavations at Giza*, 10 vols, Cairo, 1932–60

Hayes, W.C. *The Scepter of Egypt*, 2 vols, New York, 1990

Hoffman, M.A. *Egypt before the Pharaohs*, London, 1984

Hoffman, M.A., Hamroush, H.A. and Allen, R.O. 'A Model of Urban Development for the Hierakonpolis Region from Predynastic through Old Kingdom Times', *Journal of the American Research Center in Egypt* 23 (1986), 175–87

Hogg, G. *Cannibalism and Human Sacrifice*, London, 1958

Hornung, E. *Idea into Image: Essays on Ancient Egyptian Thought*, New York, 1992

Hoving, T. *Making the Mummies Dance: Inside the Metropolitan Museum of Art*, New York, 1993

Humphreys, S.C. and King, H. (eds). *Mortality and Immortality: the Anthropology and Archaeology of Death*, London, 1981

James, E.H. and Edward, F.W. *An X-Ray Atlas of the Royal Mummies*, Chicago and London, 1980

James, T.G.H. *British Museum Hieroglyphic Texts from Egyptian Stelae*, Pt 1, London, 1961

Janssen, J. *Commodity Prices from the Ramessid Period. An Economic Study of the Village of Necropolis Workmen at Thebes*, Leiden, 1975

Janssen, J. and Janssen, R. *Growing up in Ancient Egypt*, London, 1990

Jequier, G. *Fouilles à Saqqarah. Deux Pyramides du Moyen Empire*, Cairo, 1933

Kanawati, N. *The Egyptian Administration in the Old Kingdom: Evidence on its Economic Decline*, Warminster, 1977

Kemp, B.J. 'The Egyptian 1st Dynasty royal cemetery', *Antiquity* 41 (1967), 22–32

Kendall, T. *Kerma and the Kingdom of Kush, 2500–1500 BC: the Archaeological Discovery of an Ancient Nubian Empire*, Washington, DC, 1997

Kitchen, K.A. *The Third Intermediate Period in Egypt (1100–650 B.C.)*, Warminster, 1973

Lacau, P. *Catalogue général des Antiquités Égyptiennes du Musée du Caire. Nos. 28001–28126. Sarcophages antérieurs au Nouvel Empire*, 2 vols, Cairo, 1904

Lauer, J. *Saqqara. The Royal Cemetery of Memphis. Excavations and Discoveries since 1850*, London, 1976

Layton, R. *The Anthropology of Art*, Cambridge, 1991

Leca, A.P. *The Cult of the Immortal: Mummies and the Ancient Way of Death*, London, 1979

Lehner, M. *The Complete Pyramids*, London, 1997

Lichtheim, M. *Ancient Egyptian Literature*, Vols I–II: *The Old and Middle Kingdoms*, Berkeley, CA, 1975

——. *Ancient Egyptian Literature*. Vol. 2: *The New Kingdom*, Berkeley, CA, 1976

Lincoln, B. *Priests, Warriors and Cattle. A Study in the Ecology of Religions*, Berkeley, CA, 1981

Lucas, A. *Ancient Egyptian Materials and Industries*, London, 1989

McDowell, A.G. *Jurisdiction in the Workmen's Community of Deir El-Medina*, Leiden, 1985

Mahdy, El, C. *Mummies, Myth and Magic*, London, 1989

Manchester, K. *The Archaeology of Disease*, Bradford, 1983

Manniche, L. *City of the Dead, Thebes in Egypt*, London, 1987

——. *Music and Musicians in Ancient Egypt*, London, 1991

Mariette, A. *Le Sèrapèum de Memphis*, Paris, 1882

Martin. G.T. *Hidden Tombs of Memphis*, London, 1991

——. *The Royal Tomb at El-'Amarna. The Reliefs, Inscriptions, and Architecture*, Vol. 2, London, 1975

Maspero, G. *Les Momies Royales de Deir el Bahari*, Cairo, 1889

Massoulard, É. *Préhistoire et protohistoire de l'Égypte*, Paris, 1949

Meskell, L.M. 'Dying Young: the Experience of Death at Deir el Medina', *Archaeological Review from Cambridge* 13 (1994), 35–45

Michalowski, K. *The Art of Ancient Egypt*, London, 1969

Mohamed, M.A.Q. *The Development of the Funerary Beliefs and Practices Displayed in the Private Tombs of the New Kingdom at Thebes*, Cairo, 1996

Mokhtar, G., Riad, H. and Iskander, Z. *Mummification in Ancient Egypt*, Cairo, 1973

Mond, R. and Myers, O. *The Bucheum*, London, 1934

Morkot, R. 'Violent Images of Queenship and the Royal Cult', *Wepawet* 12 (1980), 1–9

Moussa, A.M. and Altenmüller, H. *Das Grab des Nianchchnum und Chnumhotep*, Berlin, 1977

Murnane, W.J. *Texts from the Amarna Period in Egypt*, Atlanta, GA, 1995

Murray, M. *The Splendour that was Egypt*, London, 1951

Murray, M.A. *Tomb of the Two Brothers*, Manchester, 1910

Naville, E. *The Temple of Deir El Bahari*, Vol. 3, London, 1906

——. *The XIth Dynasty Temple at Deir el-Bahari*, Pt 3, London, 1913

Needler, W. *Predynastic and Archaic Egypt in the Brooklyn Museum*, New York, 1984

Newberry, P.E. *Beni Hasan*, Vol. 1, London, 1893

——. *Beni Hasan*, Vol. 2, London, 1893

——. *El Bersheh*, Vol. 1 (The Tomb of Tehuti–Hetep), London, 1894

——. *Beni Hasan*, Vol. 4, London, 1900

——. *The Life of Rekhmara*, London, 1900

Nicholson, P.T. and Shaw, I. (eds). *Ancient Egyptian Materials and Technology*, Cambridge, 2000

Nunn, J.F. *Ancient Egyptian Medicine*, London, 1996

Olivova, V. *Sports and Games in the Ancient World*, London, 1984

Paabo, S. 'Preservation of DNA in ancient Egyptian mummies', *Journal of Archaeological Science* 12 (1985), 411–17

Page, A. *Ancient Egyptian Figured Ostraca*, Warminster, 1983

Parkinson, R. *Voices From Ancient Egypt. An Anthology of Middle Kingdom Writings*, London, 1991

Peet, T.E. *The Great Tomb Robberies of the Twentieth Egyptian Dynasty*, Oxford, 1943

Petrie, W.M.F. *Royal Tombs of the Earliest Dynasties*, London, 1900

———. *Shabtis*, Warminster, 1972

Pettigrew, T.J. *A History of Egyptian Mummies*, Los Angeles [1834] 1983

Piankoff, A. *Mythological Papyri*, New York, 1957

———. *The Litany of Re*, New York, 1964

Plutarch, M. *Roman Lives*, Oxford, 1999

Polhemus, E. (ed.). *Social Aspects of the Human Body*, Harmondsworth, 1973

Pringle, H. *The Mummy Congress: Science, Obsession and the Everlasting Dead*, London, 2002

Reeves, N. *The Complete Tutankhamun*, London, 1990

———. *Ancient Egypt. The Great Discoveries*, London, 2000

Reisner, G.A. *The Development of the Egyptian Tomb down to the Accession of Cheops*, Cambridge, Mass., 1936

Roberts, C. and Manchester, K. *The Archaeology of Disease*, Stroud, 1995

Romer, J. *Valley of the Kings*, London, 1981

———. *Ancient Lives*, London, 1984

Ruffer, M.A. *Studies in the Palaeopathology of Egypt*, Chicago, IL, 1921

Sagan, E. *Cannibalism: Human Aggression and Cultural Form*, New York, 1974

Sauneron, S. *Le Rituel de L'Embaumement*, Cairo, 1952

———. *The Priests of Ancient Egypt*, London and New York, 1960

Schneider, H. *Shabtis*, 3 vols, Leiden, 1977

Schwartz, J.H. *Skeleton Keys: an Introduction to Human Skeletal Morphology, Development and Analysis*, Oxford, 1995

Sheskin, A. *Cryonics: a Sociology of Death and Bereavement*, New York, 1979

Smith, G.E. *The Royal Mummies*, Cairo, 1912

Smith, G.E. and Dawson, W.R. *Egyptian Mummies*, London, 1924

Smith, J.Z. 'The domestication of sacrifice', in R.G. Hamerton-Kelly (ed.), *Violent Origins: Ritual Killing and Cultural Formation*, Stanford, CA, 1987

Taylor, J. *Egyptian Coffins*, Warminster, 1989

Thomas, E. *The Royal Necropolis at Thebes*, Princeton, NJ, 1966

Tierney, P. *The Highest Altar*, New York, 1989

Turner, B.S. *The Body and Society*, Oxford, 1984

Turner, R.C. and Scaife, R.G. (eds). *Bog Bodies*, London, 1995

Van der Sanden, W.A.B. *Through Nature to Eternity*, Amsterdam, 1996

Wilkinson, R.H. *The Complete Temples of Ancient Egypt*, London, 2000

Wilson, P. *The Domestication of the Human Species*, New Haven, CT, 1989

Winlock, H.E. *Materials Used at the Embalming of King Tut-Ankh-Amun*, New York, 1941

———. *Excavations at Deir-el-Bahari*, New York [1911], 1942

———. *The Slain Soldiers of Nebhepetre Mentuhotep*, New York, 1945

Index